# Television Access
# and Political Power

# PRAEGER SERIES IN POLITICAL COMMUNICATION

Robert E. Denton, Jr., General Editor

Playing the Game: The Presidential Rhetoric of Ronald Reagan
*Mary E. Stuckey*

Rhetorical Studies of National Political Debates: 1960–1988
*Edited by Robert V. Friedenberg*

Political Communication in America: Second Edition
*Robert E. Denton, Jr., and Gary C. Woodward*

Listening for a President: A Citizen's Campaign Methodology
*Ruth M. Gonchar Brennan and Dan F. Hahn*

Attack Politics: Strategy and Defense
*Michael Pfau and Henry C. Kenski*

Presidential Press Conferences: A Critical Approach
*Carolyn Smith*

# Television Access and Political Power

The Networks,
the Presidency,
and the "Loyal Opposition"

## Joe S. Foote

Foreword by
Newton M. Minow

*Praeger Series in Political Communication*

PRAEGER

New York
Westport, Connecticut
London

**Library of Congress Cataloging-in-Publication Data**

Foote, Joe S.
  Television access and political power : the networks, the presidency, and the
"loyal opposition" / Joe S. Foote : forewords by Newton N. Minow and Robert E.
Denton, Jr.
      p.   cm.—(Praeger series in political communication)
  Includes bibliographical references.
  ISBN 0-275-93438-1 (alk. paper)
  1. Television in politics—United States.   I. Title.   II. Series.
  HE8700.76.U6F66   1990
  324.7'3'0973—dc20          89-29763

Library of Congress Catalog Card Number: 89-29763
ISBN: 0-275-93438-1

First published in 1990

Praeger Publishers, One Madison Avenue, New York, NY 10010
An imprint of Greenwood Publishing Group, Inc.

Printed in the United States of America

The paper used in this book complies with the
Permanent Paper Standard issued by the National
Information Standards Organization (Z39.48-1984).

10 9 8 7 6 5 4 3 2 1

To Jody, Jackson, Jan, and Joseph

# Contents

# Tables

# Foreword

When John Martin, Lee Mitchell and I wrote "Presidential Television" in 1973, we knew well what impact the White House can have on the Nation's agenda when it knows how to dominate the media, especially television. What we did not anticipate back then were the incredible series of changes, both technological and societal, that would come to affect the way Presidents and their advisers use television to present and defend their points of view, and, indeed, the way television itself would affect the presidency.

In 1973, three major networks, CBS, NBC and ABC, controlled the vast majority of the American television audience. Cable television, with its scores of viewer options, was still a dream. CNN, Ted Turner's imaginative 24-hour news service, was seven years away from its debut. When people spoke about television in those days, they meant ABC, CBS and NBC. So in 1973, a President who appeared on those three networks simultaneously could realistically assume he would be seen by virtually every TV-equipped home in the nation. Indeed, we found in our research that the average presidential TV appearance was guaranteed to reach more than 70 million Americans in one broadcast.

Today, Presidents enjoy no such guarantees. ABC, CBS and NBC have lost viewers to independent stations, cable, and VCRs. Indeed, Professor Foote notes that the big three's combined prime-time audience share eroded from 91 percent in 1976–77 to 67 percent in 1988–89. Presidential television also lost significant audience; as he points out, Ronald Reagan, the Great Communicator, "seldom reached as large a share of the audience as some of his less-gifted predecessors." By the end of his eight years in the White House, President Reagan's average prime time TV

address "reached only 61 percent of the people watching television . . .
compared to 77 percent for Jimmy Carter and 79 percent for Gerald Ford
and Richard Nixon."

Obviously, the expansion of America's telecommunications industry
is one reason behind this decline. Simply put, today's viewers have a
wider spectrum of choices available to them, and more choices per
viewer mean less viewers per choice. But the changing *gestalt* of television journalism itself may have contributed as well.

In 1973, electronic journalism, or EJ, was in its infancy. Almost all the
reports seen on the evening news were shot on film and edited much
the same way newsreels of the 1930s and 1940s had been assembled.
Satellite transmissions, now a staple of almost every local TV station in
the country, were expensive. Extended live broadcasts from overseas,
such as coverage of Richard Nixon's trip to China, were so rare as to
become news events in themselves. The process of electronic newsgathering—the computer-generated character fonts, pop-up maps and
graphics, minicams, Ku-band vans and portable satellite dishes—in
other words all the bells and whistles we take for granted these days,
for the most part did not exist.

But perhaps even more significant was the way in which television
news covered the President himself back then. Presidents were still
larger-than-life figures in the 1970s. As CBS and ABC veteran anchor
Howard K. Smith told *Time Magazine* in 1971, "The Chief of State is like
the Flag. You have to be deferential." Well, don't tell that to the stalwarts
of the 1980s like ABC's Sam Donaldson, who built his reputation as the
junk yard dog of the White House press corps by shouting questions at
Jimmy Carter and Ronald Reagan. Or to CBS' leather-lunged Bill Plante,
whose bray could be heard even over the helicopter engines on the
South Lawn during White House departure ceremonies.

The problem, however, is that by braying and cat-calling at the Chief
of State, he becomes less "flag" and more "doormat." Americans may
not want an imperial presidency—but they do not believe their top
elected official should be treated like the guy next door either.

Yet confrontation, not illumination, seems to be the message these
days. And confrontation breeds airtime—especially if you want to be
seen on the nightly news. Professor Foote's research on correspondent
visibility shows us that between 1983 and 1988, the three most visible
network correspondents were ABC's Donaldson, CBS' Plante, and
NBC's Chris Wallace—all of them then based at the White House. For
years, White House image-makers tried to come up with ways in which
they could shape—or in newsgathering vernacular, put "spin" on—
stories about the President. These days, as former President Reagan,
the best public communicator since John F. Kennedy, learned during
the height of the Iran Contra affair, it's getting harder and harder to be

a successful *spinmeister*. Whenever there's a crisis: a hijacked plane, a hurricane, even a little girl trapped down a well in Texas, some reporter's sure to shout a question about it at the President, whether he's actually responsible for what's happened, or not. Familiarity breeds, well, familiarity. We see so much more of the President today than we did a couple of decades ago that a presidential TV appearance simply doesn't have the cachet it once had.

But despite all these changes—despite satellites and live White House feeds and video tape and declining network audiences—some things have not changed since 1973—and this is why Professor Foote's book is so valuable.

Foote has found, just as we discovered almost two decades ago, that the networks, despite declining audiences and increased competition, remain the primary sources for the majority of American viewers when it comes to news events. And they still deny the opposition party—whether it be Republican or Democrat—equal airtime and sufficient exposure to counteract all those videogenic White House photo opportunities.

So the status quo has not changed a whit. Indeed, just after President George Bush made his televised Oval Office address about national drug strategy in September 1989 only one of the networks—CBS—gave the Democrats equal time to speak live and unedited on an issue that is unquestionably critical to this nation's survival. ABC and NBC called their decisions not to broadcast Senator Joseph Biden's opposing viewpoint news judgement. Others, however, might choose to call it irresponsibility—or worse.

Foote's book, then, is a fascinating update of our own. It adds a wealth of new material, and draws on the author's considerable political experience as a Capitol Hill spokesman (for Speaker of the House Carl Albert) as well as an academic researcher. But this is no dry, pedantic study. Foote, it seems, isn't overwhelmingly fond of the way any of the interested parties has handled the often prickly relationship between the White House, television, and the loyal opposition. So he has written a plain-speaking book that may well outrage not only former administration officials and assorted Members of Congress and Senators, but also television executives, White House correspondents and various other political animals.

Good for him. If more of us were outraged by the status quo the way Foote is, perhaps more of us would get out there to storm the barricades so that the public is better informed.

—Newton N. Minow

# Series Foreword

Those of us from the discipline of communication studies have long believed that communication is prior to all other fields of inquiry. In several other forums I have argued that the essence of politics is "talk" or human interaction.[1] Such interaction may be formal or informal, verbal or nonverbal, public or private but always persuasive forcing us consciously or subconsciously to interpret, to evaluate, and to act. Communication is the vehicle for human action.

From this perspective, it is not surprising that Aristotle recognized the natural kinship of politics and communication in his writings of *Politics* and *Rhetoric*. In the former, he establishes that humans are "political beings" who "alone of the animals is furnished with the faculty of language."[2] And in the latter, he begins his systematic analysis of discourse by proclaiming that "rhetorical study, in its strict sense, is concerned with the modes of persuasion."[3] Thus, it was recognized over 1500 years ago that politics and communication go hand in hand because they are essential parts of human nature.

Back in 1981, Dan Nimmo and Keith Sanders proclaimed that political communication was an emerging field.[4] Although its origin, as noted, dates back centuries, a "self-consciously cross-disciplinary" focus began in the late 1950s. Thousands of books and articles later, colleges and universities offer a variety of graduate and undergraduate coursework in the area in such diverse departments as communication, mass communication, journalism, political science, and sociology.[5] In Nimmo and Sanders' early assessment, the "key areas of inquiry" included rhetorical analysis, propaganda analysis, attitude change studies, voting studies, government and the news media, functional and systems analyses, technological changes, media technologies, campaign techniques, and re-search techniques.[6] In a survey of the state of the field in 1983 by the same authors and Lynda Kaid, they found additional, more specific areas of concerns such as the Presidency, political polls, public opinion, de-bates, and advertising to name a few.[7] Since the first study, they also noted a shift away from the rather strict behavioral approach.

Then as now, the field of political communication continues to emerge. There is no precise definition, method, or disciplinary home of the area of inquiry. Its domain, quite simply, is the role, processes, and effects of communication within the context of politics.

In 1985, the editors of *Political Communication Yearbook: 1984* noted that "more things are happening in the study, teaching, and practice of political communication than can be captured within the space limita-tions of the relatively few publications available."[8] In addition, they argued that the backgrounds of "those involved in the field [are] so varied and pluralist in outlook and approach, . . . it [is] a mistake to adhere slavishly to any set format in shaping the content."[9]

In agreement with this assessment of the area, Praeger established the series entitled "Praeger Studies in Political Communication." The series is open to all qualitative and quantitative methodologies as well as contemporary and historical studies. The key to characterizing the studies in the series is the focus on communication variables or activities within a political context or dimension.

This volume examines the gatekeeping function of the television net-works in America. From a historical perspective, the author traces the evolving role of the networks as arbiters of political access. Through the system, presidents have enjoyed unparalleled access to the American people while Members of Congress and opposition leaders have largely been ignored. Today, with declining audiences and profit, the networks can only provide a forum of an interested few. As a result, Professor Foote argues that this change profoundly affects the role of broadcasting networks and the balance of political power in America.

Without doubt, this book is an important contribution to political communication and media studies. Rather than focusing on a single event or broadcast element, the study is the first to look at the role of networks in altering the balance of power between the Presidency and Congress. Clearly the impact of television upon American politics goes beyond network news, political advertising, and campaign coverage. The very structure of our communication systems influences the nature of our political process. One becomes even more sensitized, upon read-ing the book, to the symbiotic relationship between television and pol-itics in America. The perspective of the book informs us of the past and raises serious questions about the future.

I am, without shame or modesty, a fan of the series. The joy of serving as its editor is in participating in the dialogue of the field of political communication and in reading the contributors' works. I invite you to join me.

—Robert E. Denton, Jr.

## NOTES

1. See for example, Robert E. Denton, Jr., *The Symbolic Dimensions of the American Presidency* (Prospect Heights, Ill.: Waveland Press, 1981); Robert E. Denton, Jr., and Gary Woodward, *Political Communication in America* (New York: Praeger, 1985); and Robert E. Denton, Jr., and Dan Hahn, *Presidential Communication* (New York: Praeger, 1986).

2. Aristotle, *The Politics of Aristotle*, trans. Ernest Barker (New York: Oxford University Press, 1970), p. 5.

3. Aristotle, *Rhetoric*, trans. Rhys Roberts (New York: Modern Library, 1954), p. 22.

4. Dan Nimmo and Keith Sanders, "Introduction: The Emergence of Political Communication as a Field," *Handbook of Political Communication*, eds. Dan Nimmo and Keith Sanders (Beverly Hills, Calif.: Sage, 1981), pp. 12–15.

5. Nimmo and Sanders, "Introduction," p. 15.

6. Nimmo and Sanders, "Introduction," pp. 16–27.

7. Keith Sanders, Lynda Kaid, and Dan Nimmo, eds., *Political Communication Yearbook: 1984* (Carbondale, Ill.: Southern Illinois University Press, 1985), p. 284.

8. Sanders et al., *Political Communication*, p. xiv.

9. Sanders et al., *Political Communication*, p. xiv.

# Acknowledgments

When I became press secretary to Speaker of the House Carl Albert in 1972, I was dismayed that the opposition in Congress was in such an overwhelmingly inferior position to the President on network television. When the President wanted time to speak to the American people, all he had to do was ask; the opposition frequently asked but rarely received. I wondered how such a gross disparity could become an accepted practice in our American system.

In 1973, Newton Minow, Lee Mitchell, and John Bartlow Martin brought the presidential-opposition access problem into public focus with their insightful book *Presidential Television*. Minow and his colleagues forcefully argued that the gross imbalance in television coverage favored the President at the expense of the congressional opposition and created an unhealthy trend in our tripartite system of government.

In 1975, I suggested that Speaker Albert ask the Congressional Research Service of the Library of Congress to document further the President's advantage in network television access. That report, released in 1976, was prepared by a bright and dedicated young analyst in the Government division named Steve Rutkus. Eight years later, when Speaker O'Neill was experiencing the same frustration with network access as Speaker Albert, Steve Rutkus wrote another report that showed how badly the congressional opposition had fared in comparison with Presidents on network television.

By the time Rutkus was preparing his second report, I had returned to Capitol Hill as Administrative Assistant to Congressman Dave McCurdy. When I left for a teaching job at Cornell in 1983, Steve Rutkus and I decided to work jointly on a more extensive examination of the opposition access question. While we eventually decided to work in-dependently on separate projects, much of this book had its roots in our initial collaboration. I have tried to credit Steve's contributions throughout the manuscript, but these brief references do not do him justice. Steve Rutkus' imprint on this book is strong and pervasive and he understands the issue far better than anyone.

I want to thank the many people at Southern Illinois and Cornell Universities who have helped me with this project. I have been fortunate to have had extraordinarily talented research assistants whose dedication to this project has at times exceeded my own. The contributions of Cary O'Dell, Jane Biddle Cahill, and Janet Smith have been immeasurable. Likewise, I have had strong office support from Teri Davis, Rose Thorne, Lynn Pierson, Joan Payton, Marsha Leonard, and Nancy Hannula. I am indebted to department chairs Roy Colle and Don Schwartz at Cornell and Dean Keith Sanders at SIU for research assistant support and to Speaker Albert and Congressman Dave McCurdy who provided me with a bird's-eye view of the legislative process.

I am deeply grateful to Kathryn Koldehoff who injected her consid-erable talents into this project by editing the manuscript before it went to the publisher. I also gained a great deal from Kathleen Hall Jamieson, John Weisman, and David Kenney's constructive suggestions. I am thankful to the series editor Robert Denton and Praeger editor Alison Bricken who have been extremely supportive of me and my work.

Finally, I want to thank my family and friends for enduring me during this obsessive quest. My wife Jody's sacrifices on behalf of this effort have been unlimited, and I appreciate her love and encouragement. While my young children Jackson and Jan had no idea what I have been doing these past few years, their smiling faces at the end of the day propelled me to the finish.

# Abbreviations

| | |
|---|---|
| ABC | American Broadcasting Company |
| ACLU | American Civil Liberties Union |
| AP | Associated Press |
| C-SPAN | Cable Satellite Public Affairs Network |
| CBS | Columbia Broadcasting System |
| CNN | Cable News Network |
| CONUS | Continental U.S. |
| CRS | Congressional Research Service |
| DNC | Democratic National Committee |
| FCC | Federal Communications Commission |
| FRC | Federal Radio Commission |
| HUT | Houses Using Television |
| INS | International News Service |
| MFDP | Mississippi Freedom Democratic Party |
| MTV | Music Television |
| MUTUAL | Mutual Broadcasting System |
| NAB | National Association of Broadcasters |
| NBC | National Broadcasting Company |
| RNC | Republican National Committee |
| TNT | Turner Network Television |
| UIB | United Independent Broadcasters |
| UP | United Press |
| VCR | Video Cassette Recorder |

# Introduction

On July 27, 1981, Ronald Reagan was in the middle of one of the biggest fights of his political career—asking Congress for record budget cuts and $750 billion in tax cuts. He had entertained congressmen and senators at the White House and summoned them by helicopter to Camp David. Still, he felt he needed a more powerful approach to guarantee support of his proposals. Accompanied by only a few technicians and staff members, Ronald Reagan entered the Oval Office, looked into the network pool camera, and for 22 minutes talked directly to 60 million Americans.[1] At the climax of his speech, the President appealed directly to the voters to help him:

During recent months many of you have asked what you can do to help make America strong again. I urge you again to contact your Senators and Congressmen. Tell them of your support for this bipartisan proposal. Tell them you believe this is an unequalled opportunity to help return America to prosperity and make government again the servant of the people.[2]

Immediately, telephones buzzed on Capital Hill as callers rallied behind the President. *Broadcasting* magazine reported that constituents jammed the Capital switchboard with 39,000 incoming phone calls, double the normal traffic. Western Union recorded four times the normal flow of telegrams to Congress. The White House received 3,830 telephone calls, all but 709 of them supporting the President.[3] Three days later, Ronald Reagan won a major legislative victory few had thought possible.

The President's instantaneous access to the American people was made possible through the courtesy of the three commercial television networks who temporarily swept aside their prime time programming on hundreds of affiliated stations throughout the nation. The tax and budget message was like a free, prime time, program-length commercial almost as long as the evening news. Unlike network news, however, the editorial control of this program rested with the President. There would be no reporters or editors reducing Ronald Reagan's remarks to thin snippets on the evening news. With such a propitious format at his disposal, President Reagan was quick to credit television for much of his early legislative success, saying he doubted if he "could have had those [victories] without it."[4]

While President Reagan was basking in the glory of his budget victory, the Democrats in Congress were helpless. ABC, CBS, and NBC had aired the Democrat's official reply at three different times on three different days in their weakest time periods, downgrading the response to a TV throwaway. The President could get immediate access to millions of Americans at will, but the opposition in Congress had to struggle for even the most modest coverage.

Through this control of political communications which has spanned every Administration since Herbert Hoover, the networks became a powerful, pervasive force in the political system, deciding access questions that impacted political visibility and stage-managing the appearances of political leaders. As the networks propelled the rise of automatic presidential access, government on the whole did little to question independent journalistic judgments or guide broadcasters in determining when to air presidential addresses or rebuttals to the President. Broadcasters were required by law or regulation to air informative programming on matters of public interest,[5] to provide "equal time" to candidates,[6] to devote a reasonable percentage of their broadcast time to the discussion of controversial issues,[7] and to afford in such discussion a reasonable opportunity for each side of the issue to be heard.[8] They were not explicitly required by law to afford airtime to Presidents or any other governmental spokespersons.

While other countries like Britain established clear-cut rules governing the government-broadcaster relationship and mandated automatic access for the opposition, few American leaders ever questioned the unique and powerful role three private enterprises played in shaping their political access. The networks were free to exercise their own judgment regardless of the consequences for our political system. Eventually, this role of arbiters of political access gave the networks great power and placed them at the apex of the American political communication system.

This book explains the history, structure, and efficacy of the network transmission system controlled by ABC, CBS, and NBC which has delivered political voices to the American people for more than 60 years. It is a system which has brought unprecedented exposure to twentieth century Presidents and allowed them to dramatically expand their use of the "bully pulpit." Yet, it is also a system which has discriminated consistently against the opposition in Congress, and has become vulnerable to economic pressures within the broadcasting industry. Most recently, it has been a system on the edge of decline hurt by defecting audiences and advertisers, raising questions as to whether this privately-owned transmission system which has totally dominated political communication during the current century can survive into the next.

Because the high stakes issues surrounding the networks' control of the political access system have been intensively partisan, there has been little incentive for an objective examination of the subject. Both political parties at one time or another have argued passionately for reform that would expand their opposition access; yet, their voices were suddenly muted after taking control of the White House. This study transcends partisan interests to historically examine the network system beginning with the 1920s and carrying through to the beginning of the Bush Administration. It explains why the system has not worked well for either party and suggests reform.

The networks' role as arbiters of access has evolved in three phases.[9] The first phase roughly coincided with the "age of radio," from the early 1930s to the late 1940s, when the networks operated as trustees of a massive public forum in which many voices were heard. Although the networks were commercial enterprises, a significant part of network time remained unsponsored. Much of this unsponsored time was devoted to "public affairs"—to speeches by public figures and to discussions of the issues of the day. In these programs, the networks exercised benign, usually unrestrictive supervision over political access although an aversion to automatic opposition rebuttals to presidential speeches existed even in the early days.

With the advent of television broadcasting, the networks entered a second phase running from the early 1950s through the 1970s. Unlike network radio which served as a public forum available to many, the new video medium quickly became a closed vehicle committed chiefly to entertainment programs. As the public forum component began to disappear, network television journalism supplanted it as the means for presenting public affairs to national audiences.

While relatively small and untested in the 1950s, network news organizations emerged as a major force in the 1960s. They became the principal force determining the degree of access which Presidents and other public figures would have to the American people. In this second phase, the networks assumed a role almost completely journalistic. In live or other special events broadcasts, they largely ignored the pleas of the opposition for access, and thus magnified the President's stature vis-à-vis Congress and the opposition party, much more than they had during the "age of radio."

In a third phase spanning from 1981 to the present, economic factors played a larger role in the political access system as the news divisions felt greater pressure to contribute to the parent network's profitability. While the amount of access changed little, the arguments between the news and entertainment divisions over whether it should be granted became intense.

Despite the economic pressure, the networks, in an effort to counterbalance a popular President, gave the Democratic leadership in Congress more simultaneous airtime than they did in the Johnson, Nixon, Ford, and Carter Administrations combined. Shortened opposition broadcasts became a regular part of network journalism's approach to political broadcasting though access was by no means automatic.

As the twenty-first century approached, the networks, faced with declining advertising, profits, audiences, and prestige, were on the brink of a fourth phase in which new coverage models for political access would not be dominated by the three commercial television networks. A new political communication order was developing in which diverse entertainment offerings which fragmented audiences would deny a President the ability to speak simultaneously to a majority of the citizenry. The differences between the networks providing a forum which allowed a President to reach out to nearly all the people and one where he could reach only an interested few would be significant. Such a change could profoundly affect not only the role of the broadcasting networks but the balance of political power as well.

# Television Access
# and Political Power

*Chapter 1*

# Radio: Setting the Precedent

On June 21, 1923, when President Harding stepped to the microphone to deliver a speech on "The World Court" from St. Louis as part of his tour of the western United States, he spoke not just for the citizens of St. Louis, but for those in Washington and New York as well. This was the first time that a chain or network of radio stations had been assembled to carry a message simultaneously to several parts of the Nation. The speech was heard in St. Louis over KSD and in New York and Washington over AT&T stations WEAF and WCAP. Perhaps a million Americans heard the President speak, more than any President had reached before.[1] No longer was a President bound by the flatness of daily newspaper coverage or the geographical limitations of single-station radio coverage; he now had the potential to speak to the entire electorate at once, a power that would enlarge the "bully pulpit" beyond any expectation of the day. With a single flip of the switch, broadcasters could help a President rise above his adversaries in the Congress and go directly to the people.

The chain of stations assembled for the Harding speech signaled a new era in broadcasting which would profoundly change the structure of radio and television in America. The American concept of broadcasting was built on localism; individual stations were to air their own home-grown programming and each was to have its own distinctive sound. Yet, America was more than a neatly packaged collection of local autonomous entities. It was a nation with strong national interests which had united to fight a terrible World War and whose Federal Government was growing larger and more powerful. In this environment, America was poised for a broadcasting service that could bring events instantly and simultaneously into living rooms throughout the Nation.

A strong national broadcasting system contributed to a strong presidency. A politician whose voice commanded attention in every corner of such a vast land simultaneously could build a strong national constituency. Conversely, a strong presidency contributed to a strong national broadcasting system. Presidential speeches created a demand and the President provided one of the few sources of programming that could unite American interests. The American people were eager to hear their national leader over the fascinating new medium of radio, and broadcasters were pleased to be the sole purveyor of this important communication initiative. Broadcasters could also use the presidency as a springboard for building and maintaining a network of radio stations before the American people ever saw a need for such a strong national system. Given this reality, it was not surprising that presidential speeches played benchmark roles in practically every stage of early network broadcasting.

Less than half century after those early presidential broadcasts, the television networks would rival governmental institutions in their influence over public opinion. By providing Presidents with this vast national forum, broadcasters bolstered their own prestige and carved a niche for themselves that would eventually make them the dominant political communication medium. Yet, the broadcasters' political entree coincided so closely with their own fragile development, that little forethought or reflection was given to the impact their actions might have on the electorate or the political system. Spontaneous acts were establishing a system and setting precedents which would guide policy for half a century and unwittingly provide Presidents with an even greater communications advantage over the congressional opposition.

## SUCCESSFUL EXPERIMENTS IN NETWORKING

After the success of his first attempt at chain broadcasting in St. Louis, President Harding tried another in Kansas City and had scheduled still another big speech on July 31st. For the occasion, AT&T assembled its first coast to coast link-up stretching from San Francisco to New York. Radio had become such an important part of President Harding's western tour that he installed a powerful radio transmitter in his railroad car to give him a mobile broadcasting studio.

While enchanted by radio, Harding fell back on the tried and tested but rough and grueling routine of nationwide personal appearances as his mainstay of presidential communication. It may have contributed to his death. Exhausted from his extensive cross-country and Alaskan journey, President Harding fell ill before he could make his end of July coast to coast radio speech from San Francisco. Three days later, the President was dead, but the idea of chain broadcasting lived on.

Within a few days after Harding's death, the National Association of Broadcasters (NAB) was proposing to the new President, Calvin Coolidge, that he substitute radio addresses for public appearances to conserve his health and reach a wider audience.[2] By the end of 1923, as the 1924 campaign approached, President Coolidge heeded the NAB's advice and took to the airwaves regularly. When Calvin Coolidge spoke to Congress at the end of the year, AT&T assembled a chain of seven stations to carry the speech.[3] The President followed that with five additional nationally broadcast addresses. The 1924 party conventions reached an estimated 25 million and the subsequent campaign provided abundant opportunities for chain broadcasting.[4]

While the NAB was eager to promote political broadcasting, a small group of broadcasters questioned whether politicians should be turned loose without any consideration of the other side. At the first convention of the NAB in October 1923, John Shepard III of WNAC proposed that a political party applying for airtime be required to give comparable time to a speaker from the opposing party. The NAB accepted the measure and followed these "equal time" ground rules during the 1924 campaign.[5] Presidential speeches however, were not considered political except during campaigns and were not subjected to any right of reply mechanism until the campaign actually started. Still, voices were raised early to warn of the dangers of a one-sided political dialogue in which the party and congressional opposition had no standing.

By 1924, the proponents of chain broadcasting had realized that politics was the perfect bait to lure America into a permanent national system of broadcasting. The presidential election campaign that year provided ample opportunities for demonstrating the virtues of chain broadcasting. AT&T was poised to erect a permanent network of stations and believed that political speeches were an excellent way to ensure frequent use of a system that could reach 78 percent of the nation's purchasing power through the top 24 markets.[6]

The closer the fledgling broadcasting industry could bring itself to the presidency, the higher status it could bring to itself. Thus, in the early days there was no concern for the newsworthiness of presidential addresses. The broadcasters saw presidential broadcasting as a means of providing a public service and basking in the prestige of the presidency. Given the open-ended invitation extended early on to Presidents by broadcasters, it is no wonder that twentieth century Presidents since Harding have regarded their access as a right of the office.

The *New York Times* reported in 1924 that "It is a source of wonder to many listeners how a speaker can sit in the White House or stand before Congress and have his voice simultaneously enter the ether over Washington, New York and Providence."[7] The inauguration of Calvin Coolidge on March 4, 1925, showed how far chain broadcasting had come in less than two years. On that day, President Coolidge reached at least 15 million Americans over a hookup of 21 stations from coast to coast. Listeners sat spellbound to hear Presidential speech come to life. The transmission was so clear that people could hear rustling paper as the new President turned the pages of his text.

The inaugural coverage was so successful that talk circulated about broadcasting sessions of Congress. Meanwhile, "Silent Cal" Coolidge began speaking an average of 9,000 words a month over radio. Although his speeches lacked persuasive content, he was credited with being a strong and effective radio performer.[8] Soon, stations linked through chain broadcasting became known as prestige stations. While they paid a premium for the luxury of being included on the elite AT&T hookup, these special stations soon started towering over their competition as the benefits of chain broadcasting became obvious. The RCA Board of Directors met in January 1926, to approve the idea of a new national network in which RCA would own half, General Electric 30 percent, and Westinghouse 20 percent. The new venture would lease AT&T's wire under a long-term contract. On September 9th, the National Broadcasting Company (NBC) was incorporated. Four days later, it proclaimed its vision for network broadcasting in full-page newspaper advertisements saying, "The purpose of that company will be to provide the best programs available for broadcasting in the United States."[9]

The NBC advertisement also said that the new network "hoped that arrangements may be made so that every event of national importance may be broadcast widely throughout the United States." Since this announcement predated the rise of media events by several years, one can infer that "events of national importance" meant, to a large extent, politics. And, politics on a national scale was dominated by the President. Presidential addresses, congressional addresses, party conventions, and election results would provide the grist for the network mills, but the President was clearly the star attraction on which a national audience could be built. Without the President, the networks would sacrifice their chief draw.

On November 15, 1926, NBC premiered with a grand evening of live entertainment broadcast from the Waldorf-Astoria hotel in New York City. The event was a proper coming out for the nation's first broadcasting network which wanted to cultivate the right image. The 1,000 invited guests from the social register of New York, including Charles Lindbergh and Amelia Earhart, provided just the right backdrop, a sign that this was not just another corporation showing its product. This was the birth of a great institution that would rival other great American institutions. Because it provided the link that united the political communication system of the Nation, this corporation had a special, noble role which no other corporation could perform. It deserved to have the attention of every political figure beginning with the President of the United States.[10]

An estimated two million of the five million American homes equipped with radios heard NBC's first broadcast from 21 charter stations and four others. Four months later, NBC had two networks—a "red" with 25 stations and a "blue" with six affiliates. Within a year, the number of NBC stations had increased to 48.[11]

The years 1927 and 1928 were big ones for network broadcasting. In 1927, NBC covered Lindbergh's arrival in Washington after his historic transatlantic flight to Paris, and 30 million people heard President Coolidge present Lindbergh with the Distinguished Flying Cross.[12] NBC also established a west coast regional network which enhanced its ability to become a truly national network. In 1928, President Coolidge and NBC joined forces to present the first international broadcast as the President opened a Pan American conference in Havana. On December 23, 1928, regular coast to coast network service began on NBC, offering Presidents routine access to a truly national audience.[13]

While NBC had assembled an impressive list of national affiliates on paper, only a few stations cleared most programs. When cabinet members, senators, and congressmen spoke they often received little more than regional coverage. Only the President could regularly command the attention to bind affiliates together nationwide. Forty-two stations carried Coolidge's Washington's Birthday address in the House of Representatives and a full network also broadcast his Memorial Day speech that same year, further reinforcing the network dependence on presidential broadcasting.[14]

NBC received a competitor in April, 1927 when 11 stations banded together under the auspices of the United Independent Broadcasters (UIB) to form the Columbia Phonograph Broadcasting System. When the company began broadcasting in September, it had 16 stations. UIB was faltering badly when William Paley, with the help of his father's Congress Cigar Company, bought half of the network's stock. On January 23, 1929, the 28–station network became the Columbia Broadcasting System (CBS). It quickly grew to 49 affiliates in 42 cities.[15] Under Paley's leadership, the network eventually challenged NBC's dominance and prospered. By 1942, CBS would have 119 affiliates providing primary coverage to 30.3 million families.[16]

## THE DEMISE OF LOCALISM

As CBS and NBC spread their wings across the nation, the principle of localism faded fast. Every local station may have had its own transmitter and its own staff, but listeners soon wanted to hear the same singer and the same comedian that other local stations were carrying hundreds of miles away. Broadcasting historian Eric Barnouw wrote that listeners considered the move towards networking a "logical, rational step, readily accepted," but one that would have far-reaching implications for the future of broadcasting and politics as well.[17]

The advent of network broadcasting created a national message for a national audience. As the *New York Times* observed in 1928, "they [politicians] can no longer promise the western farmer higher prices for wheat without arousing the eastern factory population against higher bread prices."[18] Even in the early days it was clear that broadcasting's role in politics would be largely a national one; radio would be the cement that would create a national constituency.

Many in Washington saw how networks would change the face of American broadcasting and feared that RCA with its new radio empire would create a "radio trust" that would dominate discussion of ideas.[19] Rather than try to regulate RCA directly, Congress chose to reinforce the notion of localism which was already lost. In doing so, Congress played into the networks' hands.

Congress' refusal to deal with the ramifications of network growth made the Radio Act of 1927 obsolete before it was enacted. Naturally, anyone interested in chain broadcasting had a vested interest in perpetuating the anachronistic localism model. In a last-minute postscript, the Senate did add a sentence authorizing the Federal Radio Commission (FRC) to make "special regulations applicable to radio stations engaged in chain broadcasting," but it was an anemic effort. Congress had placed its bets on wishing the network problem away.[20]

Even though the Radio Act of 1927 ignored the trend toward network broadcasting, it did put broadcasters in a regulatory harness, conveyed legitimacy on a new industry, and cemented a close tie between government and broadcasting. The forthcoming Federal Communications Act of 1934 would rely in the end on the licensee to decide what was good for the public, greatly mitigating the problems broadcasters would face as a regulated industry.

In an environment where public service was paramount and advertising and economics were secondary, serving as a transmission belt for government communication was a natural and proper thing for a network to do. Therefore, when CBS decided to broadcast the 1928 political conventions, it cast the decision in terms of an "institutional service" for the American people and refused to seek a sponsor. Because the networks did not yet have news departments, public service rather than newsworthiness drove decision-making.

NBC took its "public trustee" cues seriously early on, behaving like an important and prestigious national institution rivaling government, religion, business, and education. NBC appointed a blue ribbon Advisory Committee whose members Barnouw described as "outshining any presidential cabinet of modern times" to show how seriously and conscientiously NBC would pursue its goal of linking the American people together through information and entertainment.

NBC President Merlin Aylesworth said that because of "the enormous power concentrated in the hands of a few men controlling a vast network," the work of the Advisory Committee was "a matter for the consideration of statesmen."[21] While such an idealistic exercise might have seemed silly for any other American corporation to undertake, network broadcasters believed they were called to a higher purpose. They had a legitimate right to overlay part of the governmental regulatory facade on their own for-profit foundation. An advisory committee might not only absorb much of the public criticism directed towards the network but enlarge NBC's aura as a powerful and legitimate American institution as well.

The NBC Advisory Committee did little, but it was an important symbol of network prestige. This was a first effort at the kind of image polishing that Frank Stanton and William Paley of CBS would refine into an art in later years. If the networks were to head off stifling government regulation and be allowed to retain their valuable frequencies, they would have to behave like pseudo governmental institutions retaining a strong public service commitment and an aura of responsible institutional power. The NBC Advisory Council, therefore, performed well in concentrating the network's image as a high-minded, public-spirited organization while the parent corporation was quickly overwhelming American broadcasting and amassing huge profits.

## NETWORK RELIANCE

By the time Herbert Hoover took his presidential oath in 1929, two powerful broadcasting companies supporting three national networks were flourishing. The depression notwithstanding, NBC's gross sales revenues leaped from $3.8 million in 1927 to $26.5 million in 1932. In 1928, CBS lost $179,000, but the next year it earned nearly half a million dollars. CBS earned $2.35 million in profits in 1931 and $2.27 million in 1934.[22]

Radio was able to amass huge profits partly because its growth was supported by a sympathetic Federal Government. As Secretary of Commerce, Herbert Hoover had championed broadcasting and had shepherded radio through its early years. He made one of the earliest radio speeches in January 1921, and demanded that private companies control American broadcasting. He rejected the European model of taxing receivers in favor of an advertising revenue base for stations and was said to favor the big stations over smaller ones. With such a background, Hoover was naturally sympathetic to network broadcasting when he became President.

Commercial broadcasting and its network offspring had become so firmly entrenched by the time President Hoover took office that it seemed almost un-American for Senator Gerald Nye in 1929 to propose that the government erect a super station in Washington to broadcast congressional debates, campaign statements, and other governmental messages. Moreover, the Nye proposal would have been technologically impossible without the government having a network of its own. Engineers estimated that it would take at least eight 10–kilowatt and five 5–kilowatt transmitters and 23 stations linked together to cover the country. The whole project would have cost more than $3 million to build and more than $1 million to maintain. Even supporters of the Nye resolution admitted it would be much cheaper for Congress to buy time from the networks than to build its own superstation.

Congressmen were also perceptive enough to appreciate the advantage of a large ready-made network audience over a government station offering no entertainment lead-in. The only station the Federal Government owned, NAA in Arlington, Virginia, had very few listeners.[23] The commercial radio networks were the only viable alternatives for political communication. Furthermore, the idea of an official broadcasting station was rendered unnecessary by the generosity of the networks which broadcast more than 100 free speeches on legislation by Members of Congress in 1929 alone. Every piece of important legislation merited a program featuring at least one congressman.

Meanwhile, President Hoover tried to keep up with his legislative counterparts by speaking on radio ten times during 1929 and 27 times the following year. By the end of 1930, he had equaled the number of talks Coolidge gave during his entire Administration.[24] President Hoover's cabinet reinforced the Administration's line by giving even more radio talks.[25] In 1929, NBC devoted from five to 25 hours per week to presidential speeches, reports on national events, and addresses by public figures. By 1930, the government was using 450 hours of broadcasting time on NBC alone.[26]

Despite his unmatched experience on the air, President Hoover was a reluctant and not particularly gifted participant in the broadcasting arena. Aides pushed him into making radio speeches. The President also had the unenviable task of selling an economic program that the American public did not want. Hoover's speeches progressively brought diminishing returns. Soon, everyone realized broadcasting was a two-edged sword; it could not only help elevate Presidents but help bury them as well. Broadcasting worked its magic best when the potential for persuasion and good feeling were at a peak, a fact not lost on Hoover's successor.

Regardless of the communication skills of the President, the networks seemed satisfied to provide time. There was, after all, substantial prestige attached to transmitting the voice of the President of the United States to the American people. Former CBS President Frank Stanton said the networks would often "fall all over themselves" to broadcast the President "because it was a recognition of radio's place in the scheme of things." Because the networks did not have serious news departments until the mid–1930s, it was important to make themselves as important as they could in the world of public affairs, and the President was their chief vehicle.[27]

## THE BIRTH OF NETWORK NEWS

Americans generally associated the networks not with journalism but with entertainment programming. The networks were, by their own definition, entertainment vehicles and were therefore not seen as serious threats to newspapers and political figures. Still, the new networks found themselves drawn willy-nilly into the public affairs arena by carrying presidential and congressional speeches as a public service.

In 1929, publicity departments controlled non-entertainment programming. Eventually, announcers and commentators entered the picture. For the Hoover inauguration, both networks prepared elaborate coverage of inaugural events. The public expected full-scale coverage, and politics quickly became a mainstay of network information programming.

News and public relations made strange bedfellows. The same people who unabashedly touted the company's achievements arranged broadcasts of national interest and fed news bulletins to the network. Yet, the arrangement had some utility. Putting a President of the United States on the air was a perfect promotion of the network. Live radio speeches propelled the networks into a superior position over their newspaper competitors. The press was relegated to amplifying an event which most of their readers had heard live hours before.

CBS took a giant step toward permanent news coverage when William Paley hired Edward Klauber in 1929. Klauber, a stern man with high journalistic standards, had been a night city editor for the *New York Times*. When he became Executive Vice-President of CBS, Klauber immediately went about bringing order to and setting standards for the network's ragtag news operation. Klauber's first actions included hiring Paul White from the United Press to be Director of Public Affairs and Special Events.[28]

By the early 1930s, the networks were already battling with each other for public affairs dominance. When NBC refused to interrupt entertainment programming for news bulletins except presidential speeches, CBS took advantage of the opportunity, claiming to beat NBC on a story by 20 to 30 minutes. By April 1931, CBS was so confident that it proclaimed itself the "dominant news network." It was beaming at least one major event per week to the nation.

Setting a trend that continues today, network news gravitated towards Washington. From one end of Pennsylvania Avenue to the other, the government churned out information for the networks. Government proceedings were abundant, easily accessible, and cheap to cover. With their Washington resources on the rise, the networks developed an insatiable appetite for presidential speeches and drew the President closer to the microphones, not vice versa. The *New York Times* claimed the networks would "vie with each other to gain the distinction of being the first to put a noted person on the air."[29] CBS announced early in May 1932 that it would carry three Hoover addresses later that month.[30] Taking the competitive challenge, NBC quickly announced it would not only carry the three Hoover addresses but add four other presidential speeches scheduled for May and June.[31] Such intramural leapfrogging sent the networks compulsively down the path of automatic presidential access.

During the 1932 campaign, broadcasting clearly showed its impressive advantage over print competitors by airing election results instantaneously to the entire nation, dooming the newspaper "election specials" on which the electorate had previously relied. The growth of news broadcasting on the networks was not lost on concerned editors. The networks were now clearly a threat.

The newspapers were particularly annoyed that the networks were building their newscasts largely on stories the newspapers had gathered and channeled into the wire services. In April 1933, the Associated Press (AP) voted to cutoff news to the networks. Stations owned by AP newspaper subscribers would get the AP service for a fee, but the networks would get nothing. The United Press (UP) and the International News Service (INS) soon followed their competitor's lead. Many newspapers dropped their listings of radio programs.[32]

Designed to run the networks out of the news business, the wire service sanctions actually had the opposite effect. The absence of easy news forced the networks to develop an infrastructure that would later become a worldwide journalistic empire. CBS' news efforts were boosted when General Mills offered to underwrite half the cost of a new Columbia News Service. Paul White opened bureaus around the country and recruited stringers. The news service soon offered scheduled news programs three times each day at 12:00, 4:30, and 11:00 P.M.[33]

During the wire service boycott, the networks realized that broadcasting held a special attraction for sources. Abe Schechter, who is credited with starting NBC's network news department, discovered that practically any American would give NBC an interview. Meanwhile, Paul White's cadre of "stringers" poised to phone in news stories from anywhere in the Nation proved to be an effective grass roots newsgathering foundation. Eventually, the networks were strong enough to force the wire services to resume selling their product to all broadcasters, but not before paying a price.[34] In what was known as the "Biltmore Agreement," the networks pledged to run no story longer than 30 words and to broadcast no more than two 5–minute newscasts each day. Fortunately for CBS and NBC, the agreement began to unravel almost immediately, and the networks found loopholes to expand their news coverage.[35]

The boycott had made CBS News stronger under Paul White and Edward Klauber's leadership and had strengthened their position over the "music box" network. NBC, however, eventually followed CBS' lead by creating a News and Special Events Division in 1936.[36] That year, George Henry Payne, a member of the Federal Communications Commission (FCC), observed that in only 15 years, radio "has achieved the position of having more listeners than the press has readers, although the press has been in existence for 500 years."[37]

## A NETWORK STAR IS BORN

Until Franklin Roosevelt became President, the networks were more captivated by the presidency than by any particular occupant of the office. The networks clung tightly to FDR's rising star and used his engaging personality on the airwaves to enhance their own status. CBS Commentator Frederic William Wile was one of the first at the networks to realize how high a priority Roosevelt placed on broadcasting. Wile emerged from a talk with the President-elect predicting that the new President would be "highly radio-minded," causing Washington to become more "radio conscious" and the American people to become more conscious of Washington.[38]

Following his success in using radio to push a recalcitrant New York legislature into action, Roosevelt told Wile that he expected to request time frequently. The new President's fascination with radio was surpassed only by the networks' fascination with him. Merlin Aylesworth, president of NBC, not wanting to miss a piece of presidential action, approached Roosevelt before he was inaugurated to offer him airtime on a regular basis. While FDR was tempted by the alluring network offer, he rejected it. The President feared overexposure and preferred to use the airwaves according to his own timing and his own priorities.[39]

Starting with his first Inaugural Address in which he told Americans the only thing they had to fear was "fear itself," the new President proved himself to be an exceptional communicator. The networks quickly realized that Roosevelt had different motivations for using radio than had his predecessors. To him, the medium was no longer a novelty for sending ceremonial greetings; it was a vital tool for persuasion. President Roosevelt used all the intimacy and directness radio could offer to rally support for his policies. Eight days after being sworn in, FDR put radio to the test. Eschewing his fiery and strained campaign oratory, Roosevelt crafted a subdued, conversational style exclusively for radio. He spoke calmly and intimately, and above all, persuasively.

As more "fireside chats" poured out of the White House, the American people responded favorably. FDR became a friend and a neighbor who could captivate a nation and develop a truly national constituency. When FDR came to office, one employee could handle all the White House mail. By March 1933, a half million letters sent the White House scrambling to hire additional staff.[40]

Franklin Roosevelt presented only 28 "fireside chats" during his four terms, but they had an extraordinary impact on a nation seeking desperately to pull itself out of depression and to win a world war. He boosted his radio speeches' appeal by making them during the "primest" of prime time (between 9:00 and 11:00 PM, EST) on weekdays when families were home together.[41] Roosevelt's political advisor Jim Farley said that radio could wash away the most harmful effects once "the reassuring voice of the President of the United States started coming through the ether into the living room."[42]

Through the Roosevelt Administration, the networks were attracting huge audiences and revenues were soaring in the midst of the depression. Popular prime time entertainment programs were developing a dedicated following which relieved FDR of the responsibility of luring Americans to their radios. The networks' popularity thus helped Presidents reach not only politically active, information-seeking listeners but the more politically inactive, passive listeners as well. The President's challenge was to mobilize this huge, ready-made national audience, a challenge made easier by America's eagerness to listen to someone offering economic hope in the midst of depression.

FDR took advantage of his platform to persuade voters to support him and his programs. Later in the century, broadcasting executives would chafe at a President using the airwaves solely to persuade voters or Members of Congress to support a particular program, but there was no such resentment of Roosevelt. On the contrary, broadcasting executives delighted in the drama and excitement Roosevelt created. Merlin Aylesworth of NBC effusively wrote President Roosevelt that "I can honestly say that I have never known a public official to use the radio with such intelligence."[43]

In his reply to Aylesworth, FDR noted what his successors also came to realize, that an address totally controlled by a President was far superior to daily journalism which Presidents could not control. As far as Roosevelt was concerned, radio speeches meant presidential control of a format in which the media could not "misrepresent or misquote."[44]

## THE LOYAL OPPOSITION REACTS

When President Roosevelt delivered his 1934 State of the Union Address he made sure that the primary audience for the nationally broadcast speech was the American people rather than congressmen and senators.[45] Naturally, the opposition party became nervous when a master communicator like Roosevelt went over their heads to the people. The Republicans soon realized that presidential domination of radio placed them in an untenable position. In 1934, Senator Arthur Robinson charged that the minority could not be heard because the Administration virtually controlled the airwaves. "American radio facilities are controlled by the government and are now practically monopolized by Administration propaganda. Difficulties are placed in the way of those who would use the air to oppose Administration policies. The Constitution itself is in danger and executive dictatorship is well on the way."[46] Senator Robinson introduced a resolution asking the Federal Radio Commission to consider government regulation to restrict broadcasters' use of the airwaves for presidential speeches, but the resolution had little support. Furthermore, the opposition was ill-prepared to rebut the President with a single voice even if they achieved access.

The opposition's grumbling in 1934 foreshadowed a half century of frustration and defeat. Precedents set during the first Roosevelt Administration would doom the opposition party in Congress to second-class status on the airwaves for years to come. As radio brought the presidency into sharper and sharper focus for the average American, it blurred perception of Congress as a coequal branch and made it more remote. While a congressman was once a citizen's most direct link to the government, Roosevelt pushed the presidency farther into that role during his 13 years in office.

As broadcasting became more sophisticated, it became more selective. By the 1930s, four networks in vigorous competition (the Mutual Broadcasting System [Mutual] had arrived on the scene in 1934) increased the incentives for more entertainment programming at the expense of sustaining public service programming—a move that meant fewer opportunities for congressional access. While broadcasters had been throwing time out to anyone in the 1920s, economic constraints changed their perspective. Advertisers were clamoring for prime time and were willing to pay a premium for it. This seductive call, according to media scholar Samuel Becker, made broadcasters "more reluctant to cancel sponsored programs to hear government officials." Becker said that while the networks could hardly refuse the President of the United States, it was "easier to refuse similar requests from Congressmen."[47]

## THE KLAUBER PRECEDENT

As Americans' appetite for information programming grew, the networks scrambled to cover every breaking story. Each time the networks carried a historic event, their prestige soared. This success also carried with it responsibility; more and more Americans were beginning to depend on the networks for information. Fortunately for CBS, Edward Klauber, with his journalistic background, had strong views about professionalism and wasted no time in educating his boss William Paley about the importance of fairness and objectivity in news coverage. Early on, Klauber instituted a training scheme to ensure a "Columbia standard of excellence" with "impersonal dignity and responsibility."[48]

By the mid–1930s, William Paley, under Klauber's tutelage, was testifying in Washington and giving speeches lauding the importance of fairness in news coverage. He asserted that CBS would never let any political party or point of view dominate all others. It was during this period of loud chest beating by Paley about fairness, however, that an important precedent for political broadcasting ran against the grain of any concept of fairness. The issue was whether the opposition party in Congress had a right to reply to the President; it surfaced before President Roosevelt's 1936 State of the Union Address.

Roosevelt scheduled his speech in prime time to achieve a maximum radio audience. The only other nighttime speech to the Congress was Woodrow Wilson's Declaration of War in 1917. Republican National Chairman Henry P. Fletcher perceptively realized that an evening speech, which would be heard by millions during an election year, was political dynamite. He knew that the Republicans had to press for rebuttal access to stay alive politically. Fletcher fired off telegrams to the presidents of NBC and CBS asking for time to respond the night after President Roosevelt spoke:

We are not objecting to the program outlined, but merely requesting an equal opportunity to place our case before the people with the same facilities, the same stations and potentially the same audience. . . .

Both sides of the vital current issues should be presented to the American jury for their own judgment. Unless the party in opposition be granted equal facilities, the dominant party can control the instrumentalities of communication in an effort to perpetuate itself in power.[49]

Within a day, NBC President Merlyn Aylesworth said his network would stand by its established policy of making time available to "responsible speakers" and would gladly give time to the Republican opposition. To him, balance required both sides to have a say on equal terms. Furthermore, competition for airtime was not yet that great, making it an easy decision economically as well.

Despite the logic of following past custom and the ease with which time for the opposition could be dispensed, CBS President William Paley said no to the Republican opposition. In a telegram to Chairman Fletcher, Paley said he did not think it was either "possible or wise for broadcasting to adopt a mathematical formula for fairness." He said such a formula would "disregard other demands of balanced programming and surrender into the keeping of others the exercise of editorial judgment and responsibility which we believe devolves upon us and which we gladly accept and seek to discharge."[50]

Paley was particularly upset that someone would try to dictate how he used "his" airtime. Giving the opposition time would be a "surrender" of his control. No matter that Paley's network was using the public's airwaves. In the end, Paley was the supreme commander. Nothing went on the air that he did not want on the air, including the highest ranking leaders of a coequal branch of government or the leaders of the chief opposition party. The network would exercise editorial judgment as "we believe befits the circumstances" and "we judge to be good broadcasting."[51] And, as Paley so proudly said in his telegram, this dictation of programming was a responsibility that he would "gladly accept and seek to discharge."

While William Paley could indeed do anything he wanted with "his" network, the opposition turndown was curious in that it violated his own self-proclaimed rule of fairness, "No discussion must ever be one-sided, so long as any qualified spokesman wishes to take the other side. The party in power must never dominate the air; nor any majority monopolize it. Minorities must always have a fair opportunity to express themselves."[52]

Although Paley would trumpet his fairness standard before Congress, guaranteed access for the opposition was out of the question. In the end, it was fairly easy for CBS to live with the double standard, which guaranteed airtime for the President whenever he wanted it but conveniently shut out the opposition. The network decision-making process was absolute. The Federal Communications Act of 1934, written just two years earlier, provided no guidance for this sensitive subject and gave the opposition no recourse. CBS was less than ten years old and already it was dictating the terms under which politicians could communicate with the American people. The Paley turndown of the opposition also brought into focus the economic pressures that were closing in on CBS.

Just a few years earlier, CBS would have welcomed practically anyone of political stature; now it was prepared to take a stand—to take something back for itself. Paley explained that now CBS had "many duties and responsibilities besides serving as a medium for the dissemination of political discussion," a subtle acknowledgement that the competition between profitable entertainment programming and unprofitable public service broadcasts was a real one.[53]

An automatic right of reply by the opposition would sap revenues and audience flows. William Paley made it clear that CBS wanted the prestige of carrying the President but it did not want the economic liability of carrying the "loyal opposition." Certainly a shrewd businessman like Paley understood the impact on the bottom line that a "mathematical formula" for opposition access would have on CBS over time. The network could justify losing money for the President on a permanent basis, but a blanket commitment to the opposition was too much. In the end, the dedication to fairness was not enough to override the fear of losing precious airtime and revenues.

According to David Halberstam's description of the 1936 controversy, CBS' Edward Klauber, speaking through Paley, was "setting a precedent that made it infinitely harder for potential presidential opponents and critics to reach the airwaves."[54] Halberstam said CBS' treatment of President Roosevelt's 1936 State of the Union message determined that broadcasting "would be to an uncommon degree, a presidential vehicle."[55]

What is remarkable is that CBS could make such a blanket judgment with no accountability to the government and with no tolerance for dissenting views. Yet, this decision seemed as logical and methodical as all the others that pushed a fledgling industry on its way into maturity. Surely there was no explicit desire either to envalue the presidency or to discriminate against the opposition. As Halberstam has written, CBS' actions formed a normal progression:

It seemed so natural at first: the President wanted to go on radio, the nation wanted to hear him, the networks themselves were delighted to be the conduit, it made their role more prestigious. Though everyone agreed that the American people really wanted to hear the President and thus he was speaking as a national leader and not simply as a politician, the ugly disturbing question always remained. At what point was the President speaking in a national emergency (in this case the Depression), and at what point was he just a very shrewd professional politician using both this new device and the nation's trauma to strengthen his own domestic political position? Was he a President or a politician? Where did you draw the line, and who could draw it, and who if anyone was permitted to answer him.[56]

With less and less access to the most formidable means of mass communication, the opposition silently watched its role in American politics diminish as the President's soared. The Republicans would put up a spirited fight during the Roosevelt Administration, but few would hear them and they would never achieve the access they sought. The actions of William Paley and Edward Klauber, while not causing the opposition's communications problems, did nothing to solve them.


## OPPOSITION AFTERSHOCKS

Less than two weeks after the State of the Union flap, the Republicans jumped into another controversy with the networks. Both CBS and NBC refused to broadcast a series of Republican skits entitled "Liberty at the Crossroads," but radio station WGN, owned by the *Chicago Tribune* and affiliated with Mutual, did. Harrison Spangler, director of the Western division of the Republican National Committee, praised WGN as one of the "great many independent radio stations in America which are not yet dominated and coerced through the great monopolistic chains, which in turn are dominated and coerced by the Roosevelt and Farley regime in Washington."[57] The GOP was frustrated. The network turndown only underscored their lack of alternatives. A *New York Times* editorial reinforced the stereotype of the opposition as a perennial second-class citizen to the President, "Under our system of government the Administration is bigger news than the opposition, at least until such a time as it begins to look that the opposition might be the next Administration. The President is always news. If he chooses in his speeches to give to the party what was meant for the State, it is the opposition's hard luck."[58]

The turmoil between the Republicans and the networks generated a new debate about fairness in political broadcasting. Representative Byron Scott, a Democrat from California, introduced legislation requiring radio stations to set aside regular periods for discussions of social problems by both sides of a controversial issue. Scott claimed this bill would have avoided the high-profile conflict between the Republicans and the networks. The bill, however, never reached the House floor. More than a decade later, the substance of Scott's proposal surfaced as the fairness doctrine, but it dealt with controversial issues rather than institutional parity.[59]

In the aftermath of the State of the Union and Republican skit controversies, the American Civil Liberties Union (ACLU) vowed to support Republican Chairman Henry Fletcher's efforts to push "freedom of the air" bills, which would set aside regular periods for uncensored discussion of both sides of social, political, and economic issues. Roger Baldwin, Director of the ACLU, said the bills "would solve the present bitter censorship problem between the networks and the Republican National Committee."[60]

A year later in March 1937, the question of presidential domination of the airwaves again surfaced during the debate over Roosevelt's proposal to reorganize the Supreme Court. Senator William King of Utah said if the networks continued to exercise their "brutal power" in "discriminating against the opposition," he would introduce a resolution to inquire into network favoritism of the Administration.[61] Meanwhile, the Scott bill was still pending in the House.

Senator King's criticism was symptomatic of the growing frustration of the Republicans. During election periods, they had the force of Section 315 (the "equal time" provision) on their side, which guaranteed balance between political candidates and threatened the loss of licenses for offenders. During the other 22 months of the two-year electoral cycle, however, the networks had no obligation to balance the political dialogue.

All of the anti-broadcasting legislation circulating through Congress naturally made the networks nervous. They dared not upset Members of Congress who wielded great control over regulation of their industry. Yet, broadcasters would never sacrifice their near absolute control over programming. Some evidence suggested that the networks tried to assuage certain Members of Congress by providing them access from time to time. A steady stream of congressional requests for airtime flowed daily into the lobbying offices of the four networks.[62] By granting the odd request, the networks could pacify specific members while holding firm in their desire to avert a mandated equal access policy for the opposition.

If the networks were sensitive to congressional reaction, they were equally sensitive to the powerful role the executive branch played in their futures. Stanley High wrote in a 1938 article for the *Saturday Evening Post* that, even though the radio networks were committed to balance between the parties in allotting airtime, "it is no part of that policy, directly, to turn down requests from those in high political places."[63] High said the networks wanted to accommodate as much administration broadcasting as possible to head off a government-owned station, which they feared would be the first step towards a British-style, non-commercial radio monopoly. This fear, according to High, made the networks "jittery" and encouraged the networks to bow and scrape for the Administration "however low the bow or loud the scrape."[64] Despite the obsequiousness of the networks, the relationship between them and the Administration was still symbiotic.

## AIRTIME FOR LEGISLATORS

Although the Republicans opposing Roosevelt never achieved parity with the President, Members of Congress from both parties had some network access. In 1935, NBC and CBS provided free time for 150 speeches made by senators and 200 by congressmen.[65] In 1937, the figures were 149 and 118 for members of the Senate and House.[66] Between 1928 and 1940, senators spoke over CBS radio 700 times and representatives 500.[67]

It was during this time of increased congressional exposure that a member of the President's own party, Senator Huey Long of Louisiana, was extraordinarily successful in securing network airtime. Long's populist, folksy ways and excellent communication skills, caused the networks to "rush to give him free time."[68] In fact, NBC provided the maverick Senator (who had broken with Roosevelt) three speaking opportunities in a two-week period.[69] An assassin's bullet on September 10th kept us from ever knowing whether Huey Long could have used radio to rival the popular President and build a nationwide political base for himself.

While some legislators like Huey Long were enjoying substantial access, few could match the President in quality or quantity. With competition for airtime growing, even mediocre time slots became difficult to secure for anyone except the President. By 1945, only 47 Republican Members of Congress and governors appeared on NBC.[70] Chester pointed out that even when a network offered rebuttal time it was usually "on the poorest night of the week" and made available optionally "only to those who wanted to carry it."[71]

In 1946 Rolf Kaltenborn, the son of the popular network commentator H. V. Kaltenborn, warned that radio "must not become the mouthpiece of the dominant party."[72] He claimed that during 1945, 56 Democratic congressmen and governors and 63 members of the administration had been given radio time compared to only 47 Republican congressmen and governors. Kaltenborn said radio executives had come to believe that they should air the opposition only in the most controversial instances.

When Price Administrator Chester Bowles made weekly radio speeches on ABC about inflation, there was no opposition rebuttal. The Network Public Service Director said, "I see nothing controversial about inflation. We are all agreed that it must be prevented." But, Kaltenborn's son strongly disagreed and lobbied for an opposition view. He reasoned that it should be the people and not the networks who decided whether a topic was controversial. He argued that if the opposition endorsed the Democrat's anti-inflation plan, it would be that much stronger. If they opposed it, Americans would learn about viable alternatives to the plan.[73] Yet, such an evenhanded solution was not to be. For the next 50 years, the networks would be making those gatekeeping decisions concerning what was controversial and what was not.

## THE GREAT CHAIN BREAKUP

By the mid–1940s, the networks were in the midst of a major crisis as their corporate power was being noticed in Washington. After conducting a major investigation of chain broadcasting, the FCC issued a report in 1941 which questioned the networks' current makeup and relationship to their affiliates. The FCC recommended that NBC sell its "blue" network and that networks be prohibited from taking over any part of an affiliate's schedule at will. The later recommendations decimated CBS' contractual agreements with its affiliates. After several months of unsuccessful legal protest, NBC sold its second network in 1943 (it would become the American Broadcasting Company [ABC]) and CBS changed its affiliate agreements.[74]

William Paley called the FCC plan a "wrecking action"; NBC said it was "illegal." Yet, both networks survived the turmoil and thrived.[75] The broadcasting giants would be allowed to operate freely during subsequent years and to collect abundant riches for themselves. It would not be until the ownership upheaval at all three networks during the mid–1980s that the networks would experience trauma as severe as they felt during the chain breakup incident.

During the chain broadcasting crisis, CBS and NBC were well served by their institutionalized public service standard. Beginning in the mid–1930s, CBS reported getting an "avalanche of praise" for its public service endeavors.[76] Realizing how important the image-building functions of their jobs were, both Sarnoff and Paley carefully positioned themselves as defenders of the highest standards for broadcasting, and eagerly enshrined journalism as a "sacred trust." As a result, few in later years would question why these for-profit corporations were so heavily involved in allocating access in the American political system.

## CLOSENESS THROUGH CRISIS

Behaviors were locked in during the World War II era that would greatly influence the way politicians communicated in the coming television age. During this time, Americans became even more dependent on the President as national leader. Cornwell has written that "a public taught to train its gaze on the Presidency will do so with increasing insistence and urgency in periods of crisis."[77] Such was clearly the case during the war. Americans became quite used to hearing the man who had led them through the crisis of the Great Depression lead them confidently through another. More importantly, they expected direct communication from the Commander-in-Chief. Radio was no longer a novelty; it was a necessity.

Prior to World War II, the President spoke over one or two networks, but during the War he always had access to all four networks—ABC, CBS, Mutual, and NBC—simultaneously.[78] Like the American people, the networks were ever-ready to respond to the President. When Franklin Roosevelt spoke to the nation two days after the bombing of Pearl Harbor, he achieved the highest rating of all time; 83 percent of American households that owned radios were listening to the President.[79]

By the end of the Roosevelt Administration, Presidents had gained a de facto right of access to all radio networks simultaneously, creating a captive audience of millions. Perhaps most importantly, the President could enjoy this radio access without worrying about a direct rebuttal by the opposition party. The precedent set during the 1936 State of the Union Address would remain intact for half a century, strengthening the presidency and weakening the party system and congressional opposition.

While the networks were cementing the patterns for presidential access, the American people were developing listening habits and expectations of political communication that would carry over into future generations. People expected government communication to arrive on the same channel as their favorite entertainment programs. They even became accustomed to having the President interrupt their favorite programs. When President Roosevelt reached out warmly to the people, they drew closer to him. Thus, young John Kennedy already had an excellent role model when he refined presidential television nearly three decades later. The path had already been cleared; the American people were ready.

## PRESIDENT VERSUS CANDIDATE

President Roosevelt was a master at inching his presidential addresses closer and closer to election periods to avoid purchasing time from broadcasters. This tactic not only increased his exposure when the voters were starting to focus on the elections but he could speak without fear of opposition reply. Section 315 of the Communications Act of 1934 required broadcasters to offer "equal time" to opposing candidates during "candidate" uses of airtime. Roosevelt insisted that he was speaking as a "President" rather than as a "candidate" and that his speeches were not subject to the reply rule.

When the President held a "fireside chat" on September 6, 1936, about drought and unemployment, the Republicans charged (to no avail) that the speech was political.[80] Roosevelt used the same successful strategy in the 1940 campaign to make as many free "presidential" rather than paid "candidate" speeches as possible. Roosevelt was particularly adamant about securing free network time for "fireside chats" because toward the end of the campaign the Democrats were almost out of money. Earlier that year, the NAB boosted the President's case by ruling that rival political candidates had to prove that FDR's speeches were political, something difficult for an opponent to do. The question of whether addresses were "presidential" or "political" continued into the Truman Administration. The Republicans were outraged on April 5, 1947, when NBC, ABC, and Mutual carried President Truman's Jefferson Day speech at a $100 per plate Democratic fund raising dinner. GOP National Chairman Carroll Reece said the networks' giving airtime constituted an illegal corporate campaign contribution. Reece also charged that "free radio time is a royal prerogative, something to be given without question whenever requested and without regard for the purpose to which it may be devoted."[81]

CBS agreed with the Republicans that the speech was political and refused to broadcast it. In its statement, however, CBS said it had "on occasion carried these broadcasts when the time was available," an admission that time and economic constraints could outweigh editorial judgments.[82] The Democrats, meanwhile, defended the three networks' contention that the speech was news that the American people wanted to hear. In an interesting twist, the Democratic National Committee (DNC) Executive Director Gael Sullivan questioned the right of a political party to protest a decision by a network. Sullivan said, "Dictation by any political party of what the radio networks shall omit or include in their broadcasts is a threat to free radio—as vital in America as to a free press."[83] Ironically, it would be the Democrats in subsequent years who would most aggressively assert their right to question the news judgments of the broadcasting networks.

In 1949, the FCC promulgated the fairness doctrine as an administrative interpretation of the Communication Act of 1934 to promote balance in broadcasting, not just during campaign periods but throughout the year. The new doctrine said that when a station presented one side of a controversial issue, it should provide a reasonable opportunity for the presentation of contrasting views. The broadcasters would decide whether a program was controversial and what groups constituted a contrasting view.

Because the focus of the fairness doctrine was issues balance rather than institutional balance, the regulation did little to help the cause of the opposition. Even when the President spoke, the networks were not obligated to present views of the opposition in Congress or the opposition party. Broadcasters could choose any group they wanted or have their own commentators provide an opposing view. As Minow, Martin, and Mitchell pointed out, to gain access to radio or television under the fairness doctrine one must be "chosen by a broadcaster as an appropriate spokesman for a point of view that the broadcaster believes to be controversial, of public importance, and not adequately presented in other programming."[84]

While the networks strongly protested the fairness doctrine until its repeal by the FCC in 1987, the regulation provided wide latitude to broadcasters. The FCC reaffirmed that its role was "not to substitute its judgment for that of the licensee ... but rather to determine whether the licensee can be said to have acted reasonably and in good faith."[85] The networks could continue airing the President as much as they liked with no comparable responsibility to give time to the opposition party as long as they balanced the issues in the President's speech. This was just another in a long line of precedents set during the early days of radio that would continue to place formidable obstacles in the path of the opposition during the rise of television.

## Chapter 2

# Television: Increasing the Dependence

President Roosevelt inaugurated NBC's first regular television service on April 30, 1939, at the New York World's Fair, but it was to be his successor, Harry Truman, who first experimented with the televised presidency. President Truman delivered the first televised broadcast from the White House on October 5, 1947, when he and Charles Luckman, the Chairman of the President's Food Conservation Program, asked for the American people's support of their program.[1] Thereafter, the networks televised all of Truman's major addresses and even began televising cabinet meetings in 1950.[2]

The new television medium began in much the same predicament as its radio predecessor—having more time to fill than quality programming. This surplus of airtime encouraged the automatic televising of Presidents. Having a President address the nation legitimized television as it had radio 30 years earlier and spurred interest in it. By the time Harry Truman entered the White House, automatic access was a given. The radio networks had been so accustomed to putting FDR on the air and had benefited so much from doing so that executives saw no reason to make radical policy changes with television.

President Truman did not have to worry about earning automatic network access; it was his birthright passed down from Roosevelt.[3] President Truman, however, faced a different and more difficult type of medium and political climate from that of Roosevelt, which mandated a different broadcast strategy. Gone were the Great Depression and World War II which galvanized public opinion and pushed Americans to the edge of their chairs when the President spoke. Supplanting that electorate unified through crisis was a more fragmented one with ever-expanding post-war expectations.

While FDR liked to broadcast a series of addresses to rally Americans around him during crisis, Truman preferred to make single addresses which did not build on a cumulative emotion. More detached than Roosevelt, Truman did not try to match his speeches with the emotional pulse of the people and the times. He used broadcasting to inform rather than to persuade and did not try to build his audience to an emotional crescendo.

By speaking each time about a different topic, President Truman unknowingly invited the networks to make coverage judgments on a case by case basis. As the news divisions matured and became more confident in their judgments, they became more concerned with the news value of each speech. Presidents continued to receive automatic coverage, but the reasons for it began to change.

President Truman's bold announcement that fired General Douglas MacArthur reinforced the networks' handling of speeches as news events. After such a bombshell, journalists jumped to record any announcement that might be front page news the next day. Missing a big presidential announcement flashed failure across the desks of network news managers. Therefore, while the networks felt less compelled to carry presidential addresses as a public service, they were more inclined to do so for fear of missing out on the big news story. Presidents picked up on this network behavior and press secretaries began to pitch speeches according to some secret nugget of newsworthiness wrapped inside each presidential speech.

President Truman's speech to the Jefferson-Jackson Day dinner in Washington in March 1952 was a perfect example of how a missed opportunity could push the networks compulsively toward automatic coverage. Fearing that the Democratic dinner might be too political in an election year or that it would set off "equal time" demands, ABC, Mutual, and NBC did not carry the Truman speech, leaving only CBS to air the broadcast.[4] But this was to be no ordinary political speech; President Truman made a surprise announcement that he would not seek re-election. Only CBS was there live to beam the message to the entire nation, catching the other networks napping.

After the Truman speech, a *New York Times* correspondent wrote that "news is news no matter what the source of its 'sponsorship'- and front-page events cannot be neatly catalogued or anticipated in advance." The *Times* said television had been given "a long overdue lesson on how its policies in regard to news coverage stand in urgent need of basic revision and much more reportorial flexibility and alertness."[5]

In such a climate where surprise newsworthy announcements could be made at any time, what broadcasters could afford to turn away, risking humiliation and defeat? In future years, the networks would waste countless hours covering the trivia of the presidency. They would unwittingly promote partisan, political causes. They would endure every kind of manipulation imaginable all to avoid the embarrassment of missing a mega-story, like President Truman's surprise announcement. From that time on, the President was always news.

## THE "CHECKERS" SPEECH

An event occurred in 1952 that left little doubt about the effectiveness of television in the political arena. Vice-Presidential nominee Richard Nixon's "Checkers" speech took television out of the novelty, ceremonial realm and established it as a serious medium for persuasive political communication. In his quest to remain on the Republican ticket, Nixon chose television to reach both General Eisenhower and the public in the wake of a potential scandal concerning a fund he used to defray office expenses while he was a member of Congress. While the "Checkers" speech was paid for by the Republican National Committee (RNC) and was not delivered by a President, it had all the aura of a presidential address. Here was a politician fighting for his political life, a fact partially disguised by television. Nixon used the speech to posture himself as an honorable U.S. Senator aspiring to the nation's second highest office who came into American homes to talk one on one, the same way Roosevelt had done so intimately on radio.

Nixon's remarks set a standard for persuasive speech-making in the television age. He was direct, forthright, and personal. Only on television could Richard Nixon maintain such firm control while exploiting the emotional context of the event. This was a commercial transformed into a news event. There would be no rebuttal, no "instant analysis," and no questions from the press. Nixon had the final word. He could set up straw men and knock them down at will. Even General Eisenhower joined the rest of the nation as a captive listener, having to accept or reject the Nixon message on its face. Had Senator Nixon held a press conference or distributed a news release, he could not have come close to equaling the persuasive advantage that television gave him. Just as FDR bypassed the media middlemen with his "fireside chats," Nixon reached for the ultimate editorial control when the stakes were highest.

## EISENHOWER'S TELEVISION INITIATIVES

The Eisenhower years will be remembered not so much for how politicians used television as for the explosive growth of television itself. Between 1952 and 1956, television sets went from a curiosity to a commodity; every American family had to have one. With the networks firmly entrenched as the chief purveyors of television programming, they rode the rising tide of the country's fascination with the new medium. The stature of television executives like Frank Stanton and William Paley of CBS rose as did that of anyone connected with television. By the mid–1950s the news divisions began to spread their wings and become more aggressive. Television anchors like Chet Huntley and David Brinkley began to attract a national following. Newspapers were still the predominant news and information medium, but network television was quickly closing the gap. Coverage of climactic political events continued to boost television's legitimacy and made voters more dependent.

The pervasiveness of network television effected every American institution, especially the presidency. With hardly any initiative of his own, President Eisenhower found his speeches increasing in importance and his reach extending. The dependence on television meant the dependence on the television networks. It was becoming impossible for a President to have popular success without a close working relationship with the networks. It was also a time when political strategists started to seek ways to make television work to their advantage.

By allowing the telecasting of parts of presidential news conferences, participating in televised cabinet meetings, and reaching millions through his addresses, Dwight Eisenhower accelerated the rise of presidential television. Still, he never exploited the persuasive potential of the medium to rally a nation to his side as Roosevelt had done on radio. Eisenhower favored vanilla ceremonial addresses on subjects like the Semi-Centennial of Oklahoma or greetings to the American Management Association more than hard-core political appeals. In a letter in 1959 to a friend, President Eisenhower confided that he was tempted to discard television from his arsenal of political weapons, complaining that it was not suited to explain complex issues, "It is difficult to dramatize the dangers of inflation and while I am willing to resort to television in an effort to talk to the people of the country as a whole, I find it very hard, even using that media, to get much coverage or interest."[6] Eisenhower lamented that an earlier talk had hardly been used by the networks.

Despite Eisenhower's frustrations with television, his Press Secretary James Haggerty had considerable success cementing a relationship with the networks. Haggerty used an informal back channel to achieve maximum access, carefully avoiding embarrassing confrontations with broadcasters. James Haggerty realized that there was a significant difference between news coverage which the media controlled and network addresses to the Nation which the President controlled. He sought formats where the President could avoid middlemen like reporters, columnists, editorial writers, and commentators.[7]

Television executives were criticized for relying too much on Haggerty's evaluation of presidential speeches. In the end, the networks were at the press secretary's mercy. Haggerty could make any speech sound attractive and could always play on the insecurity of an executive who feared the repercussions from missing a newsworthy event. Political Scientist Elmer Cornwell wrote that "it was Jim and not the networks that decided the newsworthiness of a given presidential statement."[8] Haggerty's success prompted Jack Gould of *The New York Times* to write that Haggerty "wields great influence" in a system where "the Administration can turn television on or off as it deems expedient."[9] Given his good relations with the networks, it was not surprising that ABC hired him as one of their top executives.

Contrary to conventional wisdom, Haggerty and the President often preferred that only one network carry the President's speech live. They believed they could actually get more coverage if one network carried it live and the other two delayed it. In some cases, the Administration didn't seem to mind if all networks delayed the speech. For example, when President Eisenhower made an address on Quemoy and Matsu, there was no outcry when the networks delayed the speech until the conclusion of prime time.[10] Haggerty was also sensitive to the monetary loss created by presidential speeches and wanted to spread the misery. If one network had to preempt a popular program to carry a speech, he would try to see to it that another network was tapped the next time.[11]

During the Eisenhower Administration, network television realized that presidential news could be good for business. Following the President's heart attack in 1956, network newscasts drew 300,000 more homes than usual; 12 million American households tuned in to Eisenhower's first televised news conference following his illness.[12] The networks also discovered that controversy in Congress was a good draw. When the networks televised the hearings investigating communist infiltration chaired by Wisconsin Senator Joseph McCarthy in 1954, the daytime television audience soared to 53 percent above normal.

The McCarthy hearings also gave the networks a reason to assert themselves more directly into the political process. When CBS' Edward R. Murrow used his "See it Now" program to counter the rising tide of McCarthyism, the network was wedging its own employee into the role of opposition force, a function usually reserved for politicians. It was Murrow vs. McCarthy, journalist vs. politician, and the public responded favorably. Thus, Murrow became the first of a long line of network commentators who would see their role partially as counterbalancing politicians, particularly Presidents, in order to give the American people a balanced view of the problems facing them.

In the campaign of 1956, television assumed greater importance than ever before. In 1952, only 37 percent of American homes had television. Four years later, penetration had more than doubled to 76 percent.[13] Both parties spent heavily on television with Eisenhower making 17 paid, nationwide campaign speeches and Stevenson nine.[14] The President generated controversy when he made a "non-political" speech in California close to the election which the networks carried. Naturally, the Democrats protested vigorously, but the FCC, examining the speech outside the context of a presidential campaign under the fairness doctrine, denied the request saying:

The Office of the Presidency of the United States is of such high dignity that [a station] must accept the assurance by the White House in each case whether the President's appearance is or is not non-political and . . . it is entirely inappropriate to provide time for reply to a Presidential appearance which he designates as non-political.[15]

The FCC ruling was an ominous sign for the opposition, which obviously expected more relief from the fairness doctrine. If the FCC could provide such blanket access to a President, it would be nearly impossible for the opposition to succeed in a fairness complaint as long as the President maintained that his speech was non-political. The opposition wondered why broadcasters had to accept a President's word that a speech was non-political; and why was it inappropriate to provide time for the opposition just because the President said so? Would such a double standard not foreclose the opposition from ever getting its fair share of exposure?

The most controversial incident during the campaign occurred on October 31st when President Eisenhower spoke to the nation concerning the Suez crisis. Stevenson requested time for a rebuttal, but the FCC ruled the day before the election that presidential addresses on an international crisis were not covered by Section 315, the "equal time" provision. The networks offered Eisenhower time to reply to Stevenson, but he declined.[16]

A similar incident in Britain over access during the Suez crisis ended differently. The Prime Minister, like his American counterpart, fought to keep the opposition from giving a rebuttal. In this case, however, a British rule mandating an automatic reply gave the opposition guaranteed access and provided a buffer to protect the system from partisan manipulation.

## ⱡ COVERING CAMELOT

John F. Kennedy was to television what Franklin Roosevelt was to radio. Like FDR, Kennedy whetted the network appetite, creating his own public demand for presidential programming. Also, like his predecessor, Kennedy understood the perils of overexposure. When he learned that part of Roosevelt's success with the "fireside chats" was their infrequency, he cut back on his television appearances.[17]

Even before becoming President, Kennedy proved himself to be an accomplished television performer during the debates with Richard Nixon. By making nine addresses to the nation in his first three years, opening news conferences to live television on a regular basis, and giving priority to the broadcasting media, Kennedy became a popular President in network circles.

Kennedy's ratings were good and polls showed that Americans were generally impressed with the performance of their President. When Kennedy played electronic hardball in 1961 by taking on the steel companies on national television, White House telegrams ran 2.5 to 1 in the President's favor. Aided by the television "bully pulpit," Kennedy was able to coax the steel companies to roll back their prices within 72 hours.[18]

The young President, like all other broadcasting age Presidents before him, understood the advantage of using the airwaves to bypass the press. As he once remarked, "I always said that when we don't have to go through you bastards, we can really get our story to the American people."[19] When Kennedy allowed televising of presidential news conferences for the first time in history, he was able to continue his firm control on the news agenda while appearing to be operating in an uncontrolled media environment.

As Kennedy became more and more dependent on the networks, their prestige also rose. Thus, when Press Secretary Pierre Salinger got permission to air the press conferences he found "there was . . . no question that TV was willing to preempt millions of dollars in commercial time" to carry them and carry them free.[20] By riding the wave of presidential prosperity, the networks found themselves increasingly dependent on the White House. They did not want to spoil their own success by tinkering with the President's success.

The Kennedy Administration followed Haggerty's precedent and negotiated for time through an informal three-network committee. Unlike his Republican predecessor, Kennedy aggressively sought access to all three networks simultaneously and refused to settle for less. By thinking creatively, the Kennedy people developed a much more varied arsenal than their predecessors. In addition to 19 live speeches and more than 60 televised press conferences, JFK submitted to prime time "conversations" with the networks, provided a televised tour of the White House, and allowed cameras to follow him and his brother as they discussed integration problems in Alabama. The multifaceted Kennedy strategy ensured that all media appearances complemented each other and that they relied on no one vehicle excessively.

During the Kennedy era, the networks became enamored with daily news coverage of the White House, building an infrastructure of producers, technicians, and correspondents to guarantee that this President and all future Presidents would dominate the news. The White House became the nucleus of an enormous Washington newsgathering system manned by highly visible White House correspondents. The expansion of the "CBS Evening News" to a half hour in 1963 also fed the symbiotic relationship between the White House and the networks. CBS' interview with President Kennedy on the inaugural of the program set the tone for the high priority the presidency would assume in subsequent years.

Newsmakers sensed that there was a special orbit surrounding the presidency which allowed those who entered it to make news. Publicity-conscious congressmen learned that the quickest path to network exposure was either through praise or criticism of the Chief Executive. Congressional initiatives which lacked White House interest rarely had a strong enough "spin" to break the network evening news coverage threshold.

When the full complement of network resources was in place, broadcasters could play a powerful agenda-setting role by focusing attention on the President of the United States. In many totalitarian countries, the government had to mandate that the leader be the top news story of the day, but in America the networks were doing it voluntarily. Television during Kennedy's term, according to David Halberstam, not only changed the balance of power but became a part of the new balance of power:

The Kennedy candidacy and presidency created a whole new balance of power. Not only was the influence of the opposition party diminished but in a far more basic way the whole balance of government was changed, with the presidency growing in power at the expense of the other branches of government. It was no longer Democratic President against Republican opposition, but Presidents against all else, with partisan differences muted. Truman, Eisenhower, Kennedy, Johnson, Nixon found themselves more tied to the office than to their parties, and above all bound together by the commonality of their institutional opposition. Television, given all that potential institutional opposition, became a crucial weapon.[21]

Caught in a Kennedy media whirlwind powered mostly by the television networks, the Republican opposition in Congress mustered only feeble attempts to get its message across. Their chief institutional publicity vehicle, begun just four days after the Kennedy inauguration, was the "Ev and Charlie Show," a regular news conference featuring Senate Minority Leader Everett Dirksen of Illinois and House Minority Leader Charles Halleck of Indiana. While this initiative gave Republicans a regular forum, it could in no way compete with Kennedy. Minow, Martin, and Mitchell contrasted a Kennedy news conference drawing 400 reporters with a Dirksen-Halleck production drawing only 17.[22] As hard as the opposition tried, it was running against a rising network/presidential alliance which had little use for minor league congressional figures. The "Ev and Charlie Show" disappeared in 1963.

The Republicans had endured minority status for 20 years during the Roosevelt and Truman Administrations, but had been bolstered by eight years of prominent attention in the White House; therefore, they did not take as kindly this time around to a return to media invisibility. The GOP was hungry to seize opportunities for access. When the networks simultaneously broadcast an hour-long "conversation" with President Kennedy on December 11, 1962, the GOP quickly petitioned the network for airtime. The rebuttal never took place because the Republicans could not choose whom to include in the broadcast. Such costly indecision reflected the internal conflict between younger more telegenic party members and those older members who carried the mantle of leadership.[23]

The Republican's most successful attempt to gain network access occurred during September, 1963, after President Kennedy went on the air to propose a controversial tax cut. The networks responded favorably to the Republican request for time, but would not give simultaneous access. Republican John Byrnes of Wisconsin, the ranking member of the House Ways and Means Committee, made a half hour speech Saturday on ABC (7:00 PM), CBS (7:00 PM), and Mutual (7:30 PM). A senior Republican on the Joint Economic Committee, Republican Thomas Curtis of Missouri, spoke Sunday on NBC (7:00 PM).[24] There was access, even better than expected, but on two different days and at three different times. The disparity between the President's access and the opposition's was so great that even assistant House Democratic Floor Leader Hale Boggs of Louisiana agreed that the Republicans ought to be granted simultaneous network reply time.[25]

As badly as the Republicans wanted time, they didn't always use the right arguments to secure it. In a non-presidential election year, Republican leaders knew they had a tenuous claim to "equal time" under Section 315 and yet the fairness doctrine provided them with no guarantee that the networks would choose the official Republican spokesperson to rebut the President. The GOP alluded to the problem in a statement which said it did not "contemplate a flat demand for 'equal time' but felt that in all fairness we would hope to be granted facilities for favorable and full exposure to the Republican viewpoint."[26]

In responding to the Republicans, the networks were careful to say that they were not providing "equal time" but were exercising their own independent policies of fair presentation on important and controversial issues.[27] In NBC's case, the Executive Vice-President in charge of news, William McAndrew, emphasized that the network as a "responsible news medium" would have made time available to a "representative congressional viewpoint" even if the Republicans hadn't asked for it in order for the public to "judge the merits of the issue."[28]

The Kennedy tax cut episode underscored how carefully the networks would approach opposition requests for time during the next 25 years. The networks went out of their way not to state or imply that their granting of time in any way was a response to opposition pressure or represented anything more than an isolated, independent judgment by the networks. Realizing that opposition requests fell into a vacuum between the "equal time" rule and the mainstream of the fairness doctrine, broadcasters could easily outmaneuver the opposition. In such cases, they had a vested interest in keeping the rules of access vague and ambiguous.

While the fairness doctrine was certainly no ally of the opposition, an FCC ruling issued around the time of the Kennedy tax cut speech did make their fairness requests more immediate. The Commission said it would review the fairness doctrine complaints on a case by case basis rather than cumulatively over the life of a license. This meant that a station was accountable immediately for its decisions. The new initiative also increased the likelihood that fairness complaints would receive a prompt hearing. Without such an immediate feedback mechanism, the doctrine would be useless in most political situations because of the limited life span of the issues.

During the Kennedy Administration, one network began a rare initiative to help redress the balance between the President and the opposition party. NBC in 1961 introduced "The Loyal Opposition" which would be a forum for the party out of power. NBC controlled the timing and the format of the program but usually offered the opposition great leeway. Sometimes, NBC would run the program like a network interview show and at other times turn the opposition loose to construct its own broadcast. Even though "The Loyal Opposition" fell far short of what the congressional leadership demanded, the program was a noteworthy network initiative at a time when the opposition was being buried by the weight of President Kennedy's presidential television offensive.

## ALL THE WAY WITH LBJ

If there had been any doubt concerning the submissiveness of the networks to presidential pressure, it was quickly erased during the presidency of Lyndon Johnson. Never before had the networks felt the heavy hand of governmental pressure in such a personal way. Lyndon Johnson wanted exposure when he wanted it and did not hesitate to tell the networks. His presidency would prompt the networks to rethink their closeness to the White House and devise ways to place distance in the relationship.

If Lyndon Johnson could not match the quality of John Kennedy's televised presidency, he wanted to surpass it in quantity. During his first year in office, LBJ appeared on television more times than Kennedy had in three years and more than Eisenhower had in eight.[29] By the end of his second year, LBJ had gone live on at least one of the three networks 58 times.[30] As Minow, Martin, and Mitchell said, Johnson was a "compulsive communicator."[31] In one week, *Time* reported that he made nearly two dozen speeches, held three press conferences, appeared on national television three times, and was seen in person by more than a quarter of a million people.[32] Johnson raised his exposure dramatically by broadcasting eight of his 17 addresses to the nation in prime time when viewership peaked.

President Johnson would call the networks on a moment's notice, announcing he was on his way to make a broadcast. He and his motorcade would then race toward the studios, arriving just in time to go on the air. Unlike his predecessors or successors, Johnson routinely ignored the programming constraints of the networks. He rarely told the networks what he was going to talk about, leaving them in the precarious position of interrupting valuable prime time for what might be an unimportant announcement. One of Johnson's most bizarre airwaves seizures occurred before the opening of the 1964 Democratic nominating convention. Fannie Lou Hamer, representing the Mississippi Freedom Democratic Party (MFDP), was testifying before the Party's Credentials Committee in favor of seating the black MFDP delegation. She finally broke down in tears as she emotionally recounted the blackjack beatings and other abuses she took for being actively involved in the civil rights movement.

Lyndon Johnson was furious. This was to be his convention and a dissident group from Mississippi was threatening to ruin it for him. Immediately, Johnson ordered White House aides to phone the television networks to tell them that a news conference would begin immediately. Almost as quickly as the President snapped his fingers, the networks cut off the Hamer testimony and switched live to the White House where LBJ predicted a tranquil convention.[33]

Lyndon Johnson could get away with such high-handed behavior because he was the President and network news had never been weaned from its dependence on the presidency. On the contrary, presidential dominance was the natural order. It did not hurt that two of Lyndon Johnson's friends were the heads of the two most powerful networks, Frank Stanton of CBS and Robert Kintner of NBC.

In his typical style, Johnson was not shy about calling on his friends. During the 1964 Democratic Convention, for example, Johnson called Kintner practically ordering him to get NBC cameras off the Mississippi Freedom Democratic Delegation.[34] Johnson was constantly seeking advice from Stanton on a wide range of topics from the business climate to woodworking and there were frequent murmurings in the CBS news division that Frank Stanton's relationship with Johnson seemed far too close and comfortable for a President and network executive to have.

On May 2, 1965, Johnson broke into the network news for six minutes to appeal for a truce in the Dominican Republic. Later on, he refused to wait until the top of the hour to start an address, charging on the air at 9:55 PM and cutting off the last five minutes of "Bonanza." This irritated the networks greatly. Despite the networks' obvious displeasure with Johnson's unpredictable and inconsiderate tactics, they tolerated his behavior and provided him with unprecedented exposure. Network executives soon feared that they were losing control of their own programming. President Johnson's demands for time became so frequent that the networks spent about a quarter of a million dollars to install a television studio in the White House from which the President could go on live at any time.

If President Johnson's behavior bothered network executives, it also conditioned them to accede to presidential demands. Beginning with Johnson's January 31, 1966, address on the resumption of the bombing of Hanoi, the networks carried his next seven addresses simultaneously, a trend that would continue unbroken until the presidency of Gerald Ford. David Halberstam explained Johnson's tactics:

He knew from the start that television was an enormous weapon, that he could get on whenever he wanted. Indeed, his years saw the rise of the unofficial network policy of giving the President time. In the past, the networks had always asked the reason—was the national interest involved? Now he merely asked and they gave. He knew that the Congress could not compete, that he could give whatever figures and facts he wanted and there would be no rebuttal, and that only the television correspondents themselves, and even they to a marginal degree, blocked his way. He went to great pains to have his appearances filtered as little as possible by the White House correspondents.[35]

It was also President Johnson, however, who eventually made the networks skeptical of automatic presidential access. Former CBS News President Richard Salant pointed to a speech President Johnson made to labor leaders in Florida in December, 1967, which the President led them to believe would be a blockbuster. When it was "nothing," Salant began to "worry about how we deal with this problem."[36]

After the controversial AFL-CIO speech, the networks wanted to become more vigilant, but were reluctant to turn down a President of the United States. The networks, after all, were in an untenable position. They had to ascertain newsworthiness without having access to the speech about to be broadcast. This situation nearly always gave the President the upper hand. Steve Rutkus of the Library of Congress wrote

that Johnson's policy of keeping the networks in the dark put broadcasters in a quandary:

> To air the President live without foreknowledge of the contents of his remarks
> would involve resting on the assurances of the White House that the remarks
> would be newsworthy; in effect, a network would be surrendering its journalistic
> function of covering a speech a certain way based on a judgment of its news
> value. To decline live coverage, assessing the President's address as he spoke,
> would risk missing the opportunity to televise truly momentous news as it was
> being made.[37]

Network news executives might have disagreed over treatment of
President Johnson, but they had consensus on the low priority of opposition requests. The FCC apparently agreed. When the Republican
opposition named Barry Goldwater to rebut a Johnson speech on foreign
affairs in 1964, the FCC ruled that the Republicans had no right to time
either under Section 315 or the fairness doctrine and that Goldwater's
views on foreign affairs had been adequately covered in regular news
programming.

When President Johnson was inaugurated in 1965, Republicans res-
urrected the running press conference format they had abandoned two
years earlier. With the ascension of Gerald Ford as House Minority
Leader, the "Ev and Charlie Show" became the "Ev and Jerry Show."
Unfortunately for congressional Republicans, the new program was no
more successful than its predecessor. A few excerpts from the "Ev and
Jerry Show" made the news, but it certainly was no countervailing force
to presidential communication.

The Republicans saved their biggest push for simultaneous airtime to
respond to President Johnson's State of the Union messages. A precedent for opposition airtime began in 1966 when the networks granted
Senator Dirksen and Congressman Ford a half hour five days after the
President spoke. CBS broadcast the speech at 10:30 PM while ABC and
NBC ran it an hour later.[38] These time slots were clearly inferior to the
prime time given to the President, but they were better than the opposition was used to receiving. Since the 1966 State of the Union address,
the networks have consistently provided some type of three network
exposure for the opposition, although the quality of the airtime and the
degree of simultaneity have varied greatly.

In 1967, the Republican opposition pushed not only for rebuttal access
but for simultaneous access to all three networks. Not surprisingly, the
networks went their separate ways. NBC aired Senator Dirksen and
Congressman Ford's address at 11:30 PM on January 19th while ABC
gave the Republican leaders a near-prime time opportunity at 7:30 PM
the following day. CBS refused the official Republican response alto-

gether and arranged its own network-controlled panel of GOP congress-men for broadcast on January 16th.

The CBS action was to be a harbinger of the "Other Views" policy which would characterize CBS news for years to come. By producing its own program, the network could easily satisfy its fairness obligations and still ignore the opposition in Congress. CBS' Frank Stanton said his network discharged its fairness responsibility by televising a program featuring eight Republican Members of Congress. Because six of the eight GOP members were freshmen, the Republicans countered that the CBS effort did not equal the counterbalance to President Johnson that Ford and Dirksen provided.[39] The Republicans also questioned what right the network had to define what the opposition was when an "of-ficial" opposition response had already been prepared.

House Minority Leader Gerald Ford was so upset by the network treatment of his party, especially by CBS, that he successfully added a plank to the 1968 Republican platform advocating legislation to provide free and equal time to major party spokespersons. Ford said, "Television should not be at the service of the highest bidder or the party in power. They cannot be regulated solely by the conscience or convictions of network executives and their most popular faces."[40] Calling the network treatment a "half-loaf response," Ford said that the opposition must have time to present divergent views not just in campaign periods but in the longer period between campaigns as well.[41]

Subsequently, when President Johnson made the controversial AFL-CIO speech in Bal Harbour which deceived the networks, Republicans received simultaneous access. At 7:00 PM on the night of December 15, 1967, television watchers had little alternative but to watch Senator Dirksen and Congressman Ford the same way they routinely had to settle for a presidential speech on all three channels. It was the first time since 1956 that the networks had handed free simultaneous access to the opposition. Presumably, network displeasure at the President as well as the fear of partisan attacks by Republicans motivated the networks to reshuffle their schedules to allow Dirksen and Ford on the air.

The bloom of simultaneity did not last long for the Republicans. The State of the Union message the next month brought them only limited access. Abandoning their standard Dirksen-Ford address format, the GOP substituted a 20 minute news conference the following week fea-turing Senator Jacob Javits of New York, Senator James Pearson of Kan-sas, Republican Melvin Laird of Kansas, and Minority Leader Ford. ABC televised the conference live, NBC picked up part of it but CBS did not carry it at all. Interestingly, the Republican leadership refused a CBS offer of time on the same night of the President's speech, preferring to have a full hour on the Tuesday of the following week.[42] NBC broadcast part of the Republican news conference live and also made time available nine days later as part of its ongoing "Loyal Opposition" series.

These events were not only bipolar expressions of political views by two parties, but opportunities for the networks to show off their own talent. Commentators and correspondents dominated programming on all three networks, giving views and comments on the Johnson speech. As *New York Times* television columnist Jack Gould commented, the "lesson of the evening was that in the electronic age a State of the Union message no longer stands by itself for very long." The networks' own initiative overshadowed the Republican opposition.[43] The networks also made a big effort to draw as many prominent persons as possible to interview. CBS even used the Early Bird satellite to interview economist John Kenneth Galbraith live from Geneva.[44]

By the end of the Johnson Administration, each party had labored as opposition for eight consecutive years during the television age. In each case, the opposition never matched the exposure and power of presidential television. Opposition broadcasting, which had been relegated to second-class status during the radio age, quickly assumed that role through television. Only during State of the Union messages was any trend toward sustained access evident.

## NIXON'S PERFECT RECORD

The election of 1968 brought a Republican to the White House for only the second time in 36 years, casting the Democratic congressional majority in the unaccustomed role of "loyal opposition." The party that had enjoyed such extraordinary television access under John Kennedy and Lyndon Johnson now had to sacrifice it. This feast and famine attitude toward broadcast access was the American way; there would be no middle ground.

The Democrats faced a formidable television communicator in Richard Nixon. Sixteen years earlier, Nixon had shown with his "Checkers" speech that he could be a master of persuasive television. During the 1960 debates with John Kennedy, Nixon learned how a poor television performance can devastate a political campaign. By 1969, Nixon's advisors had carefully crafted a format over which they maintained complete control; the address to the nation proved to be the perfect vehicle. In his first 18 months in office, President Nixon spoke during prime time as frequently as Presidents Eisenhower, Kennedy, and Johnson combined.[45] By moving nearly all addresses to the nation to prime time, President Nixon created an environment in which viewers saw him 50 percent more than they saw President Kennedy.[46]

Remarkably, the networks never denied Richard Nixon access during his five and one-half years in office. The President sought access 32 times and 32 times the networks gave it. Twenty-six of the speeches were during prime time, when roadblocked access on three networks provided audiences as great as 70 million Americans.[47] Even at the height of the Watergate scandal, when relations with the media were strained and the President was losing public support, the networks still provided time. No president before or since has equalled Nixon's perfect access record. A Library of Congress study in 1976 confirmed that during the Nixon Administration, "the networks have not subjected the President to a rigorous news standard before granting him access, but rather have provided access routinely."[48]

CBS Vice President Robert Chandler told the study's author, Denis S. Rutkus, that the networks made decisions before they ever saw the text of a presidential speech, making it axiomatic that an address was newsworthy. NBC Washington Bureau Chief Don Meaney told Rutkus that "If the White House asks for airtime to deliver a message, we give it." Likewise, ABC Director of News Services, Nick Archer, said, "Every time they [the White House] request time, we give it to them. It is our policy."[49]

Thus, by the network's own admission, they had let rigorous application of independent news judgment slip through their fingers, assuring presidential access. The practice of automatic access had begun midway through Lyndon Johnson's presidency and was in full stride when Richard Nixon became president. No doubt Nixon's men realized the surge of the presidential momentum and wasted no time in exploiting it.

President Nixon was particularly effective in using network access to gain support for his conduct of the Vietnam War. Nixon delivered his first address about Vietnam four months into his term and followed that with seven addresses during the 17-month period from November 1969 to April 1971. Most of these prime time addresses reached more than 50 million Americans; one reached 70 million.[50]

Pollster Louis Harris reported that Nixon's Vietnam addresses greatly boosted his favorableness rating in the face of a growing antiwar movement. After Nixon announced his phased troop withdrawals on May 14, 1969, public support for President Nixon's Vietnam policy jumped from 49 to 67 percent. Likewise, public support for use of American troops in Cambodia jumped from 7 to 50 percent after Nixon's April 30, 1970 speech defending the Cambodian incursion by American troops.[51]

Nixon's preemptive television strikes threw opponents to the war off-guard and weakened their momentum. Frustrated by Nixon's television success, a group of 16 senators who opposed the war, Republicans as well as Democrats, filed a fairness complaint with the FCC accusing the President of using his prime time television series "to present his position on the war, to discount the role of Congress in charting course in Indochina and to criticize his Senate opponents and their position on the war."[52]

Not only Senators but law students, professors, antiwar groups, and business executives lodged fairness complaints. After analyzing overall network programming on Vietnam, the FCC decided that most programming had been balanced except for Nixon's presidential addresses. The FCC ordered the networks to present a program of opposing viewpoints, the first time it had done so as a response to a presidential appearance.[53]

To comply with the FCC ruling, the three networks chose senators, Republicans and Democrats, to provide an opposition view to the Nixon addresses in a two-week period during late August and early September of 1970. Some members of the press hailed the FCC ruling as a harbinger of regular opposition access, but FCC Chairman Dean Burch quickly ended that speculation. He said the Commission had "expressly rejected any principle embodying right of reply or rebuttal to the President."[54] Thus, the opposition had won a battle that seemed to have little effect on the war. The FCC kept presidents at the top of the access hierarchy while precluding congressional access, except in extraordinary circumstances where the issues dialogue had gotten badly out of balance.

## THE STANTON INITIATIVE

At least one network executive recognized that Nixon's domination of the television dialogue was causing an unhealthy imbalance between the president and the opposition. CBS President Frank Stanton, in June 1970, announced a bold and visionary policy that would, for the first time, try to redress this imbalance between the presidency and the political opposition. He offered the Democratic Party time of its own outside the framework of replies to presidential speeches. It was a policy based not on newsworthiness of the Democrats but on the public service value of giving them exposure. In a telegram to the Chairman of the DNC, Lawrence O'Brien, Dr. Stanton said CBS would give the opposition party opportunities to present its views several times each year in programs called "The Loyal Opposition."

For the first time, the opposition could propose its own agenda instead of just responding to the president. CBS was cementing in policy the right of the opposition party to express its views regularly, a dramatic departure from anything a network had tried before.[55] Importantly, the Stanton initiative respected the constitutional equality of the Congress and the vital role an opposition party plays in the political system.

ABC President Leonard Goldenson also offered in 1970 "to make available one hour of prime time to the Congress at the beginning of each session to present to the American people a report on the 'State of the Congress.' "[56] The Goldenson proposal, however, laid down a quid pro quo in which ABC would offer time to the opposition only if the House and Senate would open its sessions to television coverage, conditions that Congress clearly was not ready to meet.

In a July 10, 1970 speech Dr. Stanton said that the power of the President "has become so great, and his right to address the nation virtually at his own terms so accepted that some balance must be provided to overcome what could become a monolithic voice on public affairs."[57] Three days earlier, DNC Chairman Lawrence O'Brien had used the party's newly found broadcast access to attack the policies of the Nixon Administration. Within 48 hours of the CBS-aired O'Brien speech, Republicans of all shades clamored for their own right to respond under the fairness doctrine which mandated that the networks seek out opposing views on controversial issues. The FCC eventually ruled that CBS had to afford "some reasonable period of time" to a Republican spokesperson to reply to the Democratic broadcast. This requirement to provide reply time to a reply, according to Dr. Stanton, was "to vitiate the series."

CBS had neither the patience nor the resources to continue bouncing back and forth between two opposition forces every time a president spoke.[58] The highly partisan Democratic broadcast had generated enough controversy to force CBS to terminate the "Loyal Opposition" series in its infancy. Dr. Stanton and CBS had been caught in such a strong regulatory and political crossfire that neither ever tried to resurrect the short-lived proposal. Ironically, the invocation of the fairness doctrine, a policy designed to promote balance, had derailed a rare network initiative to promote balance between the institutions of the president and the opposition party. The Stanton episode thus marked the beginning and the end for any sense of opposition parity in the network political broadcasting system.

Richard Salant, President of CBS News during the "Loyal Opposition" experiment, believed it was one of the few network initiatives concerned with political balance rather than issues balance. The "Loyal Opposition" was not planned and executed through the news department but through the CBS' News Executive Committee made up of the heads of the news, radio, and television divisions with the CBS president serving as chairman. It was this same committee that had contemplated a policy to promote balance between political institutions at the end of the Eisenhower Administration.

All of the maneuverings concerning opposition access were not conducted in a political vacuum. Forces in the Nixon White House were quick to exploit any perceived CBS vulnerability. Shortly after the CBS controversy with the Democrats, Presidential Advisor Charles Colson, the Nixon Administration hatchet man, met with network executives to talk bluntly about access and White House leverage over the networks.

President Nixon understood well the value of licenses to the networks' highly profitable owned and operated television stations and was not above hinting, through aides like Colson, that stations not wanting trouble should be more sympathetic to the Administration. The networks were also sensitive to this fact and did not want to enter into a running feud with the White House. Whatever the motivations and pressures were, the meeting with Colson clearly went the administration's way. In a confidential memo to President Nixon uncovered during the Watergate investigation concerning the meeting with the network executives, Colson staked out the Nixon Administration's absolute claim to network airtime:

There was unanimous agreement that the President's right of access to TV should in no way be restrained. Both CBS and ABC agreed with me that on most occasions the President speaks as President and that there is no obligation for presenting a contrasting view under the Fairness Doctrine. . . . All agree no one has a right of "reply" and that fairness doesn't mean answering the President but rather is "issue oriented." This was the most important understanding we came to.[59]

It worried the Nixon Administration that the pesky congressional opposition could actually initiate broadcasts a few times a year. This would dilute the presidential broadcast monopoly that the White House and networks had carefully crafted over the previous 30 years. Colson wanted to make sure that the Stanton initiative had not tempted the networks to go off the reservation.

As the memo clearly states, the White House had a vested interest in making sure that the fairness doctrine did not give the opposition an automatic reply. If Nixon could assure the issue orientation of the fairness doctrine, he could effectively freeze out the congressional opposition. If the focus was on issues, a network could choose whomever it wanted for a reply, including people tangential to the political process. An institution-based policy as envisioned by Dr. Stanton, however, designated the opposition party, Democrats, as the natural and legitimate counterpoint to the President.

The Colson memo only underscored how important it was to presidents to have unrestrained access to television and to have it without fear of opposition rebuttal. That the networks and Administration were in "unanimous agreement" on this point showed how deep a mark 30 years of presidential dominance had made. A one-sided point of view with no place for the opposition was the natural order, and it was sanctioned by the government's own regulatory mechanism, the fairness doctrine.

The United States Court of Appeals wrote the final chapter to CBS' "Loyal Opposition" episode more than a year after the O'Brien speech. On November 15, 1971, the Court overturned the ruling giving the Republicans time to reply to the Democrats who were replying to the president. The Court said the lower court ruling gave the Republicans "two bites of the apple." It was a policy the Court said, "strikes at the heart of representative democracy and imperils the very traditions upon which this nation is founded."[60]

The Appeals Court acknowledged that if the president became not only the "most powerful voice but the only voice" then the mechanism of public opinion could be "thrown dangerously off balance."[61] In spite of such sentiments, the Court refused to infringe on the autonomy of broadcasters. It insisted that the networks should decide opposition access questions and have wide discretion in making those decisions. The Court reminded the FCC, the independent regulatory body which had promulgated the fairness doctrine, that its rule was "not to substitute its judgment for that of the licensee, but rather to determine whether the licensee can be said to have acted reasonably and in good faith."[62]

It was clear that the FCC had no appetite for interfering with broadcasters' judgments except in the most egregious cases. Thus, not only did the Appeals Court refuse to establish any right of reply for the opposition, it solidified the right of the broadcasters to serve as powerful arbiters of access. They could hand-pick the opposition and set the ground rules for coverage, all under the protection of the fairness doctrine which they so despised.

The souring of the bold Stanton initiative drew clear battle lines for more aggressive opposition attacks on the networks. During the early 1970s, the DNC waged a legal campaign seeking "to redress the imbalance that favors the party in power in the matter of access to television and radio."[63] DNC Chairman Lawrence F. O'Brien assaulted the networks with a barrage of lawsuits to gain rulings of principle by the FCC and the courts which might spawn an automatic right of reply for the opposition.

The protracted legal battle following the Stanton initiative gave the networks a disincentive to promote institutional equality. Few would dare to venture into the firestorm experienced by Frank Stanton when he suggested that maybe the opposition deserved more than it was getting. After what Minow, Martin, and Mitchell had characterized as an "endurance contest" between the Democratic Party and the networks during the early 1970s, the courts and FCC rejected the contention that there should be an automatic right to respond to presidential appearances by the party out of power.

## THE DOOMED LEGISLATIVE ALTERNATIVE

With the fairness doctrine clearly on the side of the broadcasters, the Democrats felt compelled to pursue a legislative remedy that would mandate reply time. Senator J. William Fulbright of Arkansas introduced S. J. Res. 209 in 1970 to provide a "reasonable amount of public service time to authorized representatives of the Senate and House to discuss issues of public importance." The resolution provided for at least four occasions a year when the opposition would get time it controlled. In an eloquent statement before the Senate Communications Subcommittee, Senator Fulbright justified the need for a legislation:

There is nothing in the Constitution which says that, of all elected officials, the President alone shall have the right to communicate with the American people. That privilege was a gift of modern technology, coming in an age when chronic war and crisis were already inflating the powers of the presidency. Communication is power and exclusive access to it is a dangerous and unchecked power. I think it is a fair assumption that, if television had existed in the 18th century, the framers of our Constitution would have written something like the FCC's fairness doctrine, or the bill which I commend to you today into the basic law of the land. As matters now stand, the President's power to use television in the service of his policies and opinions has done as much to expand the powers of his office as would a constitutional amendment formally abolishing the coequality of the three branches of government.

Whatever the arguments for or against broadcast time for political parties, there can be no justification for denying equal time to the coequal branches of Government. Under our Constitution there is no paramount branch of the Federal Government; if indeed the framers regarded any branch as primus inter pares, it was not the Executive but the Congress, whose powers are spelled out in the Constitution at greatest length and in the greatest detail. If the President is regarded as having the right to communicate with the American people through the mass media whenever he wishes, the spirit and intent of our Constitution require that no less a privilege be accorded to the Senate and the House of Representatives—or, if it should claim it, to the judiciary.[64]

Senator Fulbright then related how the opposition, Democratic and Republican, had been thwarted for nearly 40 years in virtually every attempt to keep pace with the president on radio and television. While Fulbright was making an institutional argument, during the Nixon Administration the frustration was being borne by the Democrats. The Republicans, who suffered similar discrimination in previous years, were now suffering a convenient memory loss which precluded bipartisan support from forming for the Fulbright approach.

The networks, clearly in command of the presidential-opposition access question, assumed a statesmanlike detachment from the political fray and calmly explained to the Senators why broadcasters, with all their wisdom and dedication to public service, could not allow such ill-conceived legislation to pass. The strongest opponent of the Fulbright resolution was Dr. Frank Stanton, the same man who had bent over backwards to provide access to the opposition earlier in the year. The main difference was that Stanton's idea was network initiated while the Fulbright plan was being imposed on the networks from outside.

Stanton was a persuasive advocate for the broadcasting establishment. Over the years, he had become a star presence on Capitol Hill and could adroitly assuage concerns of anxious congressmen and senators. In attacking the Fulbright resolution, Dr. Stanton pounced on one of its obvious weaknesses—how do you determine who speaks for Congress? By conjuring up visions of 535 ideologues each speaking in a mass of confusion on behalf of the legislative branch, Dr. Stanton and his fellow network presidents were able to blur the issue, making the Fulbright resolution seem impractical.

When Senator Pastore, the Chairman of the Subcommittee, repeatedly asked Dr. Stanton if he would support the resolution if the spokesman problem could be overcome, the CBS executive balked. He could say only that "there was no ready place to turn in our form of government to find the spokesman to redress the political imbalance."[65] Later in his testimony, however, Dr. Stanton responded with pride to a network-inspired solution which embodied the spirit of the Fulbright resolution:

*Senator Pastore:* Let's assume for instance any President, whether he be Republican or Democrat, speaks to the American public and he becomes critical of the opposition party, again whether it is Republican or Democrat, what is the solution of your network with regard to that? Don't you think the opposition party has a right to answer that? And who does? Is that a problem that has confronted you?

*Dr. Stanton:* Certainly. Let me give you an example. In December of 1967 President Lyndon Johnson addressed the AFL-CIO convention in Miami Beach. We were told that the President was going to make an important statement and we broadcast the President's remarks. If you recall, he was pretty rough on Congress and on the Republican side of Congress in that particular address. The very next morning, we, CBS, without any request from the opposition, turned to the opposition party on the hill and offered time to respond to the President.

We had something going then that we don't have today in the opposition party on the hill. There were two spokesmen, one from the Senate and one from the House, for the Republican party, in the persons of the late Senator Dirksen and Representative Ford. On frequent occasions when there were issues between the administration and the Republican side of Congress, Senator Dirksen and Mr. Ford were the spokesmen. A pattern evolved out of our freedom to solve the problem. The Republican gave the media, if you will, spokesmen to treat with the various issues that came up. That meant we did not have to turn to a party organization to redress the situation in Florida, because we had spokesmen to who we could turn.

*Senator Pastore:* Are you taking the position that the integrity of your industry requires that you go to what you consider to be the man who can best answer to the American people, otherwise you yourself will have to answer to the American people?

*Dr. Stanton:* That is right.[66]

The Stanton testimony raises some interesting questions. When the networks, on their own initiative, wanted to find a spokesperson, the "who speaks for Congress" question disappeared. On the other hand, when the opposition insisted on naming the spokesperson, the problems became insurmountable. In the case of the Johnson AFL-CIO speech, the networks operated on the common sense approach proposed by many members of the Subcommittee—that in a partisan political system, it is usually possible to find a cohesive opposition view by working through the leadership of the opposition party in Congress. It is difficult to comprehend, therefore, the distinction Dr. Stanton made between the status of the Republican Leadership in 1967 and the Democratic Leadership in 1970. Majority Leader Mansfield and Speaker McCormack easily fit the same mold used by Dr. Stanton in 1967 when the networks relied on Senator Dirksen and Minority Leader Ford to rebut President Johnson.

Senator Fulbright refused to believe there would be any great difficulty in using the fairness doctrine to designate a suitable opposition spokesman. He believed that if the networks just used common sense and good judgment they could easily make the fairness doctrine work. On the other hand, Senator Fulbright believed that rigid enforcement could easily make a mockery of the rule. He said the Senate, like the networks, had to "function through comity" because "the rigid enforcement of our written, formal rules would soon on result in the breakdown of the legislative process."[67]

Perhaps the only real difference between the network solution and the one proposed by Senator Fulbright was Dr. Stanton's concern about the broadcasters' "freedom to solve the problem." The networks felt that if they controlled the system it would work; if the opposition maintained control it would fail. The networks had a kneejerk negative reaction ready for any initiative that smacked of government control.

To oppose the Fulbright Resolution successfully, the networks needed a system of their own to promote political balance. Dr. Stanton held up CBS' "Loyal Opposition" as an example of such enlightened network policies even though it aired only once. The question was not whether the networks could find a satisfactory solution to the opposition access problem on paper, but whether they could apply that solution regularly and consistently from year to year and from administration to administration.

One of Dr. Stanton's most disingenuous efforts during his testimony against the Fulbright Resolution was to glorify the "demonstrable advantages of diversity" (when each network broadcast a different opposition spokesman at a different time) and the "significant disadvantages of a uniform approach" (when all the networks broadcast the same opposition spokesman simultaneously). Even though anyone with a rudimentary knowledge of broadcast programming knows that a speech broadcast simultaneously over three networks is superior in impact and number of persons reached to a fragmented response dribbled out over three disparate time periods, Dr. Stanton persisted in making his point. He said, "It is that kind of freedom and flexibility that I do not want to see denied the American public. It is not for our convenience, it is to give the public a broader exposure."[68]

Programming an opposition reply in different time slots on different networks usually had far more to do with network programming constraints than a desire to provide the American people with diversity. If diversity was such a salutary goal, why did the networks always move in lock step to provide simultaneous airtime when a president wanted to speak? Would it not be better for the American people to give viewers a greater choice of programming than to force them into a captive position by roadblocking access on all three networks? Years later, in an interview, Dr. Stanton would oppose the concept of rotating coverage of presidential speeches and news conferences among the networks for fear of missing an important news event.[69] No one wanted unilaterally to loosen their grip on public affairs programming; the competition was too keen and the prestige payoff was too high. Thus, the networks saw virtue in unanimity while covering the president but virtue in diversity for covering the "loyal opposition."

The hearing on the Fulbright Resolution addressed numerous concerns that had been smoldering below the surface for years and caused the networks to think seriously about their access policies. Yet, the legislation went nowhere. It lacked bipartisan support, and few politicians in a congressional election year wanted to challenge the broadcasting industry on which they depended for much of their exposure. Perhaps most importantly, the Congress was reluctant to go against the grain of that sacred American value of media freedom. Time and again in the twentieth century, broadcasters counted on the legacy of the First Amendment as a powerful ally in their battles with Congress. Over the years, network leadership had carefully cultivated an image of respectability and responsibility, which elevated them to a special status with

Congress and allowed them to become arbiters of access who could turn away politicians at will.

## THE FOCAL POINT ISSUE

During the Nixon Administration, two groups of Democrats came at the networks: the DNC and the Democratic leadership in the House and Senate. Throughout broadcasting history, both the party apparatus and the opposition leaders in Congress had pressed for time, but it was never completely clear which group best reflected the opposition view. One of the arguments against the Stanton initiative made by the Republicans was that the Democratic congressional opposition and not the DNC (to which Stanton had given the time) was the legitimate opposition force to a president. With no universally recognized opposition to the president, the networks could question who the "loyal opposition" really was. As CBS President Stanton said when testifying against the Fulbright resolution,

And who would speak for an institution not conspicuous for its unanimity of expression even in the rare cases when there is near unanimity of view? Do the Speaker of the House and the President Pro Tempore of the Senate speak for all members of their respective houses or only for the majority in each case?[70]

From his experience, Dr. Stanton recalled how the fight for network time would intensify political rivalries within the opposition:

Lyndon Johnson, who was then Majority Leader, heard that I had talked to (Democratic National Committee Chairman) Paul Butler about [giving time to the Democrats] and he was on the phone and said, "Why are you talking to Butler about that? I'm the spokesman for the party." And I was caught between the Chairman of the Democratic National Committee and the Majority Leader and I expect that if I had gone one step farther up there on the Hill, I would have found somebody on the House side who felt the same way.[71]

The opposition argued that, on most occasions, the congressional leadership provided a clear focal point reflecting a contrasting view to the president. When there was no difference of opinion with the president, or a divided opposing voice, the opposition leadership could forfeit its right of reply.

The networks seemed more receptive to pleas from the Democratic congressional leadership; it took a more conciliatory view than the DNC, which had hit the networks hard with so many lawsuits. Still, the networks rejected the congressional leadership argument that presidential domination of television upset the balance of power between the President and Congress, and that the Democratic majority should be the natural countervailing force to the president.

## PETITIONS OF PROTEST

During the 1970s, the Democratic congressional leadership gradually assumed the role of petitioner for access from the DNC, except during campaign periods. With no hope of regulatory, judicial, or legislative relief in sight, the leadership tried to counteract its weakened position by consistently and aggressively asking for replay time. After every controversial presidential speech during the Nixon Administration, Senator Mansfield and Speaker Albert fired off telegrams to the networks. More often than not, the networks refused. Still, the leaders pressed for rebuttal access.

Frequent network refusals of opposition access created a climate between the congressional leadership and the networks distinctly different from the network–White House experience. While White House requests for airtime were marked by finesse, subtlety, and semantic games, opposition requests were often blunt and confrontational. The request process began when opposition congressional leaders sent telegrams to the heads of the three networks demanding comparable time to reply to a presidential speech. Usually, the request came before the president gave the speech. If the news division recommended an opposition reply, the network had to decide whether to clear time for both the president and the opposition, and whether the reply should come immediately following the speech or a few days later.[72]

When there was no overriding economic reason for denying the coverage, the parent network accepted the news division's recommendation based on an appraisal of the controversy surrounding the presidential speech and the opportunities for the opposition to reply during regular news programming. The network preference was to accommodate the opposition without providing a special program. Many times, the opposition had to forgo a program that they controlled and settle for being a guest on a program over which they had no control.

It is important to note that the opposition had no standing except in relation to a president's initiatives. The inability of a president to be deemed newsworthy also preempted the opposition. The networks, for example, never let the opposition on the air to explain a legislative initiative. There was no recognition of the opposition's inherent newsworthiness or its status within the political system.

## NO TIME FOR DEMOCRATS

When President Nixon decided to veto a Health, Education, and Welfare bill in 1970, the White House opted for an address to the nation in which Nixon could forcefully make his case, uninterrupted and unre-butted. After the President spoke, NBC's John Chancellor gave a two minute wrap-up while ABC returned immediately to a movie. CBS, in a 20 minute postscript, offered the kind of "instant analysis" that Vice President Agnew had severely criticized in his famous Des Moines media attack speech a few months earlier.

The President used television to put public pressure directly on Con-gress, but there was no opposition response. House Majority Leader Carl Albert and Senate Majority Leader Mike Mansfield pleaded with the networks for time. Albert made personal telephone calls and fol-lowed up with letters to the Presidents of the networks: CBS' Dr. Frank Stanton, NBC's Julian Goodman, and ABC's Leonard Goldenson. The networks still said no. The Democrats had been frozen out. The networks said they turned down Albert because opposition viewpoints to this "non-political news story" would be given ample coverage during reg-ularly scheduled news coverage. CBS said it was "at a loss to understand why Congressman Albert continues to berate us."

Two days after Nixon's speech, Congress sustained President Nixon's veto. The networks had helped the president to seize the initiative and frame the agenda on his own terms for an important legislative battle. Simultaneously, the networks had blacked out the opposition force most directly involved in the controversy. As Robert Cirino wrote, Carl Albert, stripped of network television coverage, had few viable options:

Albert had to settle for yelling on the street corner, writing an article in a magazine that has possibly 200,000 circulation, getting fifteen seconds on a newscast or having his reply buried in ten lines on Page 14 of the *New York Times*. It exemplified the establishment's idea of fairness—a 400 to 1 advantage. It is small wonder that the media is able to produce majority support for estab-lishment priorities and wars.[73]

The HEW veto episode once again showed how firmly the CBS 1936 precedent against responses held. The opposition had no right to reply; the networks would hand out limited time only when they decided it was appropriate. The congressional leadership was not amused by the total rebuff it experienced at the hands of the networks. Speaker Albert threatened to go to the FCC and the Democratic Party vowed to continue its fight for access in the courts.

The first time during the Nixon Administration that the Democrats in Congress received time to answer a presidential address to the nation came in June 1970, when ABC and NBC provided access during the noon hour on two successive days for Senate Majority Mike Mansfield to rebut a presidential address on the economy. It would be nearly four years, when a beleaguered Richard Nixon was about to resign, before the Democratic opposition would get time again on at least two networks. During the five years of the Nixon Administration, the congressional opposition never received simultaneous time on all three networks except after three State of the Union addresses (1971, 1972, 1974).

The Democrats' lack of access could not be blamed on internal division. Even when the DNC was actively involved in trying to secure airtime, Speaker Albert and Senator Mansfield never disagreed over who the proposed spokesman would be. Senator Mansfield's Counsel Charles Ferris, who would become Chairman of the FCC under President Carter, and Michael L. Reed, Speaker Albert's Legislative Assistant, formed a close working relationship which enabled the Democrats to select spokespersons easily and quickly.

Interestingly, Senator Mansfield, a man of few words not renowned as a television "star," had the greatest appeal to the networks. Both times that the networks gave the Democrats simultaneous time during the Nixon and Ford Administrations (not including State of the Union responses), Senator Mansfield was the sole spokesman. He also replied to State of the Union messages in 1971 and 1974, years that the Democrats received rare simultaneous prime time coverage.

The frustration of the Democrats in gaining network access peaked during the early months of 1973. After being reelected by one of the greatest landslides in history, President Nixon was having considerable success with his legislative program. For example, Congress sustained a presidential veto of a highly popular aid bill for the handicapped that had passed the House with hardly a dissenting vote a few days earlier. The Democrats also failed to overturn a veto of a rural water and sewer bill which directly benefitted hundreds of congressional districts.

With the Congress faring so poorly against a powerful President, questions arose about the viability of the legislative branch. How could Congress stand up to a president running roughshod over its prerogatives? Forums held throughout Washington discussed the role of the Congress in light of this "imperial presidency." Surprisingly, it was during the zenith of his presidency in early 1973 that Richard Nixon used television the least. He bypassed formal presentation of his State of the Union message in 1973 in favor of a series of low-key radio addresses laying out his blueprint for a second term.

Because the stakes were low on radio, the networks granted the Democratic leadership reply time to all of the Nixon radio messages. There was little payoff for these opposition speeches except they provided the leadership and their staffs with some glimmer of hope and momentum. Rather than being summarily dismissed by the networks, the congressional leadership found at least token recognition of their role as the natural countervailing force to the president. Speaker Carl Albert responded to the first two speeches on the budget and the environment and then passed the microphone back to the Senate.

The aura of opposition success was quickly broken on March 29, 1973, when President Nixon returned to television to criticize the Democrats in Congress for the bad state of the economy. Speaker Albert and Senator Mansfield quickly sought reply time for Senator Muskie of Maine, but the networks refused. This denial put the leadership in the embarrassing position of having chosen a spokesperson for a speech which would have no audience. Senator Muskie gave his speech anyway for news organizations willing to use parts of it. Without live coverage, however, the ill-fated speech was doomed to meager visibility.

The networks' refusal outraged and humiliated the leadership. How could they unanimously reject the Democrats' official spokesperson? The Democrats believed their legitimate role in the political system had been cavalierly and summarily ignored. Yet, broadcasters clearly had the upper hand and could exercise almost total independence. In a telegram to Senate Majority Leader Mike Mansfield, the general counsel of ABC dismissed the legitimate role of the opposition:

We respectfully take an exception to your allegation that our action [denying live airtime to Muskie] was "preventing Congress from fulfilling its co-equal role under the Constitution." We reached our decision by considering not whether the Congress should be offered live time to reply, but rather whether the Democrats should be offered time.[74]

The tone of the ABC telegram reflected the dominant position of the networks in the early 1970s. They had no compunction about saying that it was they who would decide who the opposition would be and that no one had the authority to contradict their judgments. The networks rejected the notion that a political party in Congress had institutional status in the American political system or was highly relevant to debates over public policy.

The broadcasters were on solid legal and regulatory ground; they had no regulatory responsibility toward the opposition. The broader, more basic question was whether the networks, in adhering to the fairness doctrine, were closing out the constitutionally legitimate opposition to the president from the most powerful public forum of the day.

Shortly after the networks' refusal to broadcast the Muskie speech, the Watergate scandal unfolded and captivated the American people. Still, a wounded president continued to gain access to all three networks to defend himself. President Nixon also continued making domestic policy speeches with negligible rebuttals from the opposition. The broadcast roles of the president and the opposition had become so firmly ingrained during the television age that even a political scandal of major proportions could not upset the status quo.

CBS presented a half hour of opposition views in June and another in December of 1973, the only responses broadcast over any network to three Nixon domestic policy speeches. In 1974, NBC aired one of its "Loyal Opposition" programs in April, but it was not until July 31, just a few days before Richard Nixon resigned, that the Democrats received airtime from more than one network. CBS and NBC aired Senator Lloyd Bentsen's 30 minute reply to an economic speech President Nixon had made before a Conference on the Economy in Los Angeles. ABC followed a week later with a program of its own that included a congressional spokesperson.

## CBS' "OTHER VIEWS" POLICY

While no network was eager to provide the opposition with airtime during the Nixon Administration, CBS provided a definite obstacle to access that made simultaneous access a remote possibility. The root of the problem was CBS' "Other Views" policy which mandated that the network rather than the congressional leadership define the "loyal opposition." ABC and NBC gradually began to recognize the opposition leaders in Congress as legitimate spokespersons who should be given time occasionally to rebut the presidential addresses. CBS, however, rebelled at this recognition. It would rather produce its own program of "Other Views" independent of the leadership. Naturally, such a program either excluded or minimized the "official" opposition viewpoint.

The forerunner of the CBS policy came in 1962 when President Kennedy made a speech in New York's Madison Square Garden attacking the medical establishment. CBS gave representatives of several different viewpoints an opportunity to respond to the President, a stance that would later have profound significance for the opposition party in Congress. By emphasizing issues balance rather than institutional imbalance, this initiative drew network behavior closer to the fairness doctrine and farther from any concept of institutional balance.

In 1973, CBS formally adopted the "Other Views" concept as its official "presidential reply policy." CBS said that when the president made a speech on which there was "significant national disagreement" it would decide whether disagreement existed and whether there should be a reply. CBS would produce its own program, selecting guests from a variety of sources including the congressional opposition and choosing the format, guests and length of the programs. CBS said it would schedule reply broadcasts as "soon as practicable, but generally no later than one week after the president speaks."

The opposition must have questioned how the same network that had given birth to the Stanton initiative of 1970 could adopt a policy within the same decade that severely restricted opposition access. Rather than having a broadcast which they controlled, the opposition had to settle for being guests on a program over which they had no control and in which they might not even be included. CBS, which was the first network to have a reply policy, seemed to influence the policy of one of its competitors. NBC policy states:

If the President, in a speech broadcast over the NBC radio network, or the NBC television network, or both, expresses viewpoints on major issues concerning which there is a sizable national controversy, NBC News will arrange for the broadcast of significant conflicting viewpoints.

The reply broadcast will be made available, as quickly as circumstances permit, to the NBC network or networks that carried the President's speech. NBC News will decide, in the light of those circumstances, the length, format and time period of the broadcast and which person or persons will deliver the conflicting viewpoints.[75]

In all of the reply policies, the networks are the arbiters of access; they decide whether the opposition in Congress is worthy of a reply. By the first few years of the "Other Views" policy, it was obvious that the congressional opposition was losing ground on CBS. After a Nixon speech on the economy in 1973, CBS assembled a panel consisting of the President of the National Association of Manufacturers, the President of the Teamsters Union, and Senator Hubert Humphrey. Because the labor and business leaders had become embroiled in their own controversial debate during their time to oppose the President, there was little opportunity for Senator Humphrey to rise above the babble. Contrasting views were indeed presented to the President's speech (one panel member thought the President had gone too far; another thought he had not gone far enough) but the CBS broadcast confused the public, provided no cohesive opposition response, and made all participants, including CBS, look unprofessional. Despite its ineffectiveness, the CBS program had fulfilled to the letter its obligations under the fairness doctrine.

The "Other Views" policy also reaffirmed CBS' power and individualism. Because CBS did not have to go along with the other networks, it retained more flexibility in its programming schedule. CBS could schedule replies whenever it wanted without having to relinquish control of its airtime, as its competitors did. The CBS policy was a constant reminder that the networks and not the politicians controlled the link with the public. If the opposition message got through it was only because CBS in its wisdom decided that the right person was delivering the right message at the right time.

## THE WATERGATE EXPOSURE EXPLOSION

The years 1973 and 1974 brought abundant attention to the Congress and the Democrats but not through the opposition reply mechanism.

The performance of the Senate select committee investigating Watergate and the House Judiciary Committee debating an impeachment resolution captivated the nation and elevated congressional exposure to a new high. It was one of the few times in broadcasting history that a voice on Capitol Hill resonated as loudly and fully as the President's. Day after day, live coverage from Capitol Hill exposed the American people to Congress at work. Positive public reaction to the work of the Congress soared and the "forgotten branch" of government enjoyed a renaissance.

Even those inside the Congress were not sure how the relatively unknown members of the Judiciary Committee would hold up under the intense, pervasive eye of the network cameras. Senior members urged Speaker Carl Albert to appoint a special, blue-ribbon committee of House "stars." Albert believed, however, that the caliber of the average member of the House (and the Judiciary Committee was considered no better than average) was high enough to do the job.[76] Albert's decision meant that previously obscure representatives like Barbara Jordan of Texas, William Hungate of Missouri, and Peter Rodino of New Jersey would be thrown into the spotlight. Fortunately for the Congress, these "average" members projected an image of credibility and confidence that transcended stereotypes, and they became media stars overnight. Given the Watergate experience, one wonders how increased exposure of the Congress over time would affect public perception of that institution and the party opposing the president.

For a Democratic leadership long frustrated by what it perceived as the arrogant and cavalier attitude of the television networks, the impeachment hearings provided an opportunity to turn the tables. For once, the action the networks coveted was at Congress' end of Pennsylvania Avenue. The networks desperately needed the cooperation of the opposition leadership to produce a program which captured the full drama of the Judiciary Committee. Despite advice to make access difficult for the networks, Speaker Albert cooperated fully, bending many of the House rules to accommodate coverage. As the articles of impeachment were about to be approved, Speaker Albert decided to recommend that the House allow the networks to cover the impeachment event live even though the proceedings of the House were closed to cameras.

It was during a meeting of the presidents of the three network news divisions to resolve the final questions concerning coverage that word came down that President Nixon would resign the following day. Albert aides had been amazed during the meeting at how much their boss was giving away to the networks considering his relatively hard line about preserving decorum of the House. Later, they learned that the Speaker, the man who would soon become next in line to the presidency after Nixon resigned, had known about the President's decision since early that morning and was simply playing a game with the networks until the word of the Nixon resignation leaked.[77]

Broadcasting of the Judiciary Committee proceedings no doubt hastened the opening of the House of Representatives to television cameras five years later. For one of the few times in broadcasting history, congressmen could see the positive end of media attention. When the spotlight finally turned toward the legislative branch, Members of Congress acquitted themselves well. A body accustomed to mostly negative publicity found that even network cameras could cast a friendly eye on Congress after all.

*Chapter 3*

# Network Remote Control

The ascendance of Gerald Ford to the presidency in the wake of Richard Nixon's resignation began a long healing process for the American people and for their political institutions. President Ford brought to the Presidency a distinguished political career in the House of Representatives and the goodwill of the American people who wanted a fresh start after a long Watergate ordeal. Yet, he came to office at a time when the television networks were at the peak of their power and prestige and the Presidency was not. Both the Ford and Carter Presidencies would be a time of testing between the networks and the White House in which the networks would flex their considerable muscle.

While President Ford enjoyed a honeymoon period with the networks, he never gained the special status or maintained the aura of his predecessors. During the Nixon Administration, staffers had cultivated an image of superiority and infallibility which seemed to keep the networks at bay. There was even a sense of awe at how well the Nixon people did their jobs. There was no awe of the Ford White House. Having turned down Jerry Ford at will during his congressional days, network executives felt all too comfortable with him and his style.

Years later, Ford would reflect on how a President's relations with the networks depended on his popularity. He said he had no doubts that network decision-making varied according to the perceived public strength of the Chief Executive. Weakness only brought more aggressive and less considerate network treatment.

## A FORD, NOT A LINCOLN

President Ford's first television address was the surprise announcement of Richard Nixon's pardon on a Sunday morning early in the Ford
Administration. The President quickly learned that his voice, which had
been ignored for years in Congress, could instantly captivate a nation
when coming from the White House. In his second speech before a joint
session of Congress less than a month before the congressional elections,
the President found the networks newly sensitized to the importance
of political balance. In an unusually accommodating move to the opposition, they broadcast Senator Mansfield's response simultaneously
over all three networks. Except for State of the Union responses, it was
the first time the networks had given simultaneous access since 1967
when Gerald Ford and Everett Dirksen responded to President Johnson's
partisan Bal Harbour speech.

Only a week after his major economic speech to Congress, President
Ford once again sought access from the networks, this time for an October 15th speech to the Future Farmers of America in Kansas City.
Surprisingly, the networks decided to pass on the speech, saying it was
little more than a rerun of his congressional speech a week earlier.
Suddenly, the precedent of uninterrupted simultaneous access, which
began during the midpoint of the Johnson Administration and spanned
the entire Nixon Administration, was in jeopardy.

Rarely had the networks even questioned the content of a speech
much less threatened not to carry it. The White House was puzzled and
angry. Even when Ford Press Secretary Ron Nessen circulated a revised
draft on the morning of the speech, the networks still were not stirred.
It was then that Gerald Ford and his staff deployed the ultimate weapon
in presidential television—a formal request for time. The President decided he wanted to speak directly to the American people and that the
networks were not going to get in his way. At this point, the cat and
mouse game with the White House ended. No network was willing to
tell a President that what he had to say was unimportant. Furthermore,
they also feared repercussions if the President said something affecting
national security or of vital importance to the American people. The
networks would rather give him the airtime than risk making a mistake.

Shortly before noon on the day of the speech, an assistant White House
press secretary telephoned Frank Jordan, the NBC Bureau Chief and
head of the network pool committee for that month, to make the formal
request. Jordan relayed it to the top network brass. Word soon came
back from all three network headquarters in New York that they would
indeed cover the previously rejected speech live. Network officials could
not recall any other occasion when the White House had commandeered
the airwaves by turning an informal request into a formal one.[1] Not only

did President Ford overturn network news judgments, but he managed to delay the third game of the World Series on NBC by 15 minutes, a fact that pleased few baseball fans. Furthermore, the networks were hard-pressed to get the speech on the air considering they had less than a half-day to arrange a nationwide broadcast.

Although the networks were quick to honor the presidential override and suspend their independent news judgment in deference to the President, they responded after the fact with indignation. "The big question" according to CBS News President Richard Salant was "at what point do we stop being a news organization and start being a White House transmission belt."[2] All of the networks began to rethink the ramifications of a policy that implied, according to ABC News President William Sheehan, that "any time a President flat out asks for airtime, he'll get it."[3] Among those siding with the networks was Tom Wicker of the *New York Times*:

The plain fact is the President was able to demand and get time from the networks, blanket all three of them for a period in the prime viewing hours, and impose what he had to say on the nation, even though able and experienced news executives, acting separately, had determined in advance that he had little to say that was newsworthy. Mr. Ford was able to do this, moreover, just three weeks to the day before a national election that he has been describing as of critical importance to the survival of the Republican Party.[4]

An interesting question was how the networks determined that a speech before Congress one week was newsworthy and a speech the following week to an organization in Kansas City was not? Perhaps the decision had less to do with newsworthiness than an intangible "oversaturation threshold" set by the networks beyond which Presidents should not go. An informal turn-down was a warning sign to the White House that, according to the network internal barometer, overexposure was approaching. By enforcing this regulatory mechanism, the networks could influence the tempo and velocity of presidential communication.

The Democrats demanded response time after President Ford's Future Farmers speech, but only NBC aired a response by Senator Edmund Muskie of Maine. The lukewarm network reaction to the Democratic reply was curious because the Ford speech came so close to the November elections and the networks had provided simultaneous access to the Democrats just a week earlier. Because the networks had been coerced into carrying the Ford speech, there would seem to be abundant reasons why the networks would want to provide balance through the opposition response mechanism.

That the networks' treatment of the opposition went from one extreme to the other in a two week period showed the inconsistency of network judgment and the immense latitude given the networks by the fairness doctrine. CBS, which followed its airing of a Mansfield reply with a turndown of Muskie, made it clear after the Future Farmers speech that the fairness doctrine was on its side:

Because your telegram states that your request was made under the FCC's "fairness doctrine," permit me to suggest that only last year the Court of Appeals for the District of Columbia "unequivocally" reaffirmed "that a presidential address does not automatically give rise to a special right to respond." Indeed, the Federal Communication Commission and the court have repeatedly stressed that the fairness doctrine does not impose mechanistic requirements of equality on a broadcaster's coverage of public issues. Rather, a broadcaster has fulfilled his obligations under this doctrine by presenting contrasting viewpoints on issues of public importance over a period of time.[5]

## THE "NOT READY FOR PRIME TIME" OPPOSITION

In the Democrats' battle for parity with the President on television, it was painfully obvious that the congressional leadership was no match for the White House's well-oiled publicity machine. One factor influencing the frequent network turn-downs of the opposition was the abysmal quality of congressional responses. The Democrats desperately wanted time, but had little idea of how to use it effectively. In January 1975, when the networks granted a response to President Ford's preview of his State of the Union message, it became clear that the Democrats were not up to the job.

Before his January 1975 Address to the Nation, President Ford hired former CBS News producer Robert Mead to advise him on television; Mead was the first professional television expert in the White House since Robert Montgomery, who advised President Eisenhower two decades earlier. Mead hired a 12–man CBS production unit to work with the President and rented a new VPS 100 Teleprompting system from Q-TV in New York, the state of the art technology Walter Cronkite used on the "CBS Evening News." The bill for the hardware and consultants was $25,693.[6]

Mead picked a time (another key advantage held by Presidents over the opposition) just before ABC and NBC started their highly rated movies. A full week before the speech, Mead brought the teleprompter to Washington to let the President practice. Ford then taped and retaped the 25–minute broadcast before rented CBS cameras for four days to get used to the equipment. The day before the speech, Ford had five run throughs before going live which, according to an aide, improved the delivery "about 2,000 percent."

During his many years in Congress, Gerald Ford had never been regarded as an outstanding communicator. His appearances on the "Ev and Jerry Show," in which he and Senator Everett Dirkson tried to counter President Johnson's policies, had failed to ignite great interest among the media. More often than not, Ev got the airtime and Jerry was left on the cutting room floor. The networks regarded Ford as a "bottom-of-the-barrel" choice for the prestigious Sunday talk shows.[7] Yet, as President, Gerald Ford felt the pressure to become an effective television communicator. To do so, the President opened the door to the best artistic and technological advice he could find.

After President Ford's successful State of the Union preview, *Washington Post* columnist David Broder wrote, "No President probably ever rehearsed more carefully for an address" than Gerald Ford had that night.[8] Mead not only rehearsed the speech carefully but provided the proper ambience. He chose the White House library for the event and even found a sawdust, non-crackling log for the fireplace to warm up the occasion visually. The teleprompter kept the President from losing his place in the script, a frequent problem in earlier speeches, and gave him direct eye contact with the American people. Ford clearly did the best job of communicating on television in his political career, and 70 million persons had watched him.[9]

As President Ford prepared to speak to the Nation, Speaker of the House Carl Albert and Senate Majority Leader Mike Mansfield prepared telegrams asking for time to respond to the President. Not surprisingly, no network was interested in covering the Democratic reply live. NBC said it would broadcast it later that evening at 9:00 PM. ABC agreed to run it the following night at 10:00 PM. CBS, which produced its own program of opposition voices, was not interested in Speaker Albert's "official" response. The maverick network assembled its own "Other Views" program two nights later at 10:00 PM featuring CBS' choice to speak for the Congress, Senator Hubert Humphrey.

The lax behavior of the congressional leadership heightened the already wide communication gap between the White House and Congress. Speaker Carl Albert, like President Ford, had never been fond of television. Although Albert was an excellent speaker (he had won two national oratorical championships in high school and college) he was uncomfortable on television. The Speaker actively sought network time for the opposition but shied away from it for himself. Albert believed that the chief business of Congress was conducted within the confines of the Capitol and not over the airwaves. He did not feel any strong obligation to share his opinions with the American people on a regular basis.

On the day of the speech, Albert spent five hours in the chair presiding over the House, reading his speech over only once just before the broadcast. Not only was Albert's preparation lacking compared to Ford's, but he had none of the technological wizardry available to the President.

NBC, which controlled the pool broadcast, brought only one mini-cam and a couple of lights. With no teleprompter, Albert was forced to nod up and down for more than 20 minutes during an unfamiliar speech he could hardly see under the bright lights. The Speaker's performance was predictable—clearly no match for the well-prepared Ford.[10]

Even if Speaker Albert had had all of the advantages enjoyed by the President, without simultaneous access the impact of his speech would have been minimal. Following Frank Stanton's prescription for "diversity," the networks dumped Speaker Albert into their weakest time slots (something they could not do if the speech were broadcast simultaneously). Because the speech ran at three different times and the CBS program was different, there was a partially duplicated audience. Therefore, not only did the opposition reach a substantially reduced audience of 47 million compared to the President's 70 million, it also reached a substantially different audience.[11]

Throughout the Nixon-Ford period, the Democrats could recount few victories. Typical of the frustrating negative feedback was an ABC telegram sent to congressional leaders in 1975 justifying their refusal of time:

In our judgment, the controversy concerning tax policy is a continuing issue of public importance. We have presented representative and contrasting views on this issue in the past, and we intend to cover the issue in a fair manner in our future news and public affairs programs. . . .

In conclusion, we believe that our coverage of the continuing issue of tax policy fully complies with the "fairness doctrine." Although we have no plans for a program exclusively devoted to your point of view as your wire requests, please be assured that we welcome the view of the Democratic majority of the Congress as part of our overall coverage of the tax issue.[12]

Speaker Albert was so frustrated with such a cavalier attitude toward the Democratic Leadership compared to an obsequious attitude toward the White House that he asked the Congressional Research Service (CRS) to investigate network patterns of presidential access. The CRS report, written by Denis S. Rutkus, showed that from the midpoint of the Johnson Administration to the Ford Administration, the networks had virtually abdicated their independent news judgment in favor of automatic presidential access.[13]

In releasing the report, Albert scored the networks for exercising "little or no news judgment" in dealing with Presidents but rigorous news judgments in dealing with the congressional opposition. He said, "If news judgments are relaxed, as in the case of Presidential requests for airtime, the networks relinquish their most vital journalistic prerogatives and leave themselves vulnerable to manipulation."[14]

The Congressional Research Service report requested by Speaker Albert followed a 1973 Twentieth Century Fund study headed by former FCC Chairman Newton Minow that documented the dominance of presidential access over opposition access. In their book *Presidential Television*, Minow, Martin, and Mitchell questioned whether access to television had actually shifted the balance of power in the United States even farther towards the presidency and away from the Congress.

Despite the higher profile of the opposition during the Nixon and Ford Administrations, the only headway the Democrats made was in prodding the networks into regularly providing reply time for the annual State of the Union Address. Because this speech was delivered before Congress, it was difficult for the networks to argue that the congressional leadership was irrelevant to the process. Three times during the Nixon-Ford periods (1972, 1974, and 1976) the networks granted simultaneous airtime for State of the Union replies and twice provided non-simultaneous access (1970, 1971).[15]

## PRESIDENTIAL ACCESS DENIED

While President Ford was easily winning his battle for access with the Democratic opposition, the day was approaching when the networks would finally end the nine-year streak of continuous simultaneous presidential access begun in the Johnson Administration. Shortly after President Ford announced his candidacy for re-election in October 1975, he asked the networks for television time. Even though it was more than a year before the election, both CBS and NBC refused to carry the speech. Those networks said if they granted time to Ford they would be leaving themselves open to "equal time" requests from other Republican candidates.

CBS News President Richard Salant said his network was prepared to violate the "equal time" rule "in circumstances of national emergencies or urgent presidential announcements," but he did not think the Ford speech fit in that category. NBC News President Richard Wald agreed, saying "international events affecting the national security" would be grounds for broadcasting a candidate's speech.[16]

On the other hand, ABC News President William Sheehan said he did not think that Jacob John Gordon (Ford's only announced opponent at the time of the speech) could be considered a bona fide candidate. Gordon had been a frequent candidate for state, local, and national office and had been indicted in Boston on charges of filing a false claim with the IRS and attempting to run over two IRS agents with his car.[17] Therefore, in this case ABC felt it was not bound by the "equal time" provision. In addition, ABC said the President's speech would be of "major significance," and that there was precedent for carrying an incumbent's speech when he was a candidate. President Eisenhower had been given time for a televised speech in 1956 during the Suez crisis, and President Johnson had spoken during the 1964 race concerning Chinese testing of a nuclear bomb and Khrushchev's ouster in the Soviet Union.[18]

Ford Press Secretary, and former NBC correspondent, Ron Nessen charged that the "equal time" provision which concerned NBC and CBS was not even an issue. He said the FCC exempted on the spot coverage of bona fide news events from the "equal time" provision and this was a news event.[19] Agreeing with Nessen, ABC Vice-President for Special News Programs Wally Pfister said that his network had treated the speech as "strictly an on the spot story—we made a news judgment."[20]

A source within the networks speculated that the turndown was part of a "get tough" policy against the Ford White House which they believed was too often using the networks as access channels, "The President would call up and say 'Put me on.' That's not going to happen anymore. He will now have to prove what he says is important. The balance of power has shifted to us."[21]

Some at the White House thought the dissenting networks were acting neither on regulatory nor news judgment grounds. Ford's TV adviser, Bob Mead, said that CBS' desire to boost Monday night evening ratings on its strongest night affected that network's judgment. CBS executives promptly denied Mead's charges, but the gate had been opened for second-guessing the network motivations for denying prime airtime to Presidents.

Mead also charged that CBS and NBC denied coverage to make a political point for their campaign to eliminate Section 315 of the Communications Act, the "equal time" provision.[22] While it is only conjecture to speculate that the networks were trying to boost their lobbying effort to repeal the "equal time" rule, the networks in this case were far more cautious than they ever had been before in carrying out Section 315.

ABC did carry the speech and no one petitioned for "equal time." Had President Ford not been an announced candidate, all three networks surely would have broadcast the speech. Newsworthiness was not a factor. The network decision to deny President Ford time more than a year before the 1976 election had a chilling effect on his television exposure. While the President was highly visible during the 1976 campaign, he never again approached the networks for time to address the American people during his presidency. President Ford had struck an early blow to the networks when he overrode their news judgment in 1974. One year later, the networks had scored a solid punch of their own, leaning on government regulation to put a President in his place.

## COVERAGE FOR CARTER

In 1977, control of the White House shifted again from one party to the other, bringing a new set of dynamics to the triangular relationship between the networks, the President, and the opposition in Congress. Jimmy Carter, like his predecessors, wasted little time in working the television networks to his advantage, opening his Administration with a blizzard of news conferences, speeches, and addresses to the nation. Despite his early media success, President Carter faced a television establishment growing increasingly weary of White House manipulation. As a result, the Carter Administration proved to be a time of testing on both sides. In spite of the overwhelming predisposition toward granting a President time when he wanted it, the networks were wary of abandoning either newsworthiness requirements or their First Amendment prerogatives.

Less than two years after President Ford demanded time the networks did not want to give, President Carter also strong-armed the networks. In April 1977, President Carter's TV adviser, Barry Jagoda, pitched a proposed speech on energy to the networks. Later that day, word came back to Jagoda that one of the networks would not air the speech and that the others were doubtful. This turn of events put the White House in a difficult position. Unlike the Ford Future Farmers speech, which had been before a live audience, a turn-down by the networks this time meant that President Carter would be sitting in the Oval Office talking to himself. The White House had only two alternatives: cancel the speech or formally request time. Presidential Press Secretary Jody Powell argued that the President's case should be made in two installments, a general speech to the American people stressing the urgency of the energy crisis, followed by a more specific list of recommendations to Congress two days later. Eventually, Powell's views prevailed, and Jagoda formally requested time.

The networks were already carrying President Carter's energy speech to Congress two days later; they believed that this second speech was unnecessary and did not want to be seen giving the President "carte blanche." Bureau chiefs did not like being invited to exercise their journalistic judgment only to have that judgment trumped by the White House. They saw the Carter assault as particularly ominous because the President had launched such an extensive media blitz prior to the speech. Just four months into the Carter presidency, one network executive had said, "Nothing in my experience has equalled the way the Carter White House is using television. They are playing us like a mighty Wurlitzer—and they're pulling out all the stops."[23]

The Carter demand for time brought immediate network acquiescence. Yet, there would be negative repercussions down the road. For example, when President Carter in 1978 approached the networks about making a speech about his first one and one-half years in office, ABC News President Roone Arledge said no to the White House because "it was just a speech he wanted to make about his presidency."[24] Rather than confront the networks, President Carter backed down and cancelled the speech.

Eventually President Carter, like his predecessors, learned the importance of informal negotiations to avoid embarrassing confrontations. That Presidents have had to override news judgments only twice in the past 30 years is proof that the delicate, collegial negotiations which characterize the process can work. Thus, the informal "fishing expedition" system preserves the appearance that the networks have the upper hand while assuring Presidents the airtime they want.

## CBS TRADES CARTER

A major setback for simultaneous presidential access occurred on February 1, 1978, when President Carter scheduled a live address at 9:00 PM EST to plead for public support for Senate ratification of the Panama Canal treaties. ABC and NBC carried the speech live, but CBS delayed it two and one-half hours until 11:30 PM, significantly reducing the audience. CBS said it was delaying the speech because it was a "rehash" of what the network had previously carried about the Panama Canal treaties.[25] Carter media adviser Barry Jagoda said it was ironic that the network found the talk newsworthy enough to carry at 11:30 PM but not at 9:00 PM. CBS News President Richard Salant responded that the network made a mistake in the first place by carrying the speech because it was not newsworthy.[26]

Not all CBS affiliates agreed with Salant's assessment; at least three Post-Newsweek stations affiliated with CBS bucked network judgments and carried the speech live. WTOP in Washington interrupted a popular local college basketball game between the University of Maryland and the University of Virginia to carry the speech. WTOP Vice-President and General Manager, James Lynagh, said that "when a leader of the country says he wants to communicate with the country, we are part of that process."[27]

Complicating the matter was the fact that CBS ran a heavily promoted made-for-TV movie, "See How She Runs" starring Joanne Woodward instead of the Carter speech, prompting charges that CBS was making an economic rather than a news judgment. Adding credibility to the charge was the fact that the movie came on the opening day of the important February sweeps, the quarterly local station competition for the highest audience ratings. CBS called the charges "insulting and outrageous," insisting that the judgment not to carry the speech was made solely by the news department.[28]

Paul Klein, Executive Vice-President of Programming at NBC, recalled that during the month of the Carter speech, CBS was notorious for trying gimmicks to "hype the sweeps" by running their best movies to get an abnormally high rating.[29] Given the high economic stakes involved, it was little surprise that administration officials and executives of competing networks quickly speculated about CBS' motives. Carter Press Secretary Jody Powell said that financial considerations were nothing new; the networks made every request for time into an "impending financial disaster for the network" which he said was clearly not the case.[30]

Support for Carter's contention that the network decision was economically motivated came from a surprising source, Gerald Ford's press secretary Ron Nessen. Nessen said the networks had a "misplaced concern" about losing ratings and he questioned whether it was more than coincidence that CBS, trailing in the ratings race, decided to run the Woodward movie instead of the President during a week when a national ratings sweep was being made. Nessen also said he believed that CBS cancelled plans to broadcast a Ford news conference live because it was afraid the news conference would run over into "The Waltons."[31] He criticized the networks' "near-absolute power" to determine how and when Americans hear their President, and said that the network quest for only what is new and novel robs a President of his role as educator and moral leader.[32]

Surprisingly, the distraction of a first-run TV movie broadcast on one network did not decimate the President's audience. About 40 million viewers watched President Carter's Panama Canal speech compared with 70 million for the President's State of the Union message a month earlier and more than 65 million for a one-hour interview on the three networks the previous year.[33] Still, this reduced audience was enough to out draw the CBS movie. Forty-eight percent of the viewers watched the President even though a network entertainment alternative was available. An NBC executive predicted before the speech that the movie would "over-achieve," luring 40 percent of the audience. "See How She Runs," in fact, scored only a 23.3 rating and 35 percent share of the audience. An ABC executive said the day after the movie, "If that was a business decision on CBS' part they must be gnashing their teeth this morning."[34]

The White House was aware of CBS' entertainment requirements and tried to work around them. Press Secretary Jody Powell said the White House changed the time of the speech from 10:00 to 9:00 PM just to accommodate CBS, "We attempt to avoid disrupting the network schedule any more than we have to. The networks are never happy when you ask them to give up some money to let the President be on. We chose 9 o'clock so that everybody could just slip their network schedules back 20 minutes, or whatever it was, the way they often do with special movies and football games."[35] CBS complained, however, that the White House's moving the telecast from 10:00 to 8:00 PM and finally to 9:00 PM was an example of how the speech "was mishandled from the beginning."

The denial of time by CBS set off another round of debates over how much television access Presidents should have. As with the denial of airtime to President Ford three years earlier, there were rumblings within the networks that CBS' action served notice to President Carter that he should not "abuse" his access to the American people through television. CBS New President Richard Salant declared that "Our business is journalism—not being the President's public address system. . . . If we are going to hold our heads up high, we have to draw the line somewhere. No President should take it for granted that he can commandeer us whenever he wants."[36]

For Presidents Carter and Ford, a waning public opinion rating meant sour relations with the networks. When the two Presidents began to slip in the polls, the networks started to second-guess access decisions and hint that the Presidents were becoming overexposed. Ron Nessen, Gerald Ford's press secretary and Jody Powell, Jimmy Carter's press secretary, both strongly believed that network decision-making often reflected how strong the media perceived a President to be. The press secretaries contended that when a President crossed that threshold of vulnerability, he had to struggle for what was routine in better times.

## FLASHPOINTS OF ECONOMIC PRESSURE

While network corporate executives have usually been discreet about influencing news division preemptions, such as with the Carter speech, occasionally the air of confrontation has been unmistakable. Lester Crystal, former President of NBC News, found himself in an awkward position in the late 1970s when he received a call from an angry Fred Silverman, the president of NBC, during the middle of analysis of a presidential news conference. Silverman was switching channels when he noticed that ABC was already back to its entertainment programming while NBC News still controlled his network's time.

When Silverman called, he was screaming into Crystal's ear, "Get off! Get off!" In the end, NBC held on less than two minutes more than ABC, but to Silverman it was an eternity. Silverman was so upset over the incident that he later demanded an agreement with the news division that in the future news would be off at least no longer than 15 seconds after any of its competitors.[37] As a result of such bold management encroachment, analysis of a network news conference is now a thing of the past. The conference is folded into a neat 30–minute bundle regardless of its newsworthiness.

Former CBS News President Richard Salant said he could recall only one incident when management rode roughshod over the news division—in 1978 during the funeral of former Vice-President Hubert Humphrey. Oddly enough, corporate management flexed its muscle to start a taped sports program on time. An executive ordered Salant to end the funeral special to broadcast the replay of a golf tournament played earlier in the day. Salant was furious, as angry as he had ever been during his 16–year tenure at CBS News. He said the incident would not have happened if Frank Stanton had been president of CBS. Salant said, "No matter how complex and unwieldy a company may be, and no matter what the delegation which it may require, an organization's tone—character—is set by its head."[38]

The pressures felt by Salant and Crystal during the Carter Administration were representative of an environment in which three corporations were forced to squeeze their products into just a few hours of the day. To secure additional time meant hand-to-hand combat with entertainment executives on their turf. The bottom line was that unprofitable special access by the news department had to be avoided whenever possible. Perhaps one of the best and most candid explanations of how the unscheduled news system worked came during a university seminar in the mid–1970s, when Richard Wald, former president of NBC News and later senior vice-president of ABC News, was not affiliated with any of the networks:

Institutionally, the guy who runs the news is always trying to get news on the air, and the guy who runs entertainment is always trying to get entertainment on the air. They may love each other, and outside the office they may share an identical view of the world, but in the office they fight. . . .

What you do essentially is argue it out on the basis of the various merits concerned. Everybody had prejudices. At different times in different places for different reasons, chief executive officers lean more toward news, or lean away from news. Or news people are more persuasive or less persuasive. A lot of it comes to that kind of human equation. A lot of it also comes to a question of: "For God's sake, we have not had a special on in 6 months, so we can do it," or "For God's sake, we had six specials on last week, so we cannot do it."

The question of what the competition is doing is also a main point. . . . If they're going to do it, you really want to do it, because you do not want to be beaten by them, and that's a persuasive argument. . . .

It's a finely graded series of interesting questions, all of them argued out in the space of an hour, or a half hour, because you do not have much time. Actually, winning and losing gets all mixed up because losing fights sometimes win things for you later on.[39]

## THE REPUBLICAN BACKSLIDE

Even though the Democrats opposing Presidents Nixon and Ford made little headway in their struggle for simultaneous network response

time, they fared better than the Republicans opposing the Carter Administration. In four years, the Republican congressional leadership failed
on every occasion to get a single simultaneous coverage of a reply. They
could not even get two networks to cover a reply at the same time. The
Republicans received time on 14 different occasions (about the same as
the Democrats opposing Nixon), but the replies reached low audiences
because none of them was carried on more than one network simultaneously.

The Republican leadership prepared early to counterattack President
Carter's aggressive use of television. But, less than one month into the
new Administration, the Republicans ran into a stone wall. When President Carter's "fireside chat" of February 7, 1977, reached 80 million
Americans, Republican National Committee Chairman William Brock
requested television time to express "points of view other than those
which" might be expressed by the President.[40] All three networks turned
down the opposition. After this bold rebuff, House Minority Leader
John Rhodes and his Senate counterpart Howard Baker met with the
three network bureau chiefs to find out how the Republican opposition
could improve its position. Although the networks were said to be highly
receptive to the Republicans, the coming months showed only marginal
improvement for the congressional opposition.[41]

In April 1977, the networks gave the Republicans their first reply time
after President Carter gave a "fireside chat" on energy on Monday and
gave a similar speech to Congress two days later. In response to the
President's 180 minutes of prime time exposure (60 minutes per network), the networks gave the opposition 75 minutes—15 minutes on
one network and 30 minutes each on the other two, none of it simultaneous. In fact, the responses were stretched over a 43–day period and
came in a hodgepodge of formats. CBS included the Republicans in a
television special with critics of every shape and form. ABC followed
with its own half-hour energy special that included an opposition response. Nearly two months later, NBC turned over a half hour to the
GOP to present a film reflecting their point of view.

Although the Republicans had to wait nearly two months for NBC to
give them time to respond to President Carter's April energy issue blitz,
they hailed the occasion as an opportunity to innovate. The RNC produced the film "Energy: Another View" for what it deemed "the first
time a network granted a political party complete editorial and production control over a response to a presidential message."[42] Rather than
feature the customary talking heads in a studio, the Republicans interviewed customers at a service station in Washington, DC, about high
gasoline prices, shoppers in a supermarket in Buffalo, New York, about
food prices, and farmers in Marion, Ohio, about the hazard of higher
taxes.

The Republican film broadcast on NBC was a reply to a series of presidential statements. Yet, it had overtones of the 1970 Stanton initiative in which the network gave the opposition free reign. It was an effort to strive for institutional balance without concern for newsworthiness. Since the 1960s, NBC had periodically broadcast a program called "The Loyal Opposition" (no relation to Frank Stanton's 1970 initiative on CBS) which featured Congressmen and Senators opposing the President. NBC controlled the timing, format, and sometimes the issues to be discussed. In some programs, a network correspondent would interview congressmen while on other more rare occasions the opposition would control the time as it did with the 1977 energy reply. Because of its sporadic appearance and its relegation to the poorest time slots on the network schedule, NBC's "The Loyal Opposition" seemed more like a corporate public relations effort to soothe the congressional leadership than a vehicle for achieving institutional balance. Still, the NBC initiative, unlike any other network program, recognized the institutional need of the opposition to speak and both parties heartily welcomed it.

Despite the lack of simultaneity and the disparate formats given the opposition after Carter's two energy speeches, veteran Republican aide David Gergen called this "burst of opposition programming" a "radical departure" from previous treatment of the opposition and forecast a possible "dramatic change" in the way networks viewed opposition replies.[43] Yet, the modest success described by Gergen was actually no success at all. A clear pattern of second-class exposure developed that would continue through most of the Carter Administration. Half of the time, only one network provided reply time. On only one occasion did two networks carry a Republican reply on the same day.

The Republican opposition's most glaring shortfalls came during Carter's State of the Union Addresses. Other opposition leaders had routinely achieved access during the Johnson, Nixon, and Ford Administrations, but not the Republicans opposing Carter. The GOP congressional leadership never once achieved simultaneous access. Typical of the network treatment of the GOP was the 1979 State of the Union Address. First, NBC provided a half hour during the outer reaches of prime time (10:30–11:00 PM) for four GOP congressional leaders to discuss Carter's message the same night of the speech. On Saturday night at 10:30, one of the lowest-rated time periods of the broadcast week, ABC invited six newly elected GOP Members of Congress to give their views of the State of the Union. The following Tuesday at 8:00 PM, one full week after the President's message, CBS broadcast a town meeting from Frederick, Maryland, in which the audience questioned four congressional leaders. All three formats offered the Republican leadership network television exposure, but nothing comparable to the President's. The opposition had succumbed to network judgments of what was best. If one network liked town meetings, the leadership conformed. If another network preferred a large group of congressmen to the leadership, it conformed. Clearly, these were network-produced replies that happened to invite the opposition rather than opposition replies using the networks for transmission.

## REAGAN TO THE RESCUE

The capricious nature of network decision-making greatly frustrated congressional leaders who questioned how they could receive a rush of access one year and be cut-off the next. Because there was no well-defined policy regarding the opposition, congressional leaders were vulnerable to an unpredictable case by case evaluation. Meeting every presidential address with a comparable reply in prime time would disrupt network entertainment schedules, cost sizable amounts of revenue, and remove much of the control over special access which news executives jealously guarded.

In 1978, private citizen Ronald Reagan became so frustrated with the disparity between presidential and opposition access that he questioned in a *TV Guide* article whether or not the "Loyal Opposition" was getting a "fair shake from the three commercial television networks."[44] Reagan said that during the first six months of the Democratic Administration, "President Carter completely overshadowed the opposition on television." He presented the following records of coverage time which showed that from January 20 to July 16, 1977, there was clear presidential dominance: ABC—3 hours 5 minutes, President, 12 minutes, opposition; CBS—2 hours 56 minutes, President, 8 minutes, opposition; NBC—2 hours 54 minutes, President, 6 minutes, opposition.[45]

Reagan said that even if he added in all reaction by congressional Republicans, Carter would still beat the opposition two to one.[46] Reagan questioned a fairness doctrine so "distorted" as to "consistently give the President more than three times the coverage." Because there would always be a tilt toward the President, Reagan said it would be unrealistic for the networks to do anymore for the opposition than they had to "to keep up appearances."[47] Part of the networks' motivation, according to Reagan, was economic:

Television network executives are not any more sentimental about providing time for the opposition than they are about scuttling some new fall comedy show that lands in the cellar in the season's first Nielsen ratings. Giving up golden half hours to politicians who want to grind axes with the President is not something that is done very often in the deadly serious dollar stakes played by the networks. . . . Clearly, when it comes to direct rebuttal of presidential policy statements and special messages, the networks won't give up any more time than they think they have to to keep up appearances.[48]

Reagan said that even if the Republican National Committee offered to buy prime time, the networks would still lose money. He contended that the price the network would get from a political party for a half-hour block of prime time would be far less than it would get by selling spot announcements in a regularly scheduled entertainment program, which would also produce revenues when it was rerun later in the year. Reagan said the networks could make roughly twice as much money by refusing to sell time to a political party. A mandatory requirement for opposition access, according to Reagan, would hit the networks hard financially. He said, "with so much potential lost revenue at stake," the networks "could be expected to lobby furiously against any bill to convert today's one-third-of-parity version of 'response' into the real thing."[49]

Realizing that Reagan was probably right about the Republican's chance for parity with the Administration, the congressional Republicans started to buy their own broadcasting time rather than rely exclusively on the networks for free access. In January, 1980, the GOP announced a $5 million television advertising campaign aimed at taking control of the House and Senate after 25 years of Democratic domination. One of the commercials featured a "Tip" O'Neill look-alike who ran out of gas and grumbled about it while kicking his tires. A background voice said, "The Democrats are out of gas. Vote Republican. For a change."[50] The Republicans also distributed a 15–minute weekly radio series called "On Balance" to 100 radio stations nationwide. The Republican-paid campaign showed that opposition forces with money could escape the straightjacket of limited network exposure. The Republican commercials offered total editorial control much like the speech opportunities given free to Presidents.

As the Carter Administration ended, it was clear that the Republicans had done no better, and probably worse, than the Democrats who preceded them. It was to the networks' advantage to retain the status quo which gave them complete control over requests for access. But, there was another issue emerging—the economic pressure on network decision-making. Although the economic pressures were minimal during these days of plenty, nervous executives accentuated every negative blip and pressured the news divisions for fewer preemptions. In the coming decade when financial pressures were indeed real, these economic rumblings would become a more decisive influence in determining who received access to network television.

## Chapter 4

# Economic Realities

Few Presidents have had the television experience and raw communication talent of Ronald Reagan, the quintessential "great communicator." Not only did Ronald Reagan come to the White House with considerable television skill but he came at a time when a well-entrenched legacy of automatic special television access cleared the way for his video magic. Unlike Lyndon Johnson, who brutally pushed the networks to their limits, Ronald Reagan gingerly reached for maximum exposure while leaving the networks wanting more. As Roosevelt and Kennedy before had done, President Reagan understood the pitfalls of overexposure. While Ford and Carter had lost much of their clout with the networks by appearing weak and vulnerable, Ronald Reagan retained a strong aura of confidence.

Like his predecessors, Ronald Reagan gave television priority in the media mix, surrounding himself with people who understood how powerful an agenda-setting tool television could be. As NBC diplomatic correspondent Marvin Kalb explained, television never took a back seat to anything at the Reagan White House, "This particular Administration begins its day by deciding how it will look on television at 7 o'clock that night. All activity at the White House stops at 6:59, while the three buttons are hit so that they can see the success of their work in the course of the day."[1]

More times than not, the slant of White House stories was carefully orchestrated by Administration "spin doctors" who relentlessly and aggressively pushed their company line to the major media. If White House media experts could not affect the spin of a story through selective leaks and vigilant gatekeeping, they could still affect the "bounce" of someone else's story by getting their side on the air.

The White House placed network exposure opportunities in two distinct categories: uncontrolled (which included all news programs, interview shows, and documentaries) and controlled (which included televised addresses to the nation, radio addresses, State of the Union Addresses, speeches, and paid commercials). News conferences, an uncontrolled hybrid which included dimensions of both, were not nearly as preferable as the purer types of controlled exposure. Reflecting that reality, President Reagan held an average of only one news conference every two months, about the same as Nixon and far below most of his predecessors. Kennedy, Johnson, Ford, and Carter averaged far more than one news conference per month.[2]

Some critics contended that the media were as easily manipulated during Reagan press conferences as they were during presidential addresses. The lack of opportunity for adequate follow-ups, time constraints, and the President's ability to pick and choose questioners all contributed to White House control. Yet, ABC White House correspondent Sam Donaldson insisted that Presidential press conferences were the "only time that they get to see Ronald Reagan use his mind, actually to hear a question, think about it, try to recall what it was that people suggested to him he say, or that he wants to say, and say it."[3] Donaldson argued that without the press conference the media and the American people would be subjected solely to the President's carefully crafted speeches: "When the red light goes on, no one can match him. He looks at that TelePrompTer; he reads that speech; he is, as he was trained for 45 years in Hollywood, a gangbuster performer."[4]

Realizing the importance of controlled access, Ronald Reagan was frequently frustrated when he saw his speeches chopped up into tiny little pieces for the evening news. No matter how well the "spin doctors" performed, someone outside the White House still retained editorial control. When editors matched a President's words with a critic's, the presidential aura was reduced to just another ordinary sound bite on the evening news.

With controlled exposure, on the other hand, editing was non-existent; the pure message flowed directly from the oval office to America's living rooms. No congressman, no senator, no presidential candidate could regularly achieve this ultimate level of exposure. Only the President of the United States could take over the airwaves at will and control the editorial content as well as the time and place of the address.

Ronald Reagan knew that his speeches provided a first-class opportunity to personify political problems and to establish an emotional bond by building images filled with optimism and idealism. He always said he believed in "taking the big issues to the people."[5] But, his success as a communicator, like his predecessors', depended upon the climate of public opinion. When Reagan burst on the Washington scene to promote his economic policy in 1981, television helped translate his popularity into legislative support for his programs. His speech in July 1981, urging Americans to support the largest tax cut in history immediately ignited public pressure on legislators. That one speech, along with a carefully orchestrated "grass roots" follow-up by Republicans, provided the crucial margin of victory in Congress.

Part of the genius of Ronald Reagan's first-term media strategy was the complimentary nature of the weapons in his public relations arsenal. Addresses to the nation were huge bombs to be dropped sparingly on strategic targets. The field artillery barrage of weekly radio addresses and speeches reinforced the main theme. Surrogates putting the right "spin" on the story provided strong infantry support. All initiatives—the presidential addresses, the public speeches, the interviews, the photo opportunities, the deliberate leaks, the spin control—merged into a mighty impenetrable phalanx. Few Americans could escape the company line—a prudent, patriotic, and visionary Republican Party led by Ronald Reagan rescuing a nation from Jimmy Carter's frightening legacy of double-digit inflation, high interest rates, and record deficits. The President also moved quickly to rally support after the invasion of Grenada, the bombing of Libya, the Geneva and Reykjavik summits, and the firing of air traffic controllers.

## THE DANCE OF THE SEVEN VEILS

One reason President Reagan was almost guaranteed television success was the masterful way in which his staff dealt with network executives. In both words and pictures, he played to the strength of network news while being careful not to jeopardize the network bottom line. In many ways, it is natural for networks and Presidents to get along because they have common interests; they each strive to please the same constituency, the American people. Neither can succeed without its audience. CBS executive David Fuchs said, "We have to get voted on every minute of the day, every day of the week. In a collective sense, the President has the same interest."[6] Thus, this symbiotic relationship serves both Presidents and broadcasters. After more than half a century, both seem to need each other as much as ever.

The decision-making process for special access requests usually begins when the White House speaks to the three Washington network bureau chiefs. These preliminary "fishing expeditions" determine whether the networks are willing to take the bait. Because of the importance of proving newsworthiness, the White House uses an arsenal of techniques and strategies to sell the President's remarks to the networks. Former White

House Communications Director David Gergen said the networks will agree to any request if it can be justified as newsworthy. Gergen said he often performed "the dance of the seven veils" to entice the networks without giving away sensitive information:

Sometimes, they would say, "Gee, that does not sound terribly newsy, is that really what you're going to say?" And I'd say, "Let me see if I can put some more spice in it and get more news in it." . . . You begin to know what would fly and what would not and what kind of heat they were getting from New York and what kind of heat they were not getting.[7]

Gergen said it was important that the White House never be seen asking for time but simply offering a speech to the networks. He said heavy-handed techniques usually backfired. NBC Washington Bureau Chief Robert McFarland acknowledged that the networks "play a little game of semantics with the White House" so that the President does not appear to be asking directly for time.

McFarland said the give and take also extended to scheduling which could affect the network bottom line. He said it would be inappropriate to ask a President to change the time of his speech, but the networks could subtly communicate what a good time would be for the entertainment schedule.[8] NBC News President Lawrence Grossman said that this type of network intervention actually did the White House a favor because "it does not do the President any good to deliver a message at a time when the public is not going to be happy to get it."[9]

The Reagan Administration was particularly skilled at "making points" with the networks by not interfering too much with their lucrative prime time entertainment schedules. Accordingly, the networks gave the Reagan White House high marks for dealing with television and never hinted that he abused his access to the airwaves.

David Gergen said the relationship between the White House and the networks was built on trust and confidentiality and an understanding that a President should not make the networks uncomfortable by overtly lobbying for party support from the American people. Gergan said the networks warned the White House to avoid blatant lobbying like "write your letter to x, y, or z. Here's the box number." He said he and his colleagues had to work constantly to find "a more subtle way."[10]

Although the networks can refuse access if it lacks newsworthy appeal, lobbying or anything else the President does can usually be postured as newsworthy. The White House has the added advantage of having a special back channel to the networks. Robert Kaiser of the Washington Post pointed out that the system employed by Gergen and other Reagan White House aides benefited from a two-tier system of evaluation. On one level, daily news correspondents and producers judged newsworthiness on how it compared with all other news stories. On another level, the White House secretly negotiated with network executives about the newsworthiness of a controlled communication which could only be judged against itself. Kaiser implied that the executives' criteria gave special consideration for White House requests:[11]

Consider the absurdities: the President has his man shop around for free television time on the grounds that he has something newsworthy to tell the country. So the President's man calls network news executives who—sworn to keep the secret from their own reporters—listen to a description of the speech the President proposes to give. They then consult with their superiors in New York, who debate earnestly whether what they've been leaked constitutes "news." These are the same network executives who have assigned three correspondents and three camera crews to cover the White House at all times; who have authorized the expenditure of thousands of dollars to try to get telephoto shots of the vacationing President riding a horse; who put the President or his family on the evening news programs virtually every night of the year, no matter what he is doing. These executives have to decide whether a presidential address on the economy five days after the announcement of 10.1 percent unemployment and 20 days before a national election is news instead of politicking.[12]

Former CBS News President William Leonard admitted that people "feel used and are used" by the system and that the President usually got his way, but asked "Who are we to get in the way of that communication?" On the other hand, when a speech is political, Leonard asked, "Who are we to further the Democratic or Republican Party?"[13]

As New York Times columnist Tom Wicker, observed, "Almost no Presidential appearance of any kind can be divorced entirely from its political impact."[14] Therefore, deciding whether or not a communication is political becomes difficult. Except for the time immediately proceeding an election when the assumption is that everything is political, news judgments can become highly subjective. It is the same kind of sticky problem that congressional ethics committees grapple with in determining the political use of government funds. Is sending a calendar to a constituent an official representational act or a political use of federal funds?

It remains unclear how the political versus the nonpolitical use of television squares with the criterion for newsworthiness. Cannot a highly political speech still meet the networks' test for newsworthiness? Some might argue that there is a direct relationship between partisanship and newsworthiness. If a President's remarks do not have a partisan ring, are they less likely to cross that magic newsworthiness threshold separating what gets on the news and what ends up on the cutting room floor?

## NEWSWORTHINESS AND THE EVOLUTION OF
## NETWORK POLICY

During the Reagan presidency as with others before it, the presumption was always that a President was news unless proven otherwise. Interviews with news executives like former NBC Executive Vice-President Tom Pettit reflected the socialization process that encouraged priority coverage for the White House, "The President is going to get on television just about anytime he wants to, in my opinion. I do not think that you can legitimately deny the President of the United States the right to speak to the people. What the President of the United States has to say is not unimportant."[15]

ABC Executive Vice-President Richard Wald proceeded from the same assumption—that "the President always makes news," and therefore, when "the President requested time, we always gave it." Wald said "the fact of the speech is a news event," raising the questions of whether there was but one direction those news judgments could take?[16] As the authors of *Presidential Television* wrote, "The President obviously ranks higher in the scale of newsworthiness than anyone else."[17] Edward Epstein, after observing network news operations for several months, concluded that the President ranked above all others in being able to gain exposure on the network evening news.[18]

It became a ritual of newsgathering to turn network cameras toward the White House; a daily report from the White House was automatic. Presidential coverage provided both the White House and the networks with power and prestige. When the president happened to be a "great communicator" like Ronald Reagan, the benefits derived from the White House–network connection loomed even larger.

ABC's Wald said that it was "better to err on the side of presenting the speech than not presenting it." If the networks aired a speech that was not newsworthy, Wald added, public opinion would reflect badly on the President.[19] Critics, however, charged that the entire system of reporting news was distorted by a preoccupation with the White House.[20] The presidential focus was so strong that he soon became the only personality who could play the network star role besides the anchorman.

The networks' chronic infatuation with the Presidency evolved through a series of informal, on the spot decisions. It was the nature of news that executives had the freedom to make instantaneous judgments without rigid codes or stifling bureaucracies. Yet, the routines of newsgathering imposed their own set of cues for decision-making that greatly influenced news judgments. When news executives gave a President time for special access, they reflected both the prevailing corporate culture and the legacy of their predecessors. For example, when all three networks gave simultaneous time for every presidential request from the midpoint of the Johnson Administration to the Ford Administration, newsmen were technically making a series of individual news judgments. Yet, the 100 percent consistency of these decisions among three autonomous corporations reflected a strong organizational norm.

The lack of either government regulation or network policy in this sensitive area made the networks increasingly vulnerable to a hostile external environment. Eventually, CBS News President Salant codified news policy through the "CBS Broadcast News Standards" which he drafted to guide network decision-making and explain news division policy. The other two networks soon followed suit.

Even Salant, however, admitted that executives rarely sat down and explored issues before coming to a decision, but "nibbled at the edges" before saying "let's sleep on it."[21] Likewise, NBC's Tom Pettit said the networks were never "centers of thought" which held extended seminars on policy. He said they favored ad hoc policy because they could change it as quickly and easily as they orginally made it. Then, if in the following week the networks needed a new policy, they did not have to haul out all of their dirty laundry to deal with it.[22]

## THE NEWSWORTHINESS BACKBONE

The written presidential access policies of all the networks stressed two criteria in making judgments: the newsworthiness of the speech and the network's public service obligation to allow the President to speak to the American people. All three networks claimed that newsworthiness rather than public service considerations formed the backbone of their policy. Only NBC admitted that non-news judgments by the parent network could also influence access decisions. NBC began its policy by saying that decisions are "not made solely by NBC News Division" and that the parent network "determines whether to grant access to network airtime."[23]

CBS and NBC emphasized that they used their news judgment to ascertain the importance of a speech. CBS began its policy by saying, "Presidential requests for live coverage of a Presidential speech will not be automatically granted."[24] NBC said its decisions "will not be perfunctory or without questions." Clearly, the networks considered themselves the best if not the only judge of what was important for the American people to watch. ABC, for example, said, "Should a President request time to address the nation on a matter which, in ABC's judgment, is clearly not of great national or international significance, we reserve the right to decline such requests for live coverage." The ABC policy implied that a matter was newsworthy only if it was of great national or international significance as defined by the network.

Although the networks through their policies positioned themselves as arbiters of presidential access, coverage was virtually automatic. This discrepancy was highlighted on March 17, 1986, when the *New York Times* printed a seemingly innocuous explanation about how a President automatically gets on the air entitled "Reagan: He Must Ask." It pointed out that time for the President is "almost always granted unless the content is deemed blatantly political."[25]

The *New York Times'* straightforward account of how a president gets on the air rankled the Washington Bureau Chiefs who pointedly responded in a letter to the editor that they made their own judgments independent of each other and that they carried the speeches because they "are usually newsworthy" not because "the networks are compelled or even asked to by the White House." The Bureau Chiefs were also careful to point out that they were not "required by the 'equal time' doctrine" to broadcast views in opposition to the President's "as many people believe" but did so because they thought it was "the right thing to do."[26]

The Washington Bureau Chiefs' letter illustrated how sensitive the networks were to suggestions that their judgments had become automatic and that factors other than newsworthiness influenced the process. Yet, a good White House operative could indeed "sell" a speech to the networks, and the White House was no doubt sensitive to preempting popular entertainment programs.

The Washington Bureau Chiefs were also eager to flaunt their independence from government, reminding congressional leaders that no one makes them televise the opposition; they do it only because they want to, because it is "the right thing to do." From the opposition's point of view, the "right thing" boils down to subjective judgments made by three corporate executives who must also do the "right thing" to bring in the highest ratings and profits to their companies.

One can forgive the *New York Times* for speaking of the networks collectively because they nearly always move in sync; only five times has one or more of the networks acted independently regarding presidential speeches. The White House did not have to compel all three networks to carry a speech simultaneously because broadcasters' own norms of behavior and rituals of coverage compelled them to.

## THE PRESIDENTIAL OVERRIDE

Despite all the bluster about independent news judgments, the networks always maintained a safety valve provision in their policy to abdicate those news judgments. The policy allowed Presidents who formally requested time to "override" independent news judgments. Presumably, the networks made such an exception because they believed there were times independent of newsworthiness when a President deserved airtime for the good of the American public. ABC said, "We recognize the President's unique position as Chief Executive and Commander-in-Chief, consistent with our responsibilities as broadcasters. In considering future presidential requests, we will continue to give great weight to the unique position of the Presidency in our system of government."[27] In this vein, NBC and CBS policy allowed a President to go on the air even when the networks completely turned over the reins of power to the President. The "presidential override" provision protected the networks from being accused of silencing a President during a crisis. The CBS and NBC policies were similar because Richard Salant, former CBS News president and former NBC vice-chairman, was chief architect of both. The CBS policy, written in 1974 stated:

a) Where we have sufficient reliable information, or sufficient intelligence concerning the surrounding circumstances, to permit us to make a genuine news judgment that the speech should be carried live, we should, of course, do so.

b) Where we do not have sufficient advance information or intelligence to permit us to make such a news judgment, but nevertheless we are specifically told that the reason for the absence of advance information is national security or other national interest, or we are told the speech is one of major importance to the American public, we should resolve the doubts in favor of carrying the speech live.

c) Where we are provided with sufficient information to make a news judgment, and our judgment is that live coverage is not warranted, we shall nevertheless consider such coverage if the White House explicitly states that the speech is of urgent importance to the American public. In this instance, the determination will be made on a case to case basis, with weight given to the White House assurances of urgent importance.[28]

Richard Salant and CBS President Arthur Taylor found subsection "c" of the policy the most difficult part to write. Salant said he kept the wording "fuzzy" because "it seemed best at this stage not to provide flatly that we will carry, or that we will not carry, in such circumstances."[29] Likewise, Arthur Taylor thought that in cases where the network does not think a speech should be carried but the President does, it "would require a major network decision which would not be taken lightly by either the networks or the White House."[30]

NBC's and CBS' nearly identical "presidential override" provisions implied that a President could secure airtime if he wanted it badly enough, content or newsworthiness notwithstanding. Before succumbing to the White House, the networks reserved the right to state formally that they did not believe the speech was newsworthy. NBC and CBS policy said they would broadcast a disclaimer at the beginning of such a speech saying the broadcast was being aired at the White House's request based on an assurance that the speech was of national importance.

While some could appreciate these fine distinctions in network policy, the essence was that news judgments meant nothing if the President of the United States wanted to go on the air. By institutionalizing this practice, CBS and NBC gave Presidents a formal mechanism to commandeer the airwaves even when the networks did not want to provide the time. In these cases, the news divisions suspended their "independent news judgments" and simply became quasi–official transmission belts for presidential communication.

The controversy surrounding the "presidential override" made it a rarely used option. Only Presidents Ford and Carter formally requested time from the networks. In each case, relations were seriously strained. Realizing the risks associated with the "presidential override," President Reagan wisely preferred to settle differences through back-channel communication and not to force himself on the networks.

## EXCEPTIONS TO AUTOMATIC SIMULTANEOUS ACCESS

Since Presidential access became automatic during the mid–1960s, the practice worried some network executives. In 1981 after President Reagan steamrolled the congressional opposition on the budget tax question, Richard Salant wrote:

We must be sensibly discriminating in our acquiescence to presidential requests for time on the air. . . . And we can guess wrong—as I have. But, at the least, we must not make an automatic decision. We must at the risk of charges of blacking out the President (as I have been accused of doing), or of political bias, or of lese majeste, of exercising our news judgments on what advance knowledge we can gather about a proposed presidential speech.[31]

While the exercise of independent news judgment was not particularly rigorous or discriminating, there were six occasions over 30 years when Presidents did not achieve simultaneous access, the first two of which were discussed in chapter 3: Gerald Ford's address to the nation on the economy on October 6, 1975; and Jimmy Carter's address on February 1, 1978 on ratification of the Panama Canal treaties.

Despite Ronald Reagan's stunning success in communicating with the American people via national television, four of the six network refusals came during his presidency: an economic speech on October 13, 1982; a Contra aid speech on June 24, 1986; a speech supporting Robert Bork's Supreme Court nomination on October 14, 1987; another Contra aid speech on February 2, 1988.

## ABC'S REFUSAL TO STAY THE COURSE

The first network turndown of President Reagan occurred just three weeks before the congressional elections of 1982, on October 13, when the President sought television airtime to defend his economic policies. Republicans first asked to purchase the time, but the networks declined. The White House then requested airtime for what it said would be a nonpartisan economic report to the nation. The Democrats immediately protested, claiming that the speech would be nothing more than "last-minute partisan campaigning." CBS and NBC carried the speech live, but ABC refused. Rather than basing the decision on the closeness of the address to the election and its presumed partisan overtones, ABC said the speech was not "of sufficient importance to merit live coverage."[32]

During the speech, President Reagan attacked "the hard-core opposition of a minority of Representatives who prefer continued big spending," but the most partisan statement came at the end. In closing, the President reinforced a multimillion dollar Republican advertising campaign by using the GOP's 1982 campaign slogan asking voters to help economic recovery by "staying the course." The tie-in with the ad campaign was unmistakable. The President had used "free" time which he controlled to repeat a partisan slogan to an audience of more than 50 million people three weeks before a pivotal congressional election.

*Washington Post* writer Robert Kaiser said that CBS and NBC were fooled by the President's "charade" and his utterance of "one of the great 'screw you' lines in history." Kaiser said the White House correspondents from all three networks had warned their bosses in New York that the speech would be a watered down repeat of the standard stump speech President Reagan had been making on the campaign trail. Although NBC's Chris Wallace said before the speech that he did not think "anybody is fooled" about whether the speech would be political or not, at least two of the networks considered it to be a legitimate news event rather than a political speech.[33] While CBS and NBC carried President Reagan's "stay the course" speech live, some of their affiliates did not. News executives at WBAL-TV, Baltimore; WITI-TV, Milwaukee; and WJKW-TV, Cleveland said they thought it would be inappropriate to broadcast a presumably partisan political speech so close to the November elections.[34]

There was confusion over ABC's real motivations for not carrying Reagan's speech. While ABC ostensibly rejected the speech based on its lack of newsworthiness, ABC Senior Vice-President Richard Wald recalled in an interview three years later that the network said no because the speech was "purely partisan politics."[35] ABC Washington Bureau Chief Ed Fouhy said after the speech, "If the President had something urgent to say to the nation, he could have requested prime time. He did not."[36] This remark implied that ABC would have provided the time if only Reagan had asked for it. *The Washington Post*, in an editorial after this controversial "stay the course" speech, pointed out the network dilemma in which their policy had a "built-in imbalance which can be exploited to deliver one side of a public issue with no comparable format or formula for differing viewpoints."[37]

## A CONTRA SPEECH TOO FAR

In late June 1986, President Reagan became the first President in history to be denied access by all three networks. Surprisingly, the refusal bothered neither the networks nor the White House. The incident began when the President asked Speaker O'Neill for permission to address the House of Representatives just before a vote on his $100 million aid package for Nicaraguan rebels. Saying that such an address to one house of Congress would be "unprecedented," Speaker O'Neill turned him down unless the President would speak to both the House and Senate or would answer questions from members of the House.[38] Neither alternative was acceptable to President Reagan, especially the latter. While Presidents routinely answer questions from the press, they would never consider taking questions from Members of Congress in a public forum.

President Reagan was taken aback, angered and frustrated by the Speaker's rebuff. The O'Neill decision also set off another bitter struggle within the White House over whether the President should deliver a televised presidential speech. Some argued that the ultimate PR weapon, the presidential address, should be used to push the Contra aid vote over the top. Others argued that the presidential address was a powerful tool that should be used sparingly only when public opinion was supportive. In the wrong climate, they explained, high-profile speeches could generate as much opposition as support.

When President Reagan finally decided to make the speech, he delivered it at noon rather than in prime time. This diffident approach to the Contra speech sent a signal to the networks that the President was not all that interested in drawing maximum attention to the Oval Office address. Back-channel communication between the White House and the Washington bureau chiefs reinforced that view. The networks were pleased that the President was not making a high pressure bid to have the speech carried live; NBC News President Lawrence Grossman said it was "not something worth interrupting the network for."[39]

When President Reagan stepped into the Oval Office on June 25, only the Cable News Network (CNN) was there to carry the Contra speech live. ABC, CBS, and NBC, in an unprecedented move, had decided to pass. The President gave his 27 minute speech, and his contra aid package passed the House 221–209. The *New York Times*, calling the vote a "major victory," said the President's personal lobbying, rather than his public speech, provided the margin of victory that Reagan missed just three months earlier when the House had defeated a similar aid package.[40]

## BORK RERUN

The fifth network turndown of a President was almost identical to the Contra aid speech refusal. President Reagan requested time on the afternoon of October 14, 1987, to rally support for Judge Robert Bork's quickly fading nomination to the Supreme Court. All three networks said no. The reason given was that the speech was just a rerun of the President's radio speech the previous Saturday and that it was too partisan. A more likely reason was that the President did not push for coverage. One network executive said, "Obviously, the thought occurs to you that the White House does not want this speech televised."[41]

Even though the networks claimed that the President had nothing new to say about either Contra aid or the Bork nomination, the same speeches given in prime time would have surely merited simultaneous coverage. It was as if the networks were doing the President a favor by ignoring his two speeches. Had the White House launched prime time addresses to the nation and then lost the congressional battles, the President's credibility as a great communicator and powerful persuader would have been dealt a severe blow. In the absence of the networks, CNN provided an adequate national forum for the President's views. Most American homes wired for cable had access to his views as did hundreds of local station with access to CNN feed. There was no public outcry that the networks had failed to transmit the President's speeches live.

Given the low-key way in which the Contra aid and Bork speeches were handled, it is difficult to put these episodes in the same category with the three earlier network refusals. No network executives interviewed after the speech would attach any importance to their actions. This refusal was simply a chance for the networks to flex their muscles on a low risk event that the White House really did not want on the air in the first place.

## WHO'S THE BOSS?

The most controversial network refusal to broadcast a Presidential speech came on February 2, 1988, in the twilight of The Reagan Presidency. Before another crucial congressional showdown over Contra aid, Ronald Reagan asked for airtime to make a nationally televised address.

Unlike the earlier Contra and Bork speeches, this one was for prime time and the President himself wanted to make the speech.

Using their newsworthiness criterion to measure the speech, all three networks said it came up short—just another rehash of the Contra aid message the President had given numerous times before. ABC Washington Bureau Chief George Watson said he did not know of anyone at ABC who spoke up for carrying the speech and that it did not "make sense to go on national television just to lobby a handful of congressmen."[42]

What an embarrassment to the White House! For the first time in history, all three television networks had said no to the President when he asked to speak in prime time. "Matlock," "48 Hours," and appropriately "Who's the Boss" would run as scheduled while the President spoke. Only Ted Turner's CNN would plug-in to the President live. White House spokesman Marlin Fitzwater called the network action "an incredibly narrow interpretation of their public service responsibilities and a relatively arrogant news judgment."[43]

White House Chief of Staff Howard Baker, a veteran of the network wars on both ends of Pennsylvania Avenue, said the decision "by the three over-the-air commercial networks to refuse this opportunity to the President represents an attempt to substitute their judgment for that of the President on what the country should have the opportunity to hear."[44] Baker contended that the President had a "traditional right" to communicate with the American people on important issues over television.[45]

What particularly riled Baker was that the networks seemed to be negotiating with the White House over the content of the speech. The "dance of the seven veils" has become a familiar practice in Washington, usually working to the White House's advantage. If a speech is not newsworthy enough, the networks coax the White House to spice it up. This time, however, the practice did not seem so benign. Baker charged that the networks offered a quid pro quo for coverage:

Not only do I think the over-the-air networks were substituting their judgment for the President's on what he thought he should be able to communicate to the American people, but I know firsthand that some of them said, "If you include so-and-so in the speech, we will cover it." Not only does that represent an effort by the networks to say, "We're going to decide whether the President has access to the American people but we're going to bargain on what's going to be in a future Presidential speech." I find that ludicrous and I find it totally unacceptable.[46]

As with decisions about some of the previous denials, the networks said they would have given the time if the President had either formally requested it or assured the networks that what he had to say would be newsworthy. Had that been the case, NBC News President Lawrence Grossman said, they would "undoubtedly give the time."[47] Again, the networks seemed uneasy turning down the President and were looking for excuses to turn news judgments into public service judgments.

Another familiar trend engulfing this incident was the perceived weakness of the President, which made it far easier for the networks to say no. In 1981, it would have been unthinkable to deny Reagan time. Seven years later, the decision was much easier. As ABC's George Watson said, "When a President is having problems, it's going to be harder for him to get on the air and the more times he goes to the well, the worse response he is going to get."[48] CBS had the news show "48 Hours" already scheduled in the time slot the President wanted and could have easily carried the speech. A network executive said, however, that CBS was sensitive to public opinion and felt uncomfortable being "the odd man out with the onus on them." He said in those cases it was much easier for all networks to stick together rather than have one go an opposite way.

Proponents of the fairness doctrine, whose reinstatement was vetoed by President Reagan the year before, wasted no time in citing the irony of the networks' blanket turndown of the speech. Senator Ernest Hollings of South Carolina said the network decision represented the "final demise of the letter and spirit of the fairness doctrine," and said that next time the President might think twice before vetoing a doctrine that would "give balanced exposure to all important issues and points of view." In truth, the fairness doctrine had never directly helped either Presidents or the opposition gain time, but it did stand as a symbol of government expectations of fairness in covering anything controversial, including political discussions.

While the networks were out of the coverage picture, CNN carried the President's speech and an opposition reply live. The feed was also made available to all network affiliates though hardly any used it.[49] White House spokesman Marlin Fitzwater praised "the ones [networks] . . . that have some sense of public service" for carrying the speech.[50] Those broadcasters apparently had much more influence than audience; the President's speech reached fewer than one million viewers nationwide.

The network's refusal was important. It showed how easily the three networks could black out a President from public view at will. It also showed, as Brookings Institute Senior Fellow Stephen Hess said, that "the networks determine what is news."[51] Even if it was a tactic the networks would use sparingly when Presidents were weak, the speech turndown quickly set the record straight in Washington about who was boss.

Overall, the six exceptions to automatic presidential access during the

Ford, Carter, and Reagan Administrations raised more questions than they answered. Motives other than lack of newsworthiness figured into all the decisions. CBS and NBC said they turned down President Ford because he was an announced candidate. CBS' refusal to carry President Carter was clouded by the pressure to put on a blockbuster made for TV movie during the February sweeps. ABC seemed to be reacting more to strong protests from Democrats concerned about Reagan's partisan "stay the course" address than to the newsworthiness of the speech; some CBS and NBC affiliates as well refused to carry the speech because of its partisan overtones. Meanwhile, the burying of the Reagan Contra aid and Bork nomination speeches by the networks reflected the low priority the White House gave them. Had they been given before a joint session of Congress in prime time, the networks would have been there in unison to broadcast such "newsworthy" addresses. Meanwhile, the final Contra aid speech refusal seemed to reflect the vulnerability of a lame duck President as much as it did the speech's lack of newsworthiness.

During the six network refusals to broadcast speeches several issues surfaced:

1. Should newsworthiness be the sole criterion for determining Presidential access?
2. Should a President's request be grounds for automatically granting time?
3. Is it necessary to force-feed a President to the American people by having all three networks carry a speech?
4. Do the networks sacrifice their judgment and independence when they appear to give automatic access to a President?
5. Does one network opting out of presidential coverage place too much economic pressure on the other two?
6. Do economic judgments creep into news judgments regarding Presidential access?

## THE PUBLIC SERVICE DIMENSION

The networks consistently had difficulty defining newsworthiness because almost anything a President said could be considered newsworthy. Some, for example, questioned how the networks could all agree that a speech by Ronald and Nancy Reagan on drug abuse in 1986 was newsworthy enough to interrupt prime time while a Reagan speech one day before a critical congressional vote on Contra aid was not.

The networks could justify broadcasting the Reagan drug abuse speech because their actions were not as totally dependent on newsworthiness as they claimed. Closely intertwined with the newsworthiness criterion was the network belief that they performed a public service for the American people when they covered a President. Many news executives believed as ABC's Richard Wald does that "enlightenment is newsworthy," making it all but impossible to tell where newsworthiness ends and public service broadcasting begins. Wald said that with only three major pathways to reach the American people, the scarcity issue was often enough to tip the balance in favor of a President being newsworthy.[52]

Even though the days when the networks provided the only electronic pathways to the people were long gone, the legacy of network reliance continued. Much of the legitimacy of network news depended on its ability to connect the government with its citizenry. Former CBS News President Richard Salant said the networks provided "a direct link between the White House and the people," allowing Presidents "to talk directly and simultaneously to all the people, with no reporting filter in between." Salant said it was through network television that a President "conveys the force and conviction" of his "own personality and character." NBC's Tom Pettit believed the presidential access function of the networks was "healthy for a democratic society" and essential for the electorate to size up its national leader, "I want to see the guy whose thumb is on the button. Every now and then I just want to see him. I want to see him talk. I want to see how he's doing. I want to see if he has a nervous tick."[53]

The lines between news and public service judgments were blurred from the beginning. Even though the editorial control of Presidential addresses rested clearly with the White House, the networks continued to consider these broadcasts news. These newsworthy events differed from ordinary news stories in four basic ways:

1. they were not a part of a regularly scheduled newscast;
2. the editorial control over content rested with the news source rather than with the broadcasters;
3. the news source could set time, date, and place of the broadcast;
4. the newsworthiness of the event often could not be ascertained in advance.

The only editorial control the broadcasters could exercise was whether to carry the speeches.

Despite the contrast between news programs, which the networks controlled, and televised addresses, which the White House controlled, both were placed under the same rubric of "broadcast journalism." Yet, no other journalistic endeavor usurped as much control as the Presidential address, and no other news judgment was routinely made before the news event without any evidence on which to certify the news value. Because complete control over content rested with government leaders rather than with broadcasters, the addresses took on characteristics more akin to advertisements than to news stories. For example, Fraser Seitel in *The Practice of Public Relations* listed the characteristics of advertising as follows:

1. You pay for it.
2. You control what is said.
3. You control how it is said.
4. You control to whom it is said.
5. To a degree, you control where it's put in a publication or on the air.
6. You control the frequency of its use.[54]

Presidential addresses were free, but they embodied most of the other characteristics of advertising. Certainly, the editorial control remained with the White House, and network policy could be manipulated to influence the time of the address and the frequency of airtime. When President Reagan announced his candidacy for re-election in January 1984, the Reagan–Bush Committee decided to continue the President's "free" weekly radio addresses as paid political announcements. Interestingly, no format or content change had to be made; the addresses already were tailor-made for advertising.

While the networks were willing to overlook the control issue in the case of Presidential access, they were much more vigilant regarding congressional opposition access. In 1975, CBS President Arthur Taylor rejected the opposition's request: "Fundamentally, we just respectfully reject your demand because it seeks not only to have the government dictate judgments of newsworthiness, but also to select the date, time and place of publication. We submit that the press—broadcast and print—resist such inappropriate governmental intrusion."[55]

This policy set a clear double standard because the networks denied the opposition's request for the exact type of control routinely given a President. In the case of both the President and the opposition, it can be argued that public service considerations play a larger role than the networks would admit. Even though ABC Senior Vice-President Richard Wald contended that it was the newsworthiness and not the public service catalyst that sparked the interests of the networks, broadcasters realized that they were creating an audience for a ritualistic cultural event that had become ingrained in American society. As Wald admitted, "What the President wants is not an opportunity to discuss with a few people. What the President wants is the total attention of everybody who has a television set."[56] The networks could say that the chief criterion for the access was newsworthiness, but, in fact, they were creating this massive nationwide audience first and foremost to provide a public service to the American people.

## REAGAN ON RADIO

The presidential radio addresses constituted an excellent example of the news versus public service dilemma facing the networks. The radio addresses began in April 1982 when the White House approached Mutual and other networks about the possibility of the President delivering a series of ten radio addresses. All of the networks except CBS agreed to carry the broadcasts with the proviso that the congressional opposition would be allowed to respond an hour later. The success of the first ten addresses, which prompted abundant residual exposure in the Sunday papers and weekend newscasts, convinced the President to continue them on a permanent basis. Reagan said he relished the live, controlled format because it allowed him to talk directly to the people and there was "nothing between us—no editors, no reporters, no third parties of any kind."[57]

The control Reagan had over the broadcasts bothered the networks. There was no room for them to exert their own editorial judgment and there was no way the networks could predict the content or make news judgments on a case by case basis. The addresses represented a classic case of public service judgments eclipsing news judgments. The radio addresses rocked along on and off for more than four years gathering little attention within the broadcasting industry. The stakes were so low in radio that no one seemed to mind that the networks had institutionalized carrying the President (and the opposition) as a public service. The latent radio address problem, however, burst into the headlines during the summer of 1986 when Mutual Broadcasting's Vice-President for News and Special Programs, Ron Nessen, abruptly cancelled the addresses on his network. Nessen said he had been uneasy about the "surrender" of airtime every Saturday to the President "regardless of the news value (or lack thereof). Nessen said it was the responsibility of the media to decide what is and is not news. He added, "The President and the other politicians should not be allowed to encroach on that responsibility."[58]

Nessen said that the only way his network could justify carrying the speeches was "on grounds that the statements are genuine 'news' events."[59] Nessen, who had been Gerald Ford's presidential press secretary, had a different perspective a few years earlier. In 1978, Nessen had attacked CBS for refusing to carry President Carter's Panama Canal speech. Nessen said placing all the emphasis on newsworthiness "cheats the public of television's enormous power to inform."[60]

The conflicting Nessen statements articulated both sides of the problem, showing how public service and news viewpoints could collide. The networks felt uneasy about giving the President blanket time without his earning it by being newsworthy. Politicians, meanwhile, saw education and enlightenment of the public as worthwhile goals in themselves and could see no reason to submit to the newsworthiness straight jacket. Even among broadcasters, there was ambiguity about their role. Providing time as a public service could be perceived both as a weakness and as a noble public service gesture. But, broadcasting organizations whose livelihood depended on advertising revenue had limits on how much time they could give away.

As competition for ratings grew and news developed its own bottom-line mentality, those limits began to shrink at an accelerated rate. By the mid–1980s, both unprofitable news specials and special political broadcasts in prime time were rare. The dual imperatives of public service broadcasting and profitable operations raced forward on a collision course.

## UNSCHEDULED NEWS

Predating the mid–1980s conflict between the news divisions and their parent networks was intra-network squabbling over programming with the unlikely name of "unscheduled news." These were the times when news division, usually on little notice, asked the parent network to turn profitable time into unprofitable time. Space launches, live congressional hearings, crisis events, and presidential speeches are all examples of unscheduled news. It was the parent network rather than the news divisions that decided whether these events were important and timely enough to disrupt an entertainment schedule and possibly sacrifice millions of dollars.

News executives were routinely able to convince corporate executives that unscheduled news preemptions were vital to the reputations of the networks. NBC News President Lawrence Grossman believed that what distinguished a network from another form of syndication and the one thing that linked it to its affiliates was the ability to report any time there was a major happening of national or international importance. As costly as it might have been, Grossman said such special reporting was the "cornerstone" of a network's existence. Grossman believed it would be self-defeating "to lose the network's special position not only with the affiliates but with the viewers in favor of making more money on the entertainment side and our programming executives know that."[61]

Despite the importance of unscheduled news preemptions to the viability of the networks, decisions were sometimes made more on economic conditions than the urgency of the news. News presidents had no access to television time beyond that which was normally assigned them. To get extra time, the news president had to request the time from the network president or higher. It was at this level that broadcasting executives had to balance the desire for larger profits with the desire to be responsive to the news divison.[62]

The burden of swimming upstream to interrupt entertainment programming for news puts the news division president in an untenable position with little real power. As former NBC News President Reuven Frank told Edward Epstein, "The power to preempt is the power to destroy. The president of a news division simply cannot be given the right to unilaterally preempt the programs of the network and destroy its revenues; that must ultimately be a network decision."[63]

## SCHEDULED UNSCHEDULED PREEMPTIONS

Some news preemptions were planned far in advance, such as the broadcast of a party political convention, while others, like the explosion of the space shuttle Challenger, were spontaneous. Presidential speeches and news conferences fit somewhere in between; the networks received advance notice, but not enough to make elaborate programming adjustments. While print competitors could add more pages to accommodate the unexpected, network news time was static. When a news special or a presidential speech had to be inserted into the schedule, some other program had to be deleted or delayed. The network product was a fixed, inelastic commodity.

Even the networks' "scheduled" unscheduled programming felt the iron grip of economic reality. Not all networks offered gavel-to-gavel convention coverage in 1984 or 1988. In an uprecedented move that illustrated the network withdrawal from special news coverage, two of the networks (ABC and NBC) offered scaled down election night coverage in 1986. Only CBS provided wall-to-wall coverage (8:00 P.M. to 2:00 A.M. EDT).

As one might expect, ABC's popular "Moonlighting" (27 share) and NBC's "Crime Story" (17 share) beat CBS' 1986 election coverage (14 share) in the early part of prime time. CBS eventually gained the lead when all three networks finally went head-to-head during the late evening.[64] Despite its loss of millions in revenue and third-place finish, CBS executives believed they had scored a public relations triumph while siphoning off most of the opinion leader audience.

ABC and NBC, which rationalized that the off-year elections did not warrant full coverage, said the story did not become "interesting" until after their prime time entertainment schedule was over. NBC News Senior Executive Producer Paul Greenberg said viewers "got all the information they needed."[65] CBS News President Howard Stringer, meanwhile, said that if ratings were the only reason not to offer extended coverage again "then we're as good as admitting that as a network, we have no other responsibilities but circulation."[66] Stringer said that CBS' willingness to lose millions as well as rating points during a crucial "sweeps" month showed an "extraordinary commitment" to the news division.[67] Stringer's remark was a telling commentary on the tenor of the times. In any other year, providing complete election coverage would not have been extraordinary at all; it would have been an ordinary occurrence. When Stringer said he was "very, very grateful" to corporate CBS for its generosity, he was no doubt establishing a climate in which prime time preemptions, once the right of CBS News, would now be a rare privilege.

## INSTANT NEWS SPECIALS

One flashpoint in the news struggle for preemptions was instant news specials. Former CBS News Executive Ernest Leiser said that the "near-disappearance of the 'instant special' " as well as the radical reduction in the number of prime time documentaries on all three networks, were painful signs that the news divisions had "abandoned key parts of their franchise."[68]

Leiser said that it is difficult to preempt time inside or around the prime time schedule except for ABC which has institutionalized the 11:30 P.M time slot with its "Nightline" program. Leiser said in 1985 there were only five 11:30 P.M. preemptions on CBS, down from 19 in 1981. It was even more difficult for NBC to claim the 11:30 P.M. time because of the taboo against preempting the top-rated "Tonight Show with Johnny Carson."

During a national emergency or a tragedy, network coverage was automatic and extensive, but no network could afford to assault its revenue base indefinitely. An NBC network sales executive estimated that news interrupted the network schedule between 40 and 50 times per year at a cost ranging from $20,000 to $750,000 per program.[69] Incidents like the invasion of Grenada, the bombing of Libya, the space shuttle Challenger disaster, and other unexpected events cost the networks millions.

While there was no question about going live on something like the space shuttle explosion story, marginal stories sometimes created a combat zone between the news and entertainment divisions. When the broadcasts were in prime time, these "journalistic" decisions impacted the bottom line. Unscheduled news was an unwelcome intrusion. Like a foreign object in the body, the tendency of the parent networks was to reject it. The burden of proof to justify preempting regularly scheduled programming was clearly on the news division.

Former CBS News executive Sanford Socolow said the corporate side "kept score" and was well aware when a news division president overstepped his bounds. NBC News President Lawrence Grossman, while insisting that he could take the air any time he wanted, admitted that "you do not want to abuse the privilege because it does not help the news division, your audience or your credibility with your colleagues."[70]

While unscheduled news accounted for less than two percent of the network news budget, the cost of preempting entertainment programming could make a dent in corporate earnings. The impact on the bottom line was strong enough in 1965 for Chairman William Paley to tell CBS stockholders that unscheduled news had lowered corporate earnings by six cents a share.[71]

According to former CBS News President William Leonard, a network executive would think, "Jesus Christ, no" every time news called with a request. As Leonard said, "The network *never* wants to have prime time invaded. If your job is to make the network run as smoothly and as profitably as possible, it does not do any good in the end of the year to say, 'Well, we did badly, but the reason we did badly was that we did not get on the air at all with 'I Love Lucy' or whatever it is, that the news department took it all.' That's an explanation, but the bottom line is you did not do well."[72]

## NETWORK SAFETY VALVES

To depressurize the competitive environment in which news special access must operate, the networks developed safety valves to mitigate some of the network versus news competition. These measures included providing news opportunities on the edges of prime time, preempting only lowly rated entertainment shows, and "sliding" the network, a technique that delayed all programming by at least a half hour but avoided costly preemptions.

One technique for bypassing the entertainment versus news controversy developed out of the Iranian hostage crisis in 1979–80. The networks began running special reports during the 11:30 P.M.–12:00 A.M. time period, a slot just beyond the prime time barrier. While this was a lowly rated "give away" time period for ABC and CBS, for NBC it represented the highly profitable "Tonight Show with Johnny Carson." ABC's special reports attracted such a loyal following during the hostage crisis that when it ended, ABC converted its specials into a regularly scheduled news program called "Nightline." Giving news an extra half hour beyond prime time made both news and entertainment happy; the network could avoid future preemptions during the valuable 8:00–11:00 P.M. period while the news division was guaranteed an additional half hour daily.[73] Because of the presence of "Nightline," it was rare to see an ABC news special report outside the 11:30 P.M.–12:00 A.M. period unless it was part of ongoing coverage of an extraordinary story.

While some of the networks were able to dump news specials into post-prime time hours, Presidents rarely made addresses to the nation or held news conferences out of prime time. Presidents liked to make speeches when the most profitable highly rated programs were being shown. Therefore, the networks had to be more resourceful to guard against this small but reoccurring drain on profits. One recourse that allowed them to air special news broadcasts while they preserved prime time revenue was to "slide" the network. When a President wanted to make a speech, the networks simply delayed their prime time schedule by one half hour. Prime time presidential news conferences, which consistently ran about 30 minutes, were perfect candidates for sliding the network. The White House was careful to keep the conferences under a half hour so that the networks could arrange their programming with a high degree of certainty. If the conferences habitually ran longer than 30 minutes, the networks would face scheduling nightmares and lose millions of dollars.

Because sliding the network pushed prime time programming beyond prime time, there was a limit to how long programming could be delayed. Any special broadcast running longer than an hour would certainly preclude sliding and would force a costly preemption. During the Reagan Administration, the entire network package, including the presidential speech, the opposition replies, and brief network wrap-ups, were usually under 40 minutes, allowing for an easy slide of the network.

Network contractual constraints could make a sliding difficult. NBC, for example, had a contract with Johnny Carson stipulating that his "Tonight" program not start later than midnight Eastern time. This meant that NBC could not slide the network more than one-half hour without Carson's consent. Fortunately for NBC, the "Tonight Show" host was cooperative, keeping the network from the embarrassing position of having an entertainment figure dictate news judgments.[74]

The major disadvantages of sliding the network were that if the viewer's programming routine was disrupted, audiences started dropping off towards eleven o'clock, and the affiliates' news was pushed back to 11:30 P.M. Eastern time or later. NBC Group Vice-President Raymond Timothy said that programmers did not like to lose audience flows by sliding and that viewers did not like their programs coming on at odd times. He said that programmers simply asked the news division "to do the least damage to the schedule as possible."[75]

The major opponents to sliding the networks were the affiliates which could lose substantial audience and revenues from the network practice when their evening news came on late. ABC Executive Vice-President Richard Wald said the affiliates' negative reaction was a disincentive:

Nobody ever likes sliding a network. People just do not like it. Affiliates hate it. Networks do not like it. It's not a happy thing. At no time does anybody ever feel it is a light question simply to slide the network. Affiliates' news is displaced, their ratings go down and it has a direct impact on revenue. When the ratings suffer, advertisers get very antsy and say, "Hey, I got on after midnight and 16 people in Podunk saw me." Once, sure. Twice, o.k. Three times, hmmm. Then they really get upset.[76]

Despite its disadvantages, sliding became the least painful way for the network to accommodate news division requests for presidential news conferences and speeches. It preserved network revenues, and if it did not happen too often, it was tolerated by programmers, viewing audiences, and affiliates. The sliding was predicated on the willingness of all three networks to carry the President simultaneously. As long as all delayed their programming by an equal amount of time, they maintained their competitive positions vis-à-vis competing programs. It was as if the entertainment networks were put on "freeze frame" during the presidential speech and were unfrozen 30 minutes later.

Because networks did not control huge consecutive blocks of time during the daytime hours, sliding was impossible. Furthermore, affiliates insisted that their early local news start on time. The network was left with no alternative but to preempt programming. The situation was further complicated by the fact that the networks' programs were carried at different times in each time zone.

During the day, the networks ran three separate television networks in three different time zones, one for the east coast, one for the central zone, and one for the West coast. During this programming, there were "windows" which a news division tried to hit when it preempted. For example, if Reagan began a speech at 3:00 P.M., the first window might have been at 3:07:30 P.M.. If the network missed the first window, it would have to wait for the second which might be at 3:15 P.M. News executives had to estimate how much time it would take for the broadcast and try not to join programming where the guy kissed the girl and they go to black. It was especially important that news gave up its airtime to rejoin the network at the beginning of a commercial segment. Missing a commercial break might cost the network millions.[77] Thus, there were times during the day when the networks had little control over their airtime and certain times when it would be costly and imprudent to interrupt or preempt programming.

NBC Washington Bureau Chief Bob McFarland said that if a prime time speech came on a strong night for the network, they would always slide, but if the speech was in a particularly weak time slot, they would preempt and continue with their regular programming at its usual time. An NBC vice-president told Edward Epstein in the early 1970s that it was possible to make "a clear profit" by preempting a losing show because sizable production costs and affiliate compensation could be saved while the commercials could be run in an unsalable time slot.[78]

This scenario only applied, however, when a President spoke during a network's undesirable time period. Every time there was a special news broadcast, the network in first place stood to lose real money unless it could slide programming. There was also no financial advantage in preempting a rerun or a live soap opera where the production costs could not be recouped. Network executives used printouts telling them the cost of preempting every program on the schedule. No preemption decisions were left to chance. The trick, according to one NBC executive was "to fill time that is not worth anything anyhow with news."[79]

Even when a network preempted, it may not have lost money. If the network slid its schedule, it could still charge the same amount for the commercials on the delayed programming. Rather than ask for their money back, advertising agencies usually allowed "make-goods," an opportunity to run the commercial in an "equivalent time period" later on. Epstein said that advertising agencies had a vested interest in accepting "make-goods" because they were able to keep the 15-percent rebate they received initially for placing the commercial. If "make-goods" were not allowed, the advertising agencies lost substantial sums.[80]

The networks often had little programming flexibility when a President spoke because he set the date and time of the broadcast. With the opposition, however, the networks were in complete control. Not surprisingly, they nearly always shoved an opposition broadcast into the lowest-rated time period of the week and perhaps even made money in the transaction. A scan of Nielsen ratings showed that opposition broadcasts nearly always achieved low ratings except when they followed immediately after the President.

## PRIME TIME ECONOMICS

Most presidential speeches occurred during prime time, the three hour period between 8:00 and 11:00 P.M. Eastern time when the networks made most of their revenues. This block was so precious to the networks that a 30–second commercial could cost an advertiser $200,000. With the networks facing stiffer competition every year from cable television, independent stations, and videocassette recorders (VCRs), their prime time became more important. Any disruption of the schedule, including presidential speeches and opposition replies, invited millions of viewers to switch the channel to entertainment programming. Others would be upset at seeing their favorite program preempted or delayed. At least some viewers would not return after a presidential speech, causing the network to lose audience for the entire evening.

Naturally, if the President of the United States decided to give an important speech, he would choose the "primest" of prime time for his address and news conference, usually during the 8:00–9:00 P.M.

hour on a night with high viewership. When all three networks broadcast the President simultaneously, there was the possibility the audience would top 60 million Americans. If an opposition reply, on the other hand, was broadcast at 10:30 P.M. against entertainment programming on the other two networks, a modest audience of 10 million would be considered good. Presidents from Nixon through Reagan made only five percent of their televised speeches in the outer fringes of prime time (10:00–11:00 P.M.); 54 percent of the opposition's speeches were broadcast there.

The negative economic effect of special access until recently was mitigated by all three of the networks showing the President at the same time. This practice ensured that there would be a void in entertainment programming during the speech at the network level and that no network would capitalize on the reduced audiences of the other. If all three networks came out of the speech at the same time, programmers could expect to recover most of their lost audience. If the programming was delayed too long, however, the audience for the last hour of prime time would begin to trail off, significantly diminishing the ratings. With the growing number of competitors to network television (cable, independents, VCR, etc.), however, the audience was no longer captive and began defecting. Data on the erosion of audiences for presidential speeches during the 1980's are included in chapter 7.

## WHITE HOUSE PROGRAMMERS

Presidents became increasingly sophisticated about the importance of the entertainment schedule to the networks and tried to disrupt these schedules as little as possible. Dwight Eisenhower learned a valuable lesson when he preempted "I Love Lucy" on CBS to make a political speech. The telegram he received saying, "I like Ike, I Love Lucy, drop dead" seemed to express the sentiment of the American people.[81]

Former CBS News President Frank Stanton remembered when President Johnson asked his advice on whether he would have a bigger audience if he made a speech on Sunday or Monday night.[82] *New York Times* television critic Jack Gould reported in 1965 that President Johnson "has enough respect for the 'Bonanza' popularity not to schedule a speech that could clash with such decisions as might be simultaneously reached at the Ponderosa."[83] Likewise, President Reagan wisely decided against making an address to the nation during the World Series. Presidential aids and network executives negotiated a shortened speech time that could be inserted just before the NBC baseball broadcast began.

Network executives credited the Reagan Administration with having excellent instincts about knowing the best times to deliver a speech from the networks' point of view. Former White House Communications Director David Gergen, who coordinated the timing of White House addresses during the first Reagan Administration, said he fully realized how important it was for the news division to "have credibility with their corporate people," and that the White House would have to develop a trusting relationship with the news divisions for that trust to be carried through to the corporate executives. Gergen said it would be "idiotic" to call a network to say the President was going to do a speech on Tuesday night at 8:00 P.M. without first determining how much of a problem it would be for the network.[84]

Despite the attention paid by the Reagan Administration to the network schedule, Gergen said he heard from the networks when the White House intruded on their schedule and they were not above keeping score. Gergen said he was "aware at all times what our relative standing was with the network—whether we were in good standing, bad standing." He said the worst thing you could do was to play the network for the enemy and try to gouge them.[85]

## THE 1986 FEBRUARY SWEEPS

President Reagan tried to avoid interfering with the February ratings sweeps by scheduling his 1986 State of the Union Address during the last week of January. When the space shuttle Challenger exploded on the day of his speech, however, he delayed it one week. The postponement sent shock waves through the networks because the speech would come during the crucial first week of the February sweeps. Both NBC and CBS had scheduled blockbuster mini-series that would be entering their third episode on the day of the speech.

The State of the Union Address was scheduled for 9:00 P.M. and was to last at least an hour, including the opposition reply and network wrap-up. This would make it nearly impossible for CBS and NBC to slide the network. They either had to cancel their blockbuster entertainment specials or start them at 8:00 P.M., interrupting them at 9:00 P.M. for the State of the Union and then resuming the miniseries at 10:00 P.M.. Neither of these alternatives was acceptable. To complicate matters, the networks learned that the President's second version of the speech would be 15 minutes longer than the original.

NBC Group Executive Vice-President Raymond Timothy, whose network was broadcasting the multimillion-dollar miniseries "Peter the Great," said President Reagan finally came to the networks' rescue, averting a "programming nightmare" by offering to begin his speech an hour earlier. Timothy said, "Fortunately, the President knows as much about our business as we do and understands our problems."[86]

To change the time of the State of the Union Address required a resolution passed by both houses of Congress. President Reagan apparently believed that the network entertainment schedule was overriding and asked Congress to make the change. By moving the speech from 9:00 P.M. to 8:00 P.M. to appease the networks, President Reagan sacrificed much of the West Coast audience which had not yet arrived home from work. (Senate Minority Leader Byrd's staff claimed that more people watched the Democratic reply than the President's speech, something quite possible since the network audience usually peaks shortly before 9:00 P.M.) Such an incident should leave little doubt about the importance of economics in network special broadcasts. When the President of the United States asks the Congress to pass a resolution just to preserve a network entertainment schedule and achieve higher ratings, there is ample cause for concern.

Toward the end of the February 1986 sweeps, the networks had to contend with another presidential request for time. On February 26th, President Reagan spoke to the nation about military spending. The brevity of the speech gave the networks the opportunity to package the 34-minute presentation neatly. All three networks, however, followed different strategies. NBC, which was normally in first place in the ratings at 8:00 P.M. on Wednesday with "Highway to Heaven," decided to slide the network. CBS, whose "Mary" generally finished third in the 8:00–8:30 P.M. time period, preempted the program and began "Foley Square," also a low-rated program, at 8:35 P.M. ABC, which was second at 8:00 P.M. with "MacGyver," preempted the entire hour, filling the time after the Democratic response with a live interview with Soviet commentator Vladimer Posner. The ABC decision was obviously the most costly, but the revenue loss was partially offset by ABC's placing commercials between the Democratic response and the Posner interview. *Washington Post* television writer John Carmody speculated that ABC preempted the entire hour because "it helped the network start 'Dynasty' right on time at 9:00 P.M. which was the whole point of the [news] analysis in the first place."[87]

The Reagan defense speech showed how a whole evening's prime time ratings can suffer when a President speaks. NBC's "Highway to Haven," which had a 22.2 rating the week before the speech and 22.0 the week after the speech, achieved only a 19.7 rating coming immediately after the presidential speech and opposition reply, a drop of nearly two million TV households. The cumulative ratings for the 8:30–9:00 P.M. time slot on the night of the presidential speech were 41.2 compared to 49.8 the week before and 49.5 the week after the speech which means that seven million fewer households were watching network television after the President spoke than on a normal Wednesday evening. If this were a trend, the networks would be driving away a sizable part of their viewing audience every time they put the President on.

## BETWEEN THE SWEEPS

While the sweeps periods produced the most glaring evidence that economic considerations influence news judgments, the stakes were high in non-sweeps periods as well. In April 1986, CBS was scheduled to present the second episode of its miniseries "Dream West" about the adventures of John C. Fremont when the networks interrupted prime time programming at 9:00 P.M. for a speech President Reagan was making on the American bombing of Libya. Not wanting to risk letting "Dream West" run until nearly midnight, CBS preempted it, substituting a rerun of "Cagney and Lacey" at its regular time of 10:00 P.M.

This economic decision had an effect on news programming, allowing CBS News to run 22 minutes past ABC and 11 minutes past NBC. The CBS decision raised an interesting question. Was CBS carrying on with interviews and news analysis because it has something newsworthy enough to preempt time, or was it merely coasting several minutes past its competitors to allow an entertainment program to start on time? Likewise, it could be asked if ABC had bailed out before its competitors because it badly needed to start its made-for-TV movie "A Winner Never Quits" which the *New York Times* had praised that day as "a dandy television movie" on time?[88]

Even if the dialogue between the White House and the Washington bureau chiefs went smoothly, the news division did not have the final word. Because news had no special access time beyond its normal allotment for regularly scheduled programming, it had to ask the parent network for extra time. Corporate executives evaluated the request based on programming constraints and its perceived obligation to provide time. Yet, NBC Executive Group Vice-President Raymond Timothy said the process was more of a "checklist" than a formal procedure. He said, "It's a hard thing to turn down a president of the United States. It's a fairly easy decision to put him on."[89]

Despite the trust embedded in the system, the White House occasionally violated that trust. NBC Washington Bureau Chief Bob McFarland recalled being led astray in 1985 when the White House indicated that President Reagan would speak about the Geneva arms talks (a subject NBC felt was worthy of program preemption). Instead, Reagan announced the job switch between White House Chief of Staff James Baker and Treasury Secretary Donald Regan (a story NBC felt was not newsworthy enough for preemption). McFarland said the networks were all sitting in embarrassment going "Oh, no!" for going live.[90]

The most remembered publicity ploy of the Reagan Administration was the surprise birthday party that the networks unexpectedly gave the President on national television at their own expense. The networks had granted time for a daytime presidential mini-news conference at

10:48 A.M. President Reagan was citing the drop in unemployment figures when, about halfway into the 20-minute conference, Nancy Reagan walked on camera carrying a cake with a single candle burning. The correspondents then joined the First Lady in singing "Happy Birthday" on national television.

NBC News Vice President Tom Pettit was furious. He immediately picked up the phone in New York to scream at Bureau Chief Bob McFarland, "What the hell is going on down there." McFarland, in turn, quickly phoned David Gergen to ask, "What the hell are you doing to us? This is a news conference and she's coming out with a birthday cake, for God's sake." Gergen's only reply was, "Yes, but wasn't it good television?"[91] David Gergen later admitted that the birthday cake incident was a tactical mistake by the White House and could have permanently damaged their credibility with the networks. Gergen said it was "terribly important that if we said we were going to do something, we delivered because they, in turn, had credibility with their people in New York."[92] For the system to work, both the networks and the White House had to maintain confidentiality and ensure neither side lost face.

When news was breaking, however, the network policy-making apparatus could be expedited. For example, on March 6, 1985, NBC Washington Bureau Chief Bob McFarland received airtime clearance in just minutes through a cryptic series of telephone conversations with White House spokesperson Larry Speakes, Network Executive Vice-President Tom Pettit in New York, and White House correspondent Chris Wallace. The event was a statement President Reagan planned to make concerning the veto of farm legislation:

*McFarland* [to White House spokesperson Larry Speakes]: Larry, how you doing? I need some guidance from you. What time is the man going to veto the bill? I hear between 11 and 12. O.K. I sure do. My understanding is that only one reporter is going to be in there? Well, that is fine with me. I've got no problem with that. I'll leave that up to you. No. The only person we'd have would be Chris [Wallace] and the camera crew. He's good at that stuff. Our concern is that we had heard that the bill itself is heading down to your place sometime between 11 and 12, and that you guys might decide to do it right away. O.K. Well, if you will keep me posted. I have not mentioned this to the other networks. As far as I am concerned, this is strictly unilateral, and I do not know what the other networks plan to do, but we surely want to carry it live. O.K. Thank you, Larry.

*McFarland* [to NBC Executive Vice President Tom Pettit in New York]: I need Pettit please. Mr. Speakes says nothing before 3 o'clock. That's the word from Speakes. He'll call me back when he gets a better fix on it. He says the President's schedule is such that he just does not see how he can do anything on it before 3 o'clock. O.K.? Not necessarily at 3. We do not want another time change here.

*McFarland* [to White House correspondent Chris Wallace]: I need Chris and
   Andrew. Speakes, just for your guidance only, says nothing before 3 o'clock.
   He says the schedule is just too tight. I'll let Asman the producer give you
   the details on that. Mr. Speakes did say that at some point, he's going to
   give you guys in the Oval Office a cutoff, a cut, but that's o.k. That's no
   problem. At the moment the other nets are not in on this, and I'm sure
   they will want to start getting in on this when they see the lines being run
   into the Oval Office. Larry's going to call me.

*McFarland*: Want to get me Gann? Hello. Speakes says nothing before 3 o'clock.
   Sure, sure, get the old adrenalin up, what the hell. You betcha, baby. Bye.[93]

   After all its preparation, NBC was unable to carry the President's veto
message; it came too late in the afternoon at a time when the commercial
networks no longer controlled the programming and local affiliates were
running their own programs. Still, it showed that a bureau chief's recommendation could set a chain reaction zipping through the network
bureaucracy to clear a quick path for presidential access.

## FADING MAGIC

   As President Reagan headed towards the end of his presidency, some
of his TV magic began to fade. Ronald Reagan was still popular, but
there was little reservoir of public support to bolster presidential
speeches on unpopular causes like aid to the Contras, a continued defense build-up, U.S. policy toward South Africa, and the sale of arms
to Iran. In each of these cases, Reagan's exhortations fell short. In contrast to Reagan's early broadcasting initiatives which complemented each
other, these later speeches were one-shot, isolated efforts plagued by
low momentum.
   Characterizing nearly every one of the Reagan's low-impact speeches
was a vigorous internal debate over whether the President should go
on television. Ronald Reagan had been so successful on television that
aides started using the address to the nation format like a trick play on
third and long. Whenever the President had problems rounding up the
votes he needed in Congress, aides pushed the presidential address as
a panacea. Other White House aides cautioned that the presidential
address was a highly specialized tool to be used sparingly when public
opinion had tilted toward the President's position. They argued that to
waste an address on a marginal or losing issue only diminished the
presidential credibility and media magic.
   The sharpest contrast to President Reagan's first term television success came during the fall of 1986, when the President went on national
television three times to defend selling arms to Iran. The strategy was
familiar. Go over the heads of the Washington elites directly to the

people. Take the offensive to rally the public behind the President. Let heightened positive public opinion provide a protective shield against partisan attacks. Talk to the average American. As *Washington Post* reporter Barry Sussman reported, an added value of this strategy was the control offered by the address to the nation format:

He [Reagan] was extremely selective in his comments, aiming them at average people and not those who had been following the events closely. He never mentioned Khomeini. He said the United States was not tilting toward Iran in its war with Iraq, but never explained how sending arms to one side and not the other could be read as anything but a tilt.

He likened the secret activities to the Nixon-Kissinger approach to China, denied that he was buying the release of the hostages, said that only a small amount of weapons and spare parts had been sent and made no mention of weapons that may have been sent in his name to Israel.

Many people who had been following the story were distressed by these aspects of Reagan's talk. But the President was not playing to an informed public, or to national or world leaders or lesser commentators. He was trying to keep himself up in the ratings.[94]

Unfortunately for President Reagan, even the "ultimate weapon," the televised address to the nation, could not counteract extraordinarily low public regard for Iran. Polls for the previous six years showed Khomeini to be the one person Americans liked least. A 1982 Gallup Poll done for the Chicago Council on Foreign Relations showed that the Ayatollah had a score of 11 on a "feeling thermometer" in which zero stood for the coldest feeling. Yasser Arafat scored 29.[95]

Against such odds, the White House knew the President's speech would have to be supplemented by an all-out "spin offensive" to set the agenda of American public opinion. A *Newsweek* correspondent described the process:

The current technique is first to set the White House line, then make normally aloof senior officials available to the media. Starved for contact with policy-makers and desperate for what they think are exclusives, reporters often jump at the bait. To [White House spokesperson Larry] Speakes, the press corps' follow-the-leader instincts remind him of "the starling effect—if one bird flies, then they all fly."[96]

For the Iranian speech, "spin control" seemed a natural. Just a few weeks earlier, the White House had launched its most successful spin patrol yet, organizing more than 70 events within 72 hours to turn the Reykjavik summit "failure" into a foreign policy "success" for President Reagan. After the Iranian speech, Administration officials once again unleashed a blizzard of briefings, interviews, and media appearances.

Despite the power of a national speech and the all-out spin control, the public was not persuaded. One of the first polls after the Reagan Iranian arms speech on November 13th showed that only one in five persons interviewed thought the President's statements about his dealing with Iran were essentially true.[97]

When President Reagan used the more risky press conference format a few days later to explain further his Iranian deals, negative public opinion reaction was even stronger. An ABC survey showed a ten-point drop in his approval level.[98] While many observers thought the speech had a relatively positive effect, even Republican supporters thought the "uncontrolled" news conference format hurt the President badly.

For the first time in his presidency, President Reagan was wounded. The man who could do no wrong for six years was suddenly being devoured in the press. As former Carter Press Secretary Jody Powell said, "Journalism in this town is much more likely, for a variety of reasons, to be tough on a President when he's dragging one leg and bleeding from one nostril than if he's riding high."[99] The episode was further proof of the need for a favorable public opinion environment and a strong presidential aura to make a presidential address work. It was still true that network access could work political wonders—but only at the right time, with the right person speaking about the right issue.

Not taking any chances, Ronald Reagan closed out his presidential career with only one speech during 1988, the obligatory State of the Union Message. He would provide no further opportunity for network executives to second-guess his motives or embarrass him. The Great Communicator would leave a strong legacy of success overall for gaining network access to his successor. For George Bush, it would be the waning power of the networks themselves and not the power of the presidency that would impede his effective use of the "bully pulpit."

*Chapter 5*

# Rising Opposition

The struggle for opposition access had left a long legacy of frustration among congressional leaders. Given the unsympathetic network policy and a lack of regulatory support from the FCC, the leadership over three decades reluctantly came to expect only crumbs from the network table. With no network policy guaranteeing access, the opposition during the 1960s and 1970s drifted into an insecure and untenable position. Changing political climates, changing news executives, changing competitive positions among networks, and constant economic pressure consistently kept the opposition off guard, not knowing from one year to the next what its share of prime time access would be. This network inconsistency raised an important question: Do decisions that make good journalistic sense at a particular point in time become arbitrary and inconsistent when viewed from a broad historical perspective?

The inconsistency of network judgments actually helped the opposition during the Reagan Administration. Network policy did not change, but the application of that policy did. Only nine of the 22 Democratic replies during the Reagan years were carried simultaneously by all three networks, but this was more than the opposition in the previous three Administrations combined.[1] Opposition access became as automatic as it ever could be in a system filled with so much ambiguity.

## THE REPLY PROCESS

While the opposition was completely dependent on network judgments, there was evidence to show that congressional leaders could influence their amount of access. A 1984 Library of Congress study showed a relationship between the aggressiveness of the opposition and the amount of airtime it received. During the Reagan Administration, for example, the networks gave time only when the Democratic leadership asked for it. Likewise, the only time when there was no rebuttal to a controversial presidential speech (a 1982 address on deployment of MX missiles in Wyoming), the leadership had not asked for time. It appeared that networks frequently waited for the opposition party to activate the reply mechanism and then reacted to that initiative. There were no occasions when the networks volunteered reply time the opposition did not seek.

The first months of the Reagan Administration did not appear to be auspicious ones for congressional Democrats opposing the President. By May 1981, President Reagan had addressed two joint sessions of Congress with the Democratic opposition failing to get simultaneous access for either; their only access came days after the presidential speeches. By June, frustrated Democratic leaders had drafted letters to the networks complaining about their poor access.

Previously, opposition arguments for time had meandered vaguely and inconsistently between the fairness doctrine and "equal time" demands, and requests for institutional parity. The Democrats' 1981 demands were significant because they established, for the first time, an institutional reply framework for the opposition. The Democrats asked:

1. That the networks should air reply broadcasts to major presidential addresses
2. That the Democratic Party leadership should be regarded by the networks as the focal point of the President's political opposition when preparing rebuttal broadcasts
3. That Democratic Party leadership, not the network news organizations, should determine the participants, content, and format of the rebuttal broadcasts
4. That the networks should not air Democratic response programs "at varying times" but in a way that "matches the audience of the President's presentations"
5. That broadcast rebuttals be aired immediately or close to immediately after the President's broadcast.[2]

Decisions made during the summer of 1981 gave little hope that the networks were listening to the Democrats. President Reagan's budget and tax-cutting offensive decimated the opposition. Reagan's televised speech urging Americans to contact their Congressmen and senators to vote for his $750 billion tax cut generated a huge public response. The Democrats' airtime during three different time slots on different days, could not begin to compete. Network "independent news judgment" had shut them out of the fight to sway public opinion on the most important issue of that Congress.

After President Reagan's stunning success in pushing his early economic initiatives, the media sensed the danger of a powerful President
running unchecked without a credible and visible opposition force. By
1982, both print and broadcast media were directing more attention
toward the Democrats in Congress. With the Republicans also controlling the Senate, there was a clearer media focus on the House of Representatives where the Democrats were the last bastion of opposition to
Ronald Reagan. News magazines used cover stories to cast Speaker
O'Neill as Reagan's chief antagonist. It was the first time in modern
history that a Speaker received equal billing with a President. The story
had the added personal dimension of two affable Irishmen hell bent on
pushing conflicting political philosophies to the limit.

The Reagan–O'Neill story line, the focused media attention on the
legislative–executive conflict, the aggressiveness of the Democratic opposition, and the network concern over political bias all contributed to
increased television opportunities for the Democratic opposition. While
the television networks never responded to the Democratic demands
articulated in June 1981, their actions indicated they were listening. By
the second year of the Reagan presidency, the Democrats found themselves more often than not gaining access on at least two networks
simultaneously.

During the first Reagan Administration, the Democratic leadership
received simultaneous television time on five occasions to rebut the
President, as much time as the opposition received during the Johnson,
Nixon, Ford, and Carter Administrations combined. The *New York Times*
reported after the Democratic response to the 1982 State of the Union
message that it was "the first time a party out of power was given a
chance to answer a President the same night he spoke on all three
commercial networks with a program it controlled."[3] Only CBS consistently delayed the rebuttal, scheduling its "Other Views" program more
than 24 hours after the speech and, in one case, seven days later.

When opposition access became routine during the Reagan Administration, simultaneous coverage increased. Tables 5.1 and 5.2 show just
how well the Democratic opposition to Reagan did compared to its
predecessors of both parties. The congressional leadership opposing
Reagan received five times more three network simultaneous reply time
than the opposition to Nixon, Ford, and Carter combined.

## ANTI-REPUBLICAN BIAS?

There was a significant shift by the networks in opposition exposure
patterns between the Carter and Reagan Administrations. The Republicans during the Carter Administration did far worse than the Democrats that followed them. While the opposition to Reagan routinely

**Table 5.1**
**Three Network Coverage of Opposition Responses, 1969–88**

|  | Total | 3 Network Number | % | 2 Network Number | % | 1 Network Number | % |
|---|---|---|---|---|---|---|---|
| **Nixon** | | | | | | | |
| All Speeches | 11 | 7 | 64% | 1 | 9% | 3 | 27% |
| State of Union | 4 | 4 | 100% | 0 | 0% | 0 | 0% |
| Addresses | 7 | 3 | 43% | 1 | 14% | 3 | 43% |
| **Ford** | | | | | | | |
| All Speeches | 6 | 3 | 50% | 0 | 0% | 3 | 50% |
| State of Union | 1 | 1 | 100% | 0 | 0% | 0 | 0% |
| Addresses | 5 | 2 | 40% | 0 | 0% | 3 | 60% |
| **Carter** | | | | | | | |
| All Speeches | 13 | 6 | 46% | 2 | 15% | 5 | 39% |
| State of Union | 3 | 3 | 100% | 0 | 0% | 0 | 0% |
| Addresses | 10 | 3 | 30% | 2 | 20% | 5 | 50% |
| **Reagan** | | | | | | | |
| All Speeches | 22 | 20 | 91% | 2 | 9% | 0 | 0% |
| State of Union | 7 | 7 | 100% | 0 | 0% | 0 | 0% |
| Addresses | 15 | 13 | 87% | 2 | 13% | 0 | 0% |
| **Total** | | | | | | | |
| All Speeches | 52 | 36 | 69% | 5 | 10% | 11 | 21% |
| State of Union | 15 | 15 | 100% | 0 | 100% | 0 | 100% |
| Addresses | 37 | 21 | 57% | 5 | 13% | 11 | 30% |

secured airtime on two or three networks simultaneously, the Republican opposition to Jimmy Carter never once received access to two networks at the same time. For half of President Carter's addresses to the nation, there was only one network that would carry a GOP reply.

A superficial examination of Tables 5.3 and 5.4 might result in an impression of a political bias against the Republicans, but a more plausible explanation for the wide discrepancy in opposition coverage from one administration to another was that network policy was flawed, resulting in a structural bias. The network penchant for making decisions on a case by case basis provide maximum flexibility but also subjected decision-makers to the whims of changing environments. This persistent network fear of being locked into rigid policy promoted distortion over

Table 5.2
Simultaneous Network Coverage of Opposition Responses, 1969–88

|  | Total | 3 Net. Simult. | | 2 Net. Simult. | | Non-Simultaneous | |
|---|---|---|---|---|---|---|---|
| **Nixon** | | | | | | | |
| All Speeches | 11 | 2 | 18% | 3 | 27% | 6 | 55% |
| State of Union | 4 | 2 | 50% | 2 | 50% | 0 | 0% |
| Addresses | 7 | 0 | 0% | 1 | 14% | 6 | 86% |
| **Ford** | | | | | | | |
| All Speeches | 6 | 2 | 33% | 0 | 0% | 4 | 67% |
| State of Union | 1 | 1 | 100% | 0 | 0% | 0 | 0% |
| Addresses | 5 | 1 | 20% | 0 | 0% | 4 | 80% |
| **Carter** | | | | | | | |
| All Speeches | 13 | 0 | 0% | 0 | 0% | 13 | 100% |
| State of Union | 3 | 0 | 0% | 0 | 0% | 3 | 100% |
| Addresses | 10 | 0 | 0% | 0 | 0% | 10 | 100% |
| **Reagan** | | | | | | | |
| All Speeches | 22 | 9 | 41% | 6 | 27% | 7 | 32% |
| State of Union | 7 | 4 | 57% | 0 | 0% | 3 | 43% |
| Addresses | 15 | 5 | 34% | 6 | 40% | 4 | 26% |
| **Total** | | | | | | | |
| All Speeches | 52 | 13 | 25% | 9 | 17% | 30 | 58% |
| State of Union | 15 | 7 | 47% | 2 | 13% | 6 | 40% |
| Addresses | 37 | 6 | 16% | 7 | 19% | 24 | 65% |

time. Because decisions were made in isolation and not anchored to a consistent policy, it was quite plausible that executives could unintentionally discriminate against the Republican opposition during the Carter Administration. By the standards of the times, even the Republican leadership thought it was receiving decent network treatment.

## OPPOSITION STRATEGIES

The eight years from 1981–88 gave the opposition opportunity to test the success of many of its strategies, including single-person replies. Speaker O'Neill's press spokesperson, Chris Matthews, believed that

**Table 5.3**
**Comparison of Opposition Simultaneous Access to Rebut Presidential Speeches during Republican and Democratic Administrations, 1969–88**

|  | Total | 2 or 3 Net. Simult. Coverage | | No Simult. Coverage | |
|---|---|---|---|---|---|
| Democratic Access (Nixon, Ford, Reagan) | 39 | 22 | 56% | 17 | 44% |
| Republican Access (Carter) | 13 | 0 | 0% | 13 | 100% |

**Table 5.4**
**Comparison of Opposition Three Network Access to Rebut Presidential Speeches during Republican and Democratic Administrations, 1969–88**

|  | Total | 3 Network | | 2 Network | | 1 Network | |
|---|---|---|---|---|---|---|---|
| Democratic Access (Nixon, Ford, Reagan) | 39 | 30 | 77% | 3 | 8% | 6 | 15% |
| Republican Access (Carter) | 13 | 6 | 46% | 2 | 15% | 5 | 39% |

the Democratic leadership would enhance its ability to gain airtime after the President by pushing for the live, immediate one-person response, "There is something very appealing about one person standing alone against the President of the United States. The networks will always cover one person live. There is too much uncertainty and potential news value. They'll cover it because they aren't absolutely sure that it won't be newsworthy."[4]

During the Reagan Administrations, the Democrats had opportunities to test Matthews' hypothesis. On 12 occasions from 1981–88, the Democratic leadership sent only one or two legislators to rebut President Reagan immediately after his speech. During ten of those times, their spokesperson received at least two-network simultaneous coverage in prime time, and three-network simultaneous coverage on seven occasions. As an incentive for the networks, the Democrats cut their replies to under ten minutes to meet entertainment programming constraints.

The live, single-person replies broadcast during the Reagan Administration averaged eight minutes compared to 27 minutes for the President's speeches.

Political watchers agreed that the Democrats had actually improved the quality of their replies by abbreviating them and placing them immediately after the President. Rarely did the opposition have content to match the President word for word and the shorter replies allowed the Democrats to articulate the essence of their opposition without losing rhetorical momentum. The seven-minute replies fit nicely into a 30–minute speech and response package that allowed the networks to start their next entertainment program on time. By simply delaying network programming (and commercials) for 30 minutes, the networks could avoid both financial loss and audience loss. The format also precluded the networks from doing their own commentary, leaving the Democrats as the only voice to oppose the President.

For the opposition, there was great value in coming immediately after a presidential speech. Not only did their chances of receiving simultaneous access rise dramatically but they had access to the same audience reached by the President. The only drawback to an immediate response was the lack of time to prepare a response. Opposition spokespersons either had to anticipate a President's remarks or had to make a more general presentation. Although an immediate opposition response often precluded network post-speech analysis, NBC News President Lawrence Grossman believed that to delay the opposition response made very little sense because it was a disservice to the public who may not have seen the first broadcast, and the delayed response was not as effective. In a departure from the usual network-knows-best attitude, Grossman said NBC had "an obligation to work with the opposition to find out what is in everybody's interest."[5]

There was a growing recognition within the networks, according to NBC Washington Bureau Chief Robert McFarland, that the Democrats were finally becoming more sophisticated about television, "There's no question that the Democrats are learning about the 'new TV.' They want to go live now, and they've learned that if they keep it short enough, the networks will put them on and the ratings won't go down."[6]

For years, there had been broad agreement on the poor quality of the opposition broadcasts. CBS President Frank Stanton expressed frustration that the opposition "wanted their man in there and when their man came on, he wasn't buttoned up."[7] "MacNeil/Lehrer Newshour" Executive Producer and former NBC News President Lester Crystal agreed with Stanton that giving the opposition control may have made sense, but it was lousy programming:

There was always a concern about putting on some congressman or senator who may be a terrific bore and who would not be nearly as effective as the

President. Most people at the network wanted to take control and make a program out of it so that not only would it have some journalistic character but it would be good, effective programming that maybe someone would sit down and watch.[8]

Likewise, CBS Executive Vice-President David Fuchs said the opposition needed to be aware of what it was competing against:

You used to get dreadful television, a disorganized meandering thing. They didn't realize that when you put something on the tube you are competing with everything else on it and the American public are used to this enormously sophisticated style of communication in commercials and programs of all kinds. When they suddenly see something primitive, it drains the energy right off the screen.[9]

One reason why the Democratic responses were so poor was that leaders tended to sacrifice television quality to accommodate all of the senior congressmen who wanted to participate in them. Eventually, they had to face the reality that the people who were adept did not always have political power and the people who had power were not always adept on television.[10] For Democratic strategists to agree to send only one representative before the cameras, as they did during the Reagan Administration, required considerable self-control and sophistication about television.

## RECALCITRANT CBS

Throughout the Reagan Administration, the CBS "Other Views" policy remained the single biggest obstacle to simultaneous opposition access and gave CBS the reputation as the most difficult network to deal with on these matters. A 1984 Library of Congress study concluded that CBS was "the network which most often rejected the Democratic Leadership as the focal point for broadcast rebuttals to President Reagan."[11] As a counterpoint to six of the seven televised addresses by Mr. Reagan to the nation during the first three of the Administration, CBS televised programs of its own exclusively devoted to contrasting viewpoints rather than give airtime to spokespersons selected by the Democratic Leadership.

CBS' non-simultaneous scheduling of its opposition broadcasts successfully kept the opposition leadership from roadblocking time on all three networks. Rarely during the first five years of the Reagan Administration did CBS join its competition to give the opposition simultaneous access. In one case, CBS turned down official Democratic spokesperson Michael Barnes after a Reagan speech on El Salvador but ran its "Other Views" program at the same time the other networks were presenting

Table 5.5
**Inter-Network Comparison of Prime Time Coverage of Opposition
Replies by Time of Broadcast, 1969–87**

| Time | ABC | CBS | NBC |
|------|-----|-----|-----|
| 8:00 – 8:30 | 6 | 7 | 8 |
| 8:30 – 9:00 | 6 | 7 | 5 |
| 9:00 – 9:30 | 2 | 1 | 2 |
| 9:30 – 10:00 | 2 | 2 | 1 |
| 10:00 – 10:30 | 6 | 10 | 6 |
| 10:30 – 11:00 | 8 | 11 | 9 |
| Total | 30 | 38 | 31 |

Barnes' official reply, giving the Democrats simultaneous but different and fragmented access.

When the "Other Views" policy was exercised in a volatile political climate, it significantly diminished the opposition's ability to communicate. For example, when President Reagan delivered his all-out plea for the American people to influence their congressmen to support his controversial tax-cut proposal in 1981, CBS ignored the "official" reply and countered the next evening with a correspondent posing questions to invited congressional Democrats, labor leaders, and economists. After the Democrats lost the crucial tax vote, DNC Chairman Charles Manatt protested. He said the opposition's message became "obscured by the multitude of faces" and the "unclear line of thought." Manatt charged that the format was not conducive to "a clear and lucid response to the President's one-voice, one-message speech on behalf of his tax program."[12]

Table 5.5 shows that while CBS broadcast more replies than the other two networks, they also provided poorer time periods on the fringes of prime time. By 1985, a consistent pattern was emerging in which ABC and NBC would present an opposition reply live after the President while CBS would present its "Other Views" program in a 10:30–11:00 P.M. time slot that evening or a few days later. In April 1985, CBS rejected the official Democratic reply by Senate Minority Leader Robert Byrd of West Virginia which was broadcast live by ABC and NBC, choosing instead to present its "Other Views" program two hours later. The CBS program, facing network entertainment shows, finished 71st out of the

71 programs rated by the Nielsen Company with a meager 5.7 percent of the households with television watching it.[13] Not only did the CBS "Other Views" program fare badly but it deprived the congressional opposition of the opportunity to roadblock three networks simultaneously as President Reagan was able to do.

Before President Reagan's address to the nation on May 29, 1985, the Democratic leadership anticipated CBS' maverick scheduling and protested. When ABC, NBC, and CNN announced they would carry the speech, House Speaker O'Neill and Senate Minority Leader Byrd told CBS that they found it ironic that CBS had scheduled a program called "America Censored" at 8:30 P.M. in lieu of the Democratic response, and pointed out that "the three major networks, ABC, NBC, and CNN" were carrying the Democratic message live. CBS News President Edward Joyce offered to include the Democrat's official spokesperson, Chairman Dan Rostenkowski of the House Ways and Means Committee, in their "Other Views" program three days later but the Democrats refused and demanded that the reply be shown live. CBS defended itself by saying "we've been following that policy for more than ten years."[14]

The Democratic leadership twitted CBS after the Rostenkowski speech when they learned that Chairman Rostenkowski received higher ratings on NBC than the President. Speaker O'Neill's spokesperson, Chris Matthews, claimed that the President had a 12.2 rating with a 22 share while Rostenkowski had a 13 rating and a 23 share. Matthews said the ratings victory was a slap in the face for CBS which he described as "believing in the three-network system, but not the two-party system."[15]

The CBS "Other Views" program, broadcast on Friday at 10:30 P.M., meanwhile, finished 57th among the 62 programs included in the Nielsen ratings. It was scheduled in a giveaway time slot against the seventh most popular network television program, "Miami Vice." Not surprisingly, CBS' "Other Views" received only a 7.1 rating and a 13 share of the audience, making it one of the four lowest rated programs of the entire week.[16]

The President's May 1985 tax reform speech once again underscored how different CBS' "Other Views" program could be in substance as well as in timing. During its 30–minute program, CBS included six politicians and industry leaders and four network journalists. Like the 1973 program described earlier, this program featured an odd assortment of "opposing views": spokespersons were Republican Congressman Jack Kemp of New York; Alexander Towbridge, President of the National Association of Manufacturers; Ted Balesteri, President of the National Restaurant Association; and J. McDonald Williams, a Dallas real estate developer. Representing the Democrats were Representative Richard Gephardt of Missouri, co-author of a major tax reform plan, and Senator Daniel Moynihan of New York. During the second half of the program, the quests were shunted off the air to let three network correspondents and anchor Dan Rather give their observations about tax reform.

Viewers watching Chairman Rostenkowski and those watching the CBS' parade of voices on tax reform no doubt got different messages. In the CBS format, the two Democrats had little opportunity to present their case, had to compete with a multitude of disparate voices, and had no control whatsoever over the broadcast. The CBS program, like all the "Other Views" programs that preceded it, did a better job than those of the other two networks in meeting federal regulatory requirements; it presented a variety of opposing viewpoints on a controversial issue. Yet the babble did little to help the opposition compete with the powerful voice from the White House. ABC Vice-President David Burke, before becoming President of CBS News, believed that CBS went too far in asserting its right to pick opposition spokespersons and ignored a logical institutional counterpoint to the President, "Why should we say to the leader of the opposition, 'I'm sorry but we don't accept your point of view? We'll pick the guests.' Why should we do that? The Congress is an equal branch of government and the leaders represent that equal branch. And they have every right to expect us to keep our editorial nose out of their point of view."[17]

Despite the logic of Burke's remarks, the networks generally felt uneasy about relinquishing their journalistic prerogatives and turning over airtime to a politician. As NBC Executive Vice-President Tom Pettit said, "Good journalists ordinarily control the content of what they put out— either in the wire service or the newspaper or the television network." He said that when the opposition was given time it was "like their buying it, but without having to pay for it."[18]

The CBS' "Other Views" program conformed to that view, returning control to the networks while at the same time providing them with the aura of journalistic enterprise. All of the networks might have wanted to inject themselves deeper into defining who speaks for the opposition, but only CBS did so. The other two networks recognized the congressional opposition as the natural counterpoint to the President and provided the leadership with the freedom to craft whatever response it felt was effective.

Between 1986 and 1988, even CBS conformed to the behavior of its competitors, joining ABC and NBC for simultaneous coverage of all opposition replies to Reagan televised speeches. CBS seemed to be fulfilling Chris Matthews' prediction that the networks would not be able to resist covering the opposition if one person spoke live immediately after the President.

## THE NOT-SO-LOYAL MOSCOW OPPOSITION

An incident in February 1986 on ABC showed that CBS was not the only network that could attract criticism for its airing of opposing views. After President Reagan presented his nationally televised speech urging more defense spending, all networks broadcast a short Democratic response. While two networks resumed their entertainment programming, ABC allowed Radio Moscow commentator Vladimir Posner to provide a further rebuttal to the Reagan speech. The Posner appearance was supposed to be an interview with David Brinkley, but turned into a seven-minute monologue by the Soviet spokesperson.

White House Communications Director Patrick Buchanan was "astonished" that ABC had turned over its airwaves to a "trained propagandist for the Soviet Union" and wrote a letter of protest to ABC News President Roone Arledge. Buchanan said ABC gave Posner "a standing he does not merit, a legitimacy he does not deserve."[19] Meanwhile, President Reagan told a bipartisan congressional leadership group that he did not "know why the hell the media is so willing to lend support to the Soviets."[20]

The *Washington Post* reported that the incident precipitated an "anxious discussion" at ABC and a statement the next day by Senior Vice-President Richard Wald admitting that Posner "was allowed too much scope on our program." Wald said ABC's error was allowing the Soviet commentator to push on too long without an "opposing voice to point out the errors and the inconsistencies in what he said."[21] Roone Arledge wrote a letter to President Reagan admitting that Posner's appearance "was a deviation from good American common sense and the standards of fairness for which ABC news is known."[22]

The reverberations from Posner's rebuttal were so strong that FCC Commissioner James Quello was still talking about the ABC interview six months later. In a speech to Pennsylvania broadcasters in October 1986, Quello said, "ABC's faux pas, allowing a Soviet journalist eight minutes of prime time coverage to propagandize a strong refutation of a major address by the President of the United States, is blurring the line between journalistic 'scoops' and irresponsible decision-making."[23]

The Posner incident underscored the importance of the quasi-official role the networks play when they decide who will rebut the President. In these cases, more than news judgments are being made; the networks are setting the agenda for the "official" responses to presidential speeches. Chances were that the Posner "interview" was meant to be no more than a postscript to the Democratic rebuttal and was used partially to fill time until the start of the next hour. Even though Posner's appearance may not have been meant as a serious network statement about who should rebut the President, the context of the speech defined it that way.

ABC clearly underestimated the repercussions its editorial control over rebuttals could have and the difference between this kind of special program and its regular news programming. The Posner incident exposed one of the pitfalls of the network practice of making a Presidential speech an "XYZ Special Report." The advantage of such a practice is that the networks maintain editorial control over most of the broadcast and give the appearance that the news division is packaging the event. The disadvantage, however, is that the networks take more of the responsibility on themselves to be arbiters of political access and are held responsible if they err in judgment. As ABC quickly learned, it bore the responsibility for tilting the rhetorical balance on a political subject of national importance.

## "DYNASTY" OVER DEMOCRACY

The opposition traditionally gained its strongest institutional foothold by replying to presidential State of the Union addresses. The Democrats opposing Reagan strengthened that precedent.[24] From 1982–84, the networks carried the opposition replies simultaneously, accounting for three-fifths of the simultaneous opposition access during the first Reagan Administration. Except for 1985, the networks provided the opposition with simultaneous access on every occasion.

Rather than using their newsworthiness criterion to justify granting time for opposition replies to the State of the Union, the networks carry rebuttals as a tradition. CBS said that it "has for many years provided the out-of-office party with an opportunity to present its views of the State of the Union in connection with the President's address."[25] ABC cited its "traditional practice" to give response time to the Congressional leadership of the opposition party.[26] While only ABC specifically acknowledged the congressional opposition, all three networks accepted it as the natural counterpoint to State of the Union Addresses.

The lone Reagan State of the Union address that did not receive simultaneous three-network opposition access came in 1985 when ABC decided not to join CBS and NBC in carrying the Democratic response live. Media critics and network competitors quickly noted that the reply would have come during ABC's most popular entertainment program "Dynasty." Moreover, it would have come during the beginning of the February sweeps which were crucial to ABC's lagging programming fortunes.

Despite the criticism, ABC's decision did indeed boost ratings during the sweep month. According to overnight Nielsen ratings in nine large cities, 43 percent of the audience watched the first part of "Dynasty" when CBS broadcast the Democratic reply; "Dynasty" rose to 48 percent of the audience when NBC broadcast the reply from 10:30–11:00 P.M. EST. Meanwhile, the Democratic reply was viewed by only 7 percent of the audience on both CBS and NBC.[27] Not only was ABC able to position itself well in the ratings but it also earned two million dollars in revenues by selling six minutes of advertisements valued at $165,000 per 30 second commercial.[28] Despite ABC's success compared to the Democratic opposition, many network analysts were surprised that "Dynasty" did not pull a larger audience. One NBC executive said the ABC action appeared to be "a quick and easy run for the ratings" which should have fared far better than it did.

Speaker "Tip" O'Neill's spokesperson, Chris Matthews, dubbed ABC's actions " 'Dynasty' over Democracy." Matthews said, "Our response is going against the most powerful show on TV, then ABC is going to bury us the next night after Hugh Downs [host of '20/20']." Rumors within ABC and the other networks said that the news division strongly fought to carry the Democratic reply after the President's State of the Union message but was overruled by the entertainment division.

In an interview a week before the controversy, ABC Vice-President David Burke, the News Division's point man in the " 'Dynasty' over Democracy" episode, acknowledged that the money men do have a right to intrude on programming, "They are, after all, in a competitive business and they are, after all, responsible to a board of directors who are ultimately responsible to the stockholders. So the network feels it has some say . . . as to when the reply will take place."[29]

Burke said that while the rank and file news people can still operate with an immunity from economic pressures, "We in management know that we are in business and we know that we are a contributing part of the higher corporation. I am as attuned to their programming problems as they are."[30] Affiliates are also attuned to programming demands and sometimes ask to substitute entertainment programming for a presidential speech or news conference. In the case of the "Dynasty" episode, however, two west coast stations, including ABC owned and operated KABC in Los Angeles, requested permission to show the Democratic response and "Dynasty" as well. ABC denied the request, refusing to discuss their reasoning.[31]

Reaction from the other networks to ABC's programming decision was critical. News executives saw the incident as a setback for the ABC news division. NBC spokesman Curt Block said he thought the sweeps played a big role in the ABC decision. Noting that ABC carried the State of the Union and the Democrats on the same night last year Block said, "That was a Wednesday night, too, what changed: It was in January and not during the sweeps and they're in third place now."[32] Press reaction was also critical. *USA Today* called ABC's action an obvious "ploy for ratings."[33]

The 1985 State of the Union controversy underscored the frustration felt by the opposition in dealing with a network's substitution of economic judgments for entertainment judgments. In the "Dynasty" episode, ABC news executives, not entertainment executives, were left to explain and execute the decision as well as take criticism for it. The argument began and ended with the news division, but it had very little to say in the matter. Network executives were really calling the shots. This placed the news division in the untenable position of explaining a programming decision they strongly opposed. Former CBS News President Richard Salant said this misplaced responsibility problem also extended to policy decisions when "network lawyers have had an unfortunate tendency to cloak network policy decisions in news judgments."[34]

The " 'Dynasty' over Democracy" experience illustrates the conflict that can occur when the network and the news division have different priorities. While there has been a strong tradition historically at the networks to insulate the news division from economic pressure, corporate needs now predominate. When a network is under economic pressure, as third-place ABC clearly was in February 1985, the news division may have to bend to satisfy the needs of its revenue-generating counterpart. This kind of elastic judgment tied to economic considerations bothers those in opposition who realize that their communication link to the American people rests upon the vicissitudes of the network balance sheet.

## PERILS OF THE "CANNED" RESPONSE

Beginning in 1982, the Democratic leadership substituted prepared films for live responses to the President's State of the Union Address. By the Democrats' own admission, the programs were "not a response to the President's speech," but a "Democratic view of the State of the Union."[35] These "canned" presentations prompted chronic network dissatisfaction over the way the congressional leadership handled their "gift" of airtime. ABC Vice-President George Watson wrote to Speaker of the House Thomas P. "Tip" O'Neill in 1983 complaining that the Democrats' taped response had "seriously departed" from the principles of pertinence and timeliness and "called into doubt the definition of the word 'response.' " Watson reminded the Speaker that the networks had no legal obligation to give the opposition time but were doing so "in an effort both to be fair to the congressional opposition and to elevate the level of political debate."[36]

Two years later, NBC News President Lawrence Grossman, in a letter to Speaker O'Neill, renewed the attack on the Democrat's reply format.

The Grossman letter indicated NBC's reluctance to take a passive approach to congressional replies and its desire to influence editorial content:

Are we right in simply turning over our time to the opposition party for its own production, even if it has very little if any relevance to the President's report that night? Should we in the future invite leading exponents from the other side to respond to the President's positions? Should we offer prime time for a live address by a single opposition party leader in response to the President's appearance?[37]

Grossman said he felt compelled to intervene because the leadership's initiatives were "backfiring in a sort of awful exchange of ideas." He said he did not think that leaving the replies in the hands of the opposition party the way they were being handled "was serving anybody's cause."[38] Grossman met privately with House Speaker O'Neill and Majority Leader Wright, warning them that NBC would dump the opposition in favor of its own hand-picked spokespersons unless the Democrats' replies conformed to network expectations.

The Grossman initiative could be seen as an effort by NBC to stage-manage Democratic congressional replies and inject itself into the colloquy between the President and the Congress. While Grossman did not want to be seen as telling "other people how to do their work," he saw it as his network's "journalistic responsibility to sharpen the issues" by setting parameters within which the opposition should operate.[39]

Grossman's initiative underscored the control the networks could exert over those who used their airwaves and the closeness of the networks to the machinery of the American political system. In the last half of the twentieth century it has been impossible for political leaders to operate without negotiating with the leaders of broadcasting corporations, usually on the networks' own terms. One might question, however, whether a network would ever apply the same standard to a President. Traditionally, presidents have had complete control of airtime during their addresses to the nation without network intervention. The conventional wisdom at the networks was that the American people should decide if a President presented himself and his arguments well. While the opposition has expected the same autonomy given the President, it has rarely received it.

From a television production standpoint, the Democrats agreed with NBC's Lawrence Grossman. Democratic political consultant Joseph Rothstein claimed that a live reply would make a "deeper impression" than a "canned commercial."[40] The Democrats also wanted to create the impression that the State of the Union was a single event—not only the President's speech but the congressional opposition response as well.

Being obviously pleased that the Democrats decided to abandon their taped reply in 1986, all three commercial networks agreed ahead of time to carry the State of the Union response live. Ironically, the space shuttle Challenger tragedy postponed the State of the Union by a week, forcing the Democrats into another taped message.

It was not until the 1987 State of the Union reply that the Democrats had a chance to employ the live strategy the networks so strongly wanted. Less than five minutes after President Reagan's State of the Union Address, the new Speaker of the House, Jim Wright of Texas, and the new Senate Majority Leader, Robert Byrd of West Virginia, were in the Speaker's office ready to address the same television audience reached by the President.

The half-hour live Democratic reply won favorable reviews. *Time* said the Wright-Byrd reply "proved more effective than the slickly produced Democratic responses of past years."[41] *U.S. News and World Report* reported that it "was rated by even White House staffers as the best Democratic response in the Reagan era."[42] Not only were the two opposition leaders credited with going live but with putting in the time necessary to perfect the writing and presentation of the speech. Both leaders sought consultants to help them restrain their flamboyant oratorical styles and to define the issues more clearly and succinctly.

The success of the 1987 Democratic State of the Union reply reflected the same kind of symbiotic relationship Presidents had enjoyed with the networks for years. The unsolicited Grossman initiative forced the opposition to become better television communicators. By abandoning the "canned" presentations, the Democrats were able to secure more and better time from the networks and have an immediate agenda-setting impact.

By the end of the Reagan Administration, the lone case in 1985 in which ABC rejected the opposition to run the highly rated entertainment program "Dynasty" seemed to be an aberration. The networks were ready to suspend independent news judgment consistently to designate the congressional opposition as the sole official counterpoint to the President. Outside of this State of the Union framework, however, the spell of "network tradition" was broken along with the guarantee of the opposition's extraordinary access. There were some, like *New York Times* columnist James Reston, who said Congress was only kidding itself if it believed it could compete on a coequal basis with Reagan by going on television because "he's so good at it, and there are so many of them, so divided in what they want to say."[43]

## THE RADIO PRECEDENT

When the three commercial radio networks agreed to broadcast a series of ten weekly radio addresses by President Reagan in 1982, the

Democratic ledership also received time. By the time President Reagan had to suspend his radio talks temporarily after announcing his candidacy for re-election in January 1984 (he continued them on a paid basis until the election with no Democratic response), he had made 85 radio broadcasts; the Democrats in Congress had received 85 opportunities to reply one hour after the presidential speech. When President Reagan resumed his radio talks in 1985, the Democrats began another four years of uninterrupted, automatic access.

By granting reply time to the Democrats, the broadcasters who participated in the radio experiment (CBS did not) had tied their policy to institutional parity rather than issues parity. This action was important because it marked the first time the networks had taken a reply out of the news category and placed it in the public service category. The radio policy gave the congressional opposition unprecedented, guaranteed access. Unfortunately, this important precedent had no carry-over to television; broadcasting executives still made those decisions on a case by case basis. The radio-television inconsistency had an economic basis; granting the opposition time on radio cost hardly anything while the same type of access on television cost hundreds of thousands of dollars.

## THE BRITISH WAY

The radio speeches provided the opposition for the first time with the kind of institutional access British broadcasters routinely gave their opposition party. Since 1947, British broadcasters and the political parties have operated under Aide Mémoire (1947 and 1968) which guaranteed access to the Prime Minister and an automatic response to the opposition. The British system not only provided a one-for-one equality of access but the automatic opposition reply served as a deterrent to over use of broadcasting by the government. Another advantage of the British system was the consistency it provided from government to government, eliminating the wide swings in opposition access often observed in America. Such explicit, longstanding policy proved useful in a difficult political time like the Suez crisis in 1956. BBC executive Grace Wyndham Goldie credited the Aide Mémoire with providing a firm foundation for decision-making when Prime Minister Anthony Eden tried to block an opposition reply to a Ministerial address at the height of the crisis:

Suez is, therefore, a salutary warning of the lengths to which a political party may go, when in power, to prevent the broadcasting of any opinions but its own. It also reveals the importance of maintaining procedures, agreed to in advance by broadcasters and the Opposition as well as by the Government, to which the broadcasting organizations can refer when refusing to submit to government pressures exerted at moments of tension when emotions are running high.[44]

Americans, without the benefit of a structure like the Aide Mémoire, are more subject to the vicissitudes of the political environment and the inconsistencies caused by news executive turnovers. With the networks making decisions on a case by case basis, the opposition has little institutional clout. Complicating the problem was the fairness doctrine, which for more than 30 years reaffirmed broadcaster control over the dialogue of issues and concerned itself only with the balance of issues.

## COMMUNICATION AS CONGRESSIONAL PRIORITY

Even though national exposure would seem to be invaluable to the congressional leadership, many leaders worked actively to avoid network television. Traditionally, the leadership preferred to concentrate on internal rather than external relationships. Leaders born in the early part of the century were uncomfortable in the television age. Having little confidence in their ability to perform, they delegated media responsibilities to younger, more articulate members.

Speaker Rayburn, who dominated the House leadership from the postwar years until his death in the early 1960s, set a strong precedent for inwardly focused congressional leadership, keeping cameras out of Congress and virtually ignoring television. Rayburn also had little need for the "showhorses" who courted media attention. Speaker Rayburn's immediate successors, John McCormack of Massachusetts and Carl Albert of Oklahoma, largely followed their mentor's media avoidance, although Albert aggressively fought for institutional exposure for the opposition.

During the 1970s and 1980s, the leadership of Congress found itself in an important transition period which began during the Watergate period and ran through the Reagan era, a time when television was the chief offensive political weapon. While Speaker O'Neill was as personally reticent about television exposure as his predecessors, the Reagan–Democratic budget battle propelled him into the limelight as the most televised Speaker in history. Speaker O'Neill averaged 120 exposures on the evening network news a year compared to 46 for Speaker Albert and 20 for Speaker McCormack.[45] Gone were the days when a Speaker could hide behind his gavel in the House chamber without venturing into the media spotlight.

It was also during the Reagan Administration that Members of Congress became more critical of their leaders' media performance. The *New York Times* reported in 1984 that, "there has long been grumbling in the back benches that neither the House Speaker, Thomas P. O'Neill, Jr., nor the Democratic leader in the Senate, Robert C. Byrd, suits the politics of the television era."[46] The criticism was particularly harsh on Senator Byrd. Senator Lawton Chiles, who opposed Senator Byrd for the Minority Leader's post, told a *New York Times* reporter in 1984, "I think we need somebody who can communicate like Robert Dole can, who can articulate ideas and concepts and is ready to do that. We're talking about a new media day, where you've got to be pro-active, thinking about getting our messages out there. You've got to be quotable enough and colorful enough so that you get invited to the weekend shows and morning shows and have a presence."[47]

Both as Majority Leader from 1977 to 1981 and as Minority Leader from 1981–85, Byrd did not compare favorably with either his predecessors or successors. A study of network television coverage of congressional leaders from 1969–85 showed that Senate majority leaders averaged 107 mentions a year; Senator Byrd averaged 80. Senator Byrd's successor Robert Dole of Kansas received almost three times more coverage than Byrd during his first year as Majority Leader. As Minority Leader, Byrd received less than half the coverage of his predecessors.[48] While Senator Byrd was elected Majority Leader without opposition for the 100th Congress which convened in 1986, he was under considerable pressure to give television a higher priority. Some congressional insiders believed that Senator Byrd's inability to serve effectively on the media stage was a factor in his stepping down as Majority Leader in 1989.

There was also the opportunity for middle tier leaders to be propelled into national prominence. After House Ways and Means Committee Chairman Dan Rostenkowski replied to President Reagan's tax message in May 1985, U.S. News and World Report reported that he was the "biggest winner" in the tax battle. The magazine said his seven-minute rebuttal paid off "in heightened respect from colleagues" and "instant recognition."[49] Syndicated columnists Evans and Novak said Rostenkowski's "stellar performance, which surprised even close friends," elevated his national prestige "to a record high."[50] During the speech, Chairman Rostenkowski had asked viewers to write him and said if they could not remember how to spell his name just write "Rosty, Washington, DC." Surprisingly, the Chairman received 24 cartons of mail from throughout the country which took eight persons working full-time to open.[51]

When Speaker O'Neill retired in 1987, Speaker Jim Wright worked hard to fulfill the media role he believed a twentieth century speaker was expected to perform. Speaker Wright decided a year in advance of his election that he would make a live reply to the State of the Union in 1987 if he had the chance.[52] The new Speaker, long noted as an excellent orator but considered too "hot" for television, also worked diligently with consultants to learn the requirements for video success.

Although Wright was a protégé of Sam Rayburn and, like his predecessors, was generally uncomfortable with television, he made a special effort during his early days as Speaker to accommodate the broadcast media. For example, he began giving broadcasters interviews after his daily "pad and pencil only" news conference. When he boldly took the lead position in negotiating a peace accord in Central America, Wright benefitted from heavy media exposure. Speaker Wright's problems in 1989 that led to his resignation, however, obscured whatever progress with the media he had made.

Presumably, the external role of the congressional leadership will become more important as leaders feel compelled to be effective spokespersons for their party and their colleagues. Clearly, the networks have been more likely to respond favorably to the opposition when a highly visible, articulate person is offered for a rebuttal to a presidential address. The election of Tom Foley as Speaker and Richard Gephardt as Majority Leader of the House of Representatives paved the way for a new generation of leaders who developed during the television age. By the twenty-first century, media should be a prime prerequisite for congressional leadership.[53]

## THE WINNING COMBINATION

To a new generation of media managers, opposition access was just another in a long line of profit-draining burdens which had to be minimized. Strangely enough, the Democrats in Congress opposing Reagan were short-term beneficiaries of this bottom line pressure. Because they understood and appreciated the intensity of the prime time financial squeeze, the leaders of the Democratic opposition tailored their access strategy to meet network economic constraints.

Congressional leaders used a combination of consistent political pressure and creative programming techniques to increase their access. First, they promptly and forcefully asked for time. Second, they willingly sacrificed the length of time they received in order to get time immediately after the President's speech, trading seven minutes in reply time for Reagan's 30. In this way, the opposition boosted its chances to gain coverage by at least two networks simultaneously and reached most of the same audience the President did. The networks, meanwhile, had to disrupt programming only once for a tolerable period in economic terms.

The Democrats' recognition of network programming considerations paid huge dividends. All opposition replies since 1986 have been carried live simultaneously by three networks, giving the Democrats unprecedented access. For more than eight years, the networks had given the Democrats in Congress practically everything they wanted, except a guarantee of airtime. It looked as if the de facto automatic reply policy begun during the Reagan Administration would continue for some time.

Thus, by conforming to the economic constraints of the networks, the opposition received far more prime time television exposure in eight years than their predecessors had during the previous 12. Yet, the congressional leadership understood full well that the same economic values that had worked to their advantage with shortened opposition replies could quickly and easily steal away their coveted prime time once again. The " 'Dynasty' over Democracy" episode proved that in a competitive race for money and ratings, nothing is sacred, especially access for the opposition.

The precedents set by radio, the tradition of State of the Union address responses, and the success of the congressional opposition during the Reagan Administration all pointed to increased emphasis on institution-based responses. Yet, this progress could be as ephemeral as the day's news; "independent news judgment" traditionally has looked neither kindly nor consistently on the opposition. The opposition would have to be aggressive, tenacious, and vigilant if it was to penetrate the network policy making apparatus and influence change from the status quo. The challenge was to consolidate gains into an institutional protection like that guaranteed in the British system. Leaders had to push for balance between institutions as well as issues and position themselves as the natural counterpoint to presidential initiatives. They also had to oppose any network initiative which blurred the clarity of the tri-polar focus envisioned in the Constitution.

*Chapter 6*

# The Networks as Loyal Opposition

The closing of the 1980s found the networks in an uncertain, tentative position, grasping for an identity that would restore them to their former glory. Though shaken from their own internal revolution, the networks still held a certain cachet with the American people which grew partly from their own close involvement with the political system. The American people still looked on the networks as a faithful friend in times of crisis and as an organization that even represented their views and asked their questions in the halls of power. Thus, the congressional opposition operated in an environment where the networks held as much institutional clout as they did. In the end, the opposition was competing not only with the White House for access but with the networks as well. But the opposition's quest for access was tied to a broader issue—the symbolic power of the television networks as institutions, and their influence on the American political system. This chapter shows how the networks have used their entree to the political system to forge a powerful role as a de facto opposition force.

For more than half a century, three American corporations have focused a national electorate on a series of media events which helped define the political agenda. Party conventions, debates, press forums, and presidential speeches have become touchstones to political involvement. Hardly any major political event is structured without significant attention paid to the network involvement in it. When all three networks broadcast a political event at the same time, cues are sent to the American people that this is something of utmost importance. In times of crisis, simultaneous broadcasts become a vehicle for forging national unity and consensus.

When network involvement dominates a political event, as it often has, the broadcasters can assume roles traditionally assigned to political and governmental institutions. In the case of the President and congressional leaders, the networks inadvertently arrogate new power to themselves by taking on the role of a non-partisan opposition force. Media critic Michael Robinson, Director of Georgetown University's Media Analysis Project, wrote that network news emerged as the new "Loyal Opposition" which acted as the "shadow cabinet" in the American political system.[1] In such a role, the networks presented themselves on a commanding national stage off-limits to traditional opposition forces. A major outgrowth of the networks "Loyal Opposition" role, according to Christopher Matthews, Press Spokesperson for former Speaker Thomas P. O'Neill, Jr., was the eclipse of the power of political parties:

At a dizzying pace, the TV news networks have absorbed many of the democratic functions traditionally held by political parties: the elevation of key public issues, the promotion of new leaders, the division of executive and legislative authority, and the constitution of political opposition. It was once the parties that bally-hooed the causes, touted the candidates, and aroused the nation. Today network executives make these decisions, based not on ideology but on a rational mix of "news judgment" and commercial savvy. For better or worse, the nation's dogged two-party system has been challenged by a three-network system that runs at a much higher voltage and delivers at a speed approaching light itself. Even in the reign of the Great Communicator, there is one force that holds supreme power: the networks that carry him.[2]

## CONTROLLING THE ARENA

In many ways, the networks were the chief beneficiaries of the decline of the political parties and the rise of the presidency. As millions of Americans huddled around their radios and televisions to listen to the President of the United States, network media messengers basked in the glow of the presidential aura. The rising popularity of network television and of the televised presidency paralleled each other, blessing the networks with badly needed prestige and legitimacy, camouflaging the inter-network competitive battle for the biggest bottom line, and whetting network appetites for a larger role in politics.

The networks liked political television because they were the stage directors; they threw the switches and set the rules. Network executives griped about giving away so much profitable airtime, but in the end, they did not want to sacrifice their prestigious connection to the United States Government, especially if that prestige could be had without sacrificing profits. The network tie to powerful institutions helped elevate them to a comparable status. In less than 70 years, the networks found themselves compared favorably in public opinion polls alongside

Congress, business, labor, the military, religion, and other more established American institutions.

Almost from the beginning of broadcasting, the networks aggressively used political events as a springboard for prestige and competitive advantage. Presidential elections, political conventions, presidential speeches and news conferences, and daily White House coverage provided an ideal focal point for showcasing network talent and vying for the public's respect and trust. Decisions about who would anchor the conventions and the election night broadcasts and who would travel with the candidates were among the most important decisions made by news executives.

As the networks relied more and more on the political arena as a source of raw material for news, they also exercised greater control over the events they covered. The networks had such a tight grip on political broadcasting that it was impossible to follow a presidential campaign without running into the mediating hands of the networks. Many observers of American politics, including some journalists, believed that the system became imbalanced. Max Kampelman, lawyer, author, and Chief Arms Negotiator under President Reagan, wrote in 1979 that the setting of the nation's political agenda, traditionally a prerogative of politicians, had been assumed by the media. British journalist Henry Fairlie wrote that the primary activity of Washington "is no longer the government of the country through its political institutions; it is now the sustaining of the illusion of government through the media and in obedience to the media's needs and demands."[3] Likewise, Robert MacNeil, co-anchor of the "MacNeil/Lehrer Newshour" said that television cast a spell over the nation, which convinced people that its own imperatives must govern, "If television does not like something as it is, it is assumed that the wide public won't either. Therefore, change it so that television will like it. Television viability becomes the viability that matters. Television is American politics in the way that television is American sports."[4]

Politicians responded to the power of television and its personalities by showing proper deference to an institution that Max Kampelman claimed was second only to the presidency in power.[5] For example, just before President Carter made his surprise announcement giving diplomatic recognition to the People's Republic of China, he invited network anchors Walter Cronkite, John Chancellor, and Frank Reynolds to Washington for a special briefing one hour before the speech. Reynolds, who was suffering from terminal cancer, rose from his sickbed for the occasion. This incident was tacit recognition that network anchors had assumed a status comparable to congressional leaders for whom this special type of briefing was usually reserved. The media stars had become a powerful force who deserved special handling.

## UPWARD MOBILITY

As the networks became more powerful, their correspondents and anchors reflected that power through increased visibility. Network anchors frequently turned up in polls naming America's movers and shakers. CBS' Walter Cronkite became such an authority figure in the 1960s that his commentary opposing the Vietnam War was said to be the principal turning point in tilting American public opinion against the war.

Adding to the networks' aura of power was the constancy of their personnel and their privileged position above the partisan fray. Presidents came and went, but the David Brinkleys, Ted Koppels, Dan Rathers, and Mike Wallaces lingered. When America faced both crisis and triumph, the network stars guided Americans through traumatic events, explaining their repercussions. The more urgent the information, the more the country depended on them. Whether it was conventions, news conferences, addresses to the nation, speeches, interviews, special events or daily news coverage, network news reporters were the interpreters for these events.

Accompanying the increased clout of network correspondents were their wealth and social standing. For years, there was a natural and healthy social distance between the media and the people they covered, partly because of a disparity in incomes. News people were notoriously underpaid. When network stars commanded six- and seven-figure incomes and celebrity status, they became major players in the Washington social circuit, populating elite dinner parties and power tennis matches throughout the city.

Social distance between news reporters and newsmakers had been erased. Former CBS anchor Walter Cronkite claimed that at one time, "We knew Archie Bunker better than the bankers" but a "better class of reporters" meant the "loss of the common touch."[6] Less complimentary of this trend was Michael Leeden who in an article in *Public Interest* claimed that since the 1960s, the media have taken on "all the trappings of other elite institutions; high salaries, luxurious perks, status, top billing on the society pages," and have developed a "new style and a new mythology to protect their privileges."[7]

The networks used the popularity and visibility of their journalists to consolidate competitive positions. The networks increasingly based news promotions on the personalities heading their newscasts. When anchor Dan Rather replaced Walter Cronkite, CBS promoted him like a political figure. In a tape strongly resembling a political commercial, an announcer lauded Rather's "experience, integrity, and leadership," implying that Rather possessed some extraordinary personal traits that could help him exercise "leadership."

Active promotion of network correspondents brought the inevitable comparisons between politicians and journalists. Author David Halberstam wrote that Lyndon Johnson resented network correspondents who "had not earned the Presidency, and yet there they were pretending to be his equal. . . . Who had elected them?" Halberstam quoted Johnson as telling one of his aides, "I can't compete with Walter Cronkite. He knows television and he's a star."[8] Not only was Cronkite a better communicator than Johnson, but Cronkite, except for presidential speeches, controlled the airwaves. ABC's Ted Koppel's interviewing mechanism symbolizes that control. When Koppel interviews guests on his popular "Nightline" program, he stays in a different room making it far easier to cut them off at will and control their access. Under such circumstances, it is not surprising that politicians often find themselves in a submissive position when they enter the networks' turf.

Despite the politicians' reputation for equivocation on the issues, it is they, not the journalists, who in the end must make a stand and take the heat. Politicians believe it is all too easy for network journalists to breeze in and out of the political world without bearing the burden of solving the problems. Perhaps this immunity from unpopular decision-making explains why a *Times Mirror* poll in 1985 showed network anchors Peter Jennings (90%), Dan Rather (89%), and Tom Brokaw (88%) all had a higher favorability rating than Ronald Reagan (68%), one of America's most popular Presidents.[9] Network personalities could have it both ways, sharing the prestige and glamour of political life while avoiding the tarnish of political reality.

## NETWORK SELF-SUFFICIENCY

Accompanying the network personification of its "stars" as infallible supermen and superwomen was an increasing insularity and resistance to material from the outside world. For years, networks relied exclusively on their own talent and expertise, distrusting anything they did not produce. It was common for network news departments to refuse outside film, even routine stock footage. This network policy gained attention in 1960 when CBS rejected the David Wolper documentary "Race for Space" produced in cooperation with the Department of Defense. CBS President Frank Stanton, sensitive to the risks of airing material the networks had not produced, told a Senate Committee that the network could best discharge its duties if it required that all material come from "employees of, and hence accountable to, CBS News." Wolper countered to the FCC that, "If the networks could only open the window you would find that a lot of fresh air . . . would blow into the television scene and the public would get the advantage of the exposure to new and exciting programming."[10] The Wolper episode, whose aftershocks are still being felt, led CBS and its competitors down a route towards deeper insularity and distrust of outsiders.

Columnist Jack Anderson recalled an experience similar to Wolper's when the networks rejected a packaged interview he had done with President Ford during the bicentennial celebration. The program was financed by Philadelphia businessman Edward Piszek, who was willing to sponsor it at commercial rates. Anderson felt the networks turned down the interview out of an unwillingness to air productions with roots outside of their studios, "Each network explained, in effect, that it doesn't carry interviews with the President unless he is buoyed up by a supporting cast of network personalities. In other words, it is not so much the President's answers that matter; it's who asked the questions."[11]

Veteran CBS commentator Eric Severeid believed that the television-age emphasis on self-sufficiency induced the networks to break ties with their constituencies, and ultimately sowed the seeds of anti-network sentiment which surfaced in the 1980s. Severeid said he told CBS executives on several occasions that he felt uncomfortable being the only voice giving commentary on CBS and that some mechanism should be developed to allow people from outside the network to have some input. He saw public access as a safety valve against the networks becoming arrogant and insular.[12]

Echoing Severeid's view was "Sixty Minutes" Executive Producer Don Hewitt who said that opening network doors to public response is the "one place we fall down badly." Hewitt said he suggested giving six of CBS' documentary hours each year to the public including cameras, videotape, and editors "so they can do as slick a job of answering as we do in our pieces."[13] Hewitt's "Sixty Minutes" colleague, Mike Wallace, said television "cannot complain about libel trials, and preach the necessity of free and full discussion of issues of public controversy, and then fail to make our facilities available for that discussion."[14]

"Sixty Minutes" has provided a limited public response outlet by making time each week for a sampling of viewers' letters. By opening the network door to even a symbolic access, "Sixty Minutes" received more than 150 thousand pieces of mail in two years. CBS occasionally broadcasts "Your Turn: Letters to CBS News," but little sustained effort has been made by any of the commercial networks to open their doors wider to the public. Perhaps the most ambitious effort to provide criticism of the media has been ABC's "Viewpoint" which is scheduled to air quarterly in the "Nightline" time slot.

The Chairman of Accuracy in Media, Reed Irvine, said that if "enlightened people" were running the networks, they would charge ahead voluntarily to let people "have their say" as a means of heading off public discontent.[15] The British did just that on their newest broadcasting outlet, Channel 4, by installing "The Video Box," a device through which the public could record a one-minute message about television programming. Several of the messages were regularly incorporated into the weekly "Right to Reply" program which answered and amplified many of the complaints.

## ANTI-MEDIA BACKLASH

By locking out public expression, the networks left themselves vulnerable to public attack. During the early 1980s an anti–media backlash developed, partially related to the smug insularity and arrogance of the networks. A wave of anti–press sentiment surfaced in 1983 when the Pentagon barred reporters from the Grenada landing force. NBC commentator John Chancellor warned his audience that "The American Government is doing whatever it wants to, without any representative of the American public watching what it is doing."[16] But the American people did not buy the networks' "representatives" premise. NBC viewers supported the press ban in Grenada five to one. ABC anchor Peter Jennings said his mail was running 99 percent in favor of President Reagan. *Time's* letters were eight to one against the press.[17] Almost as quickly as the polls hit the street, national news coverage of the Grenada invasion turned positive. Thus, it appeared that while the public had little input in setting the initial media agenda, the media's self-inflicted slavery to ratings and polls opened the way for the public to have a strong, indirect voice in editorial affairs. Like the politicians, broadcasters sometimes found it all too easy to go with the flow of public opinion.

The highly publicized Westmoreland and Sharon libel trials against CBS and *Time* magazine in 1985 gave Americans another opportunity to vent their frustrations with the media. A poll commissioned by the American Society of Newspaper Editors around the time of the libel trials found that 78 percent of the 1600 adults questioned thought reporters were only concerned about getting a good story and did not worry about hurting people, while 63 percent thought the media took advantage of ordinary people who became victims of circumstance.[18] Similar polls showed that the public respected the job the media were doing, but resented the callousness and arrogance they displayed in their dealings with individuals. In a 1987 *Times Mirror*/Gallup poll, 59 percent of respondents said the press had too much influence in determining a party's Presidential nominee while only 31 percent said it had the right amount.[19]

The public opinion backlash of the mid–1980s did not go unnoticed by media executives. Throughout the nation, newsrooms buzzed with concern about public perception of journalism's short-comings. NBC Anchor Tom Brokaw told the International Radio and Television Society

in 1984 about an increasingly "hostile environment" because "there has
been an abuse of privilege."[20] According to W. Vincent Burke, Vice-
President of News for the ABC-owned television stations, broadcast
journalists became the "brash brats who intrude."[21] ABC executive
George Watson, admitting that the public has the impression that "we
arrogantly don't give a damn," said the media could not protect a free
press by only invoking the First Amendment; it must provide "an at-
tentive ear and an open mind" to public concerns.[22] Likewise, NBC News
President Lawrence Grossman told affiliates during the Reagan Administration that journalists must be sensitive to the charges of appearing
"arrogant, impolite, and even smugly superior with our insider's knowledge and our privileged access" and must be "more open than we have
been to the views and concerns of the public we serve."[23]

## THE PEOPLE'S REPRESENTATIVES

During the 1970s, the networks not only closed themselves off from
outside input but conformed to what Schudson called a "new political
reality." Under this system, a journalist was no longer the relater of
news but the interpreter of news as well.[24] NBC's Chief Political Correspondent, Roger Mudd, said, "What the national media, and mainly
television, have done is to believe that their chief duty is to put before
the nation its unfinished business. . . . The media have become the nation's critics, and as critics no political Administration, regardless of how
hard it tries, will satisfy them."[25] Likewise, ABC White House correspondent Sam Donaldson cited the "critical oversight function" of the
media as their reason for "taking on the political process."[26]

The networks took their adverse critics role a step farther, implying
that the media were "representatives" of the people much like Members
of Congress represented a constituency. Max Kampelman has written,
"In addition to looking upon himself as a defender of people, the journalist now looks upon himself increasingly as a spokesman for the people."[27] CBS' "Evening News" anchor Dan Rather once said at a press
conference that he was protecting his sources "not for the benefit of
reporters. It is for the benefit of listeners and viewers and readers. . . .
The cause is America."[28] Rather's statements reflected what journalists
called "the people's right to know," a battle cry frequently used to justify
journalistic inquiry.

As representatives of the people, the media not only had the First
Amendment to stand behind but also the fairness doctrine, which gave
the networks power to select the opposition forces in America. By requiring broadcasters to seek out opposing views on controversial issues,
the fairness doctrine left the definition of the opposition to broadcasters.
While broadcasters considered the fairness doctrine an offensive in-

fringement on their press freedom, it actually legitimized their power to select who the political opposition in America would be. In the case of rebuttals to Presidential addresses, the networks could ignore the opposition views of the congressional leadership, the political parties, and any other group.

Another criticism associated with the implementation of the fairness doctrine was that the networks gravitated toward conventional, mainstream opposition forces associated with the existing power structure and away from the political and social extremes. Minority groups have frequently accused the networks of "rounding up the usual suspects" for opposition viewpoints rather than exploring new perspectives and ideas. Media scholars contended that broadcasting was a powerful force for preserving the status quo in society and discouraging discordant viewpoints.

Broadcasters have been so accustomed to hand-picking the televised opposition that any suggestion that this arbitrary selection is unfair meets with outrage. Typical of the view toward government-mandated control was in a 1970 *Broadcasting* editorial responding to a suggestion that the networks provide more time for the opposition, "Whatever broadcasters choose to do about covering those in and out of power, they must never yield their rights to do the choosing, unless they wish to demote themselves from journalists to messengers."[29]

Central to the networks' avoidance of becoming little more than messengers has been their power to choose opposing views. When the FCC repealed the fairness doctrine in 1987, it relieved broadcasters of an onerous regulatory burden, but it also deprived them of a mandate to enter the political communication system. Now, they will be setting the ground rules for access with neither prodding nor hindrance from the Federal Government.

## INSTANT ANALYSIS

Not only did the networks allocate opposition time under the fairness doctrine, but they retained part of the opposition role for themselves, using their own correspondents and anchors to rebut the President. When Presidents Johnson and Nixon accelerated their televised media blitzes in the 1960s and 1970s, the networks developed "instant analysis" as a first-line defense against the power of the electronic Presidency. After a presidential speech, one or more network commentators would discuss the speech, review the highlights, and add interpretation. The network commentators would usually be the only alternative voice heard. More often than not, instant analysis was heavy on recap and light on analysis.

Regardless of how tepid the commentary, instant analysis displeased

Presidents. It undercut the impact of a President's remarks and rein-forced the notion that the networks controlled the airtime. Several con-servative groups protested loudly during the Nixon Administration at what they perceived as biased commentaries after network speeches. The criticism became so vocal that CBS Chairman William Paley sus-pended instant analysis for five months.

Instant analysis provided an influential reaction to a presidential speech. Was the speech effective? Did the President look good? Was he forceful? Were there any flaws that the audience might not detect? Dur-ing these crucial minutes after the speech, the White House staff as well as the public, were watching. When the networks disallowed immediate congressional reaction, the networks' instant analysis became the most immediate counterbalancing force influencing the success or failure of the speech. As one aide in the Carter Administration said, "You really don't have any way to know how it went over. Your first barometer is TV. If they say it was monstrous, many people think it was. If they say it was good, then it becomes good."[30] This agenda-setting mentality was evident at the 1984 presidential debates where campaign aides for both Reagan and Mondale madly scrambled to the anchor booths after the debates to be the first to proclaim victory. Campaign strategists believed that the network-controlled analysis and interviews after the debates were almost as important as the debate themselves.

The advent of instant analysis postured the networks as a non-partisan, de facto "Loyal Opposition" to the President. The networks were not trying to seize control of the political communication system or make themselves the centers of political debate; their behavior was more akin to that of the western hero who surveys the environment and smugly but reluctantly decides that he is the only one big enough and courageous enough to clean up the town. In trying to provide balance to an unbalanced situation, a group of journalists backed into a role never envisioned by the Constitution and never demanded by the American people. Instant analysis had impact because of its proximity to the presidential speech and because it came in prime time. In poten-tially ambiguous situations, network analysis could channel the audi-ence's attention or put a positive or negative cast on a political figure.

Instant analysis gained favor partly because it was far more efficient and predictable to use network commentators than outsiders after pres-idential speeches and there was never a shortage of network people who wanted to get on the air. The correspondent hierarchy began with regular beat reporters and rose to those privileged few who could anchor or participate in a special broadcast. The networks were so confident about their abilities that it was difficult to imagine anyone becoming a better countervailing force to the President. Network personnel were perceived internally at least as being more adept than congressional leaders at communicating on a par with Presidents. Most television executives in the 1970s shared the sentiments of NBC Washington Bureau Chief Donald Meany who felt that their own commentators were best suited to deliver "informed, fair, honest comment. We prefer pure analysis to partisan discussion or pro and con comment."[31]

Correspondents and analysts were trained to speak succinctly, forthrightly, and authoritatively. The good ones had a firm grasp of the issues facing the American people. Perhaps most importantly, the network people were controllable and predictable and understood the constraints on the medium. In the end, there was no capital to be made from bringing in outsiders, but considerable liabilities.

While a network commentator might overstep the boundaries once in a while, he or she was far more predictable than an outside source. It would be embarrassing to invite a well-known public figure and then cut that person off after 30 seconds because it was time for the next entertainment program to start. Network commentators, however, were quite used to being shouted at through concealed earphones and rudely cut off. Competition between networks, competition within the networks, the status associated with presidential television, and the communication advantage of using professional broadcasters provided ample incentive for the networks to attach their own postscript to Presidential addresses. Yet, this analysis was further evidence to Americans that the networks, rather than the politicians, were their real representatives in Washington.

Instant analysis gradually disappeared largely because of programming constraints, which shortened the time the news division had for comment, and because the quality of comment was not always high. After repeatedly having to come on after the President without having seen copies of the speeches until the last minute, Eric Severeid of CBS finally told management he could no longer do instant analysis because, given the time constraints, he had nothing substantive or insightful to say.[32]

## NEWS CONFERENCES

A whole generation of viewers grew up watching the President of the United States being challenged regularly, not by the opposition, but by the media during presidential press conferences. That these conferences were broadcast simultaneously on all three networks gave them a special importance and provided a visible, prestigious stage for those who asked the questions.

By the end of the Kennedy presidency, viewers were accustomed to watching network personalities question the President and analyze his remarks, further reinforcing the key network position as intermediary in the political process. Correspondents were, after all, protecting the "people's right to know." When Dan Rather became a folk hero by confronting President Nixon at the height of Watergate, it was clear that news reporters had a special role in the political system.

Until the presidency of John Kennedy, news conferences had been relatively private affairs between Presidents and newsmen. There was little posturing because there was no one to posture to except other journalists. Kennedy changed the rules when he allowed press conferences to be televised, making them the principal forum for hand-to-hand public combat. Televised news conferences gave the networks another ideal opportunity to intrude into the political arena. It was a format that the networks produced and also starred in, and one which made the American people comfortable with news journalists acting as presidential counterpoints. Just as Members of Parliament had a right to question Prime Ministers in England, network journalists in America assumed a "right" to question Presidents regularly in a forum controlled by the networks.

Presidents were under pressure to perform, but so were journalists. Print reporters were personifying their bylines for the first time. Although their questions were supposed to be intelligent, lucid, and somewhat aggressive, one had the feeling that print reporters practiced their "spontaneous" questions for hours in front of a mirror before the conference, wanting to look and sound good for their national audience. In contrast, network reporters confidently stood before a national television audience and boomed out questions. This was the networks' show. The American people could get the broadcast only through them.

A network anchor introduced the broadcast and handed the audience over to the President. Sometimes, the network anchor would give his own correspondent a build-up before the conference started. When the network correspondents were called on (and they invariably were, often by name), there was instant recognition in homes throughout America. These familiar correspondents were doing something that few Americans, including Congressmen and Senators, could ever do—confront the President of the United States.

## POLITICAL CONVENTIONS

The political conventions are still another example of how networks control political events. A visitor's attention when entering a convention hall would probably focus on two things—the huge podium and the three imposing network anchor booths perched above the convention floor displaying the huge neon logos of ABC, CBS, NBC, and most recently CNN. The anchor booths' physical domination of the convention floor symbolizes the networks' editorial domination of the proceedings. Don Hewitt, Executive Producer of CBS' "Sixty Minutes" and longtime convention producer, said the networks have taken too much control:

There is no doubt whose convention this really is. The politicians meeting there are now extras in our television show. My job for more years than I want to remember was to oversee the CBS floor reporters. In truth, my job was not all that different from a circus ringmaster. I was given responsibility of seeing that my ring was more exciting than NBC's or ABC's. And if Ed Bradley had to get into a contretemps with the Mayor of Chicago to keep my show moving, so be it. When I first went to political conventions, we were observers and reporters. Now we're participants. And there's something a lot wrong with that.[33]

As the networks took greater control of the conventions, they not only injected themselves farther into the political process but pushed legitimate participants farther from it. A study analyzing the 1980 Republican and Democratic conventions found that the networks showed the official proceedings of the conventions only half of the time, filling the rest with their own coverage.[34] Jack Valenti, president of the Motion Picture Association of America, said that when the conventions veer from the podium they distort reality and the political process:

If ever you wanted a revealing example of how powerful the networks are now, you could see it during the Democratic convention and you can see it again during the Republican convention. The networks dictated the shape and form of the convention. The speaking alignment was built around the two-hour coverage by the three networks. One network turned its cameras off the Speaker of the House of Representatives, who was speaking on the convention rostrum, and turned them on their own newspeople. This display of raw muscle was a bit scary since it was evident that Speaker O'Neill had been summarily dismissed from the national audience by someone whose name and face are unknown to the American public. Three people, one in each network, unelected and unseen, decided who went on the air and who didn't.[35]

The party conventions would be a logical area for the networks to disengage as "representatives" of the people; technology has boosted opportunities for organizations like the Cable Satellite Public Affairs Network (C-SPAN), as well as local stations to provide coverage without the big three. Yet, the conventions represent a competitive intramural challenge for the networks that has little to do with the business of the parties. Conventions are the network equivalent of the Paris Air Show where they can periodically show off their technology and stars. To withdraw from such a media event would be painful indeed.

## PRESIDENTIAL DEBATES

Another trend toward network dominance could be seen developing around the Presidential primary and general election debates. Even though most of the debates have been controlled by third parties like the League of Women Voters, the network presence has certainly been felt to control them and to supply moderators and panelists. During the 1988 primary debates, the networks scrambled for a front-row position. NBC started the competition on December 1, 1987, when it organized and broadcast its own Democratic forum live from the Kennedy Center in Washington. As could be expected, NBC had total control over the format, giving its own moderator Tom Brokaw a major role in the proceedings.[36]

For the 1988 general election, the political parties arranged to take control of the debates themselves, putting some distance between politicians and the networks. They realized that debates predated television and could be staged independent of it. Politicians feared that having journalists serve as participants and testers of the political winds risked significant distortion of important electoral events and unnecessary network control. Even Don Hewitt of CBS, the producer of the first televised debates in 1960, condemned the practice of having journalists participate in debates, preferring to let candidates "go at each other." Hewitt said the reporters all sat there saying "what can I ask that will make me look smart but not partisan."[37]

## THE NETWORKS AND DIPLOMACY

In recent years, the networks have used sophisticated telecommunication operations rivaling those of some nations to thrust themselves into American diplomacy. The foreign policy door sprang open when the networks became brokers in the Egyptian–Israeli peace process in the late 1970s. As Egyptian President Anwar Sadat made his historic visit to Israel, network anchors like Barbara Walters and Walter Cronkite fell into the role of intermediary, relaying important diplomatic messages between the governments.

Both Prime Minister Begin and President Sadat were keenly aware of the importance of the networks in defining the issues and placed extraordinary importance on communication with network representatives. Likewise, the networks delighted in the prestigious position conferred upon them by world leaders. In 1986, the networks' intense coverage of the Philippines elections once again elevated them to a special status on both sides of the Pacific. The networks swarmed into the Philippines, covering the election, according to a congressional aide, like "an American primary out in the hinterlands."[38] President Marcos spent almost as much time on American TV as he did campaigning in his own country and his remarks quickly reverberated back to the Philippines. Marcos could not reach President Reagan directly, but he could reach him through the networks. The energized Philippines coverage created a heightened awareness by Americans rarely seen on a foreign story and changed the way the White House and Congress approached the whole Philippines issue. As New York Congressman Stephen Solarz said, "It was another example of how TV creates a political reality of its own."[39]

John Corry, a television writer for the *New York Times*, believes that the networks have grown "increasingly supernational, roaming the world like sovereign powers." He charges that when network cameras rush in like imperial armies, the scene becomes the center of public opinion and political debate. When the networks throw their full resources into an area, they become a powerful force to be reckoned with, often throwing the U.S. Government off balance and forcing it to deal with them like they were a foreign power themselves. Likewise, NBC anchor Tom Brokaw said technology that brings instant access to world events tempts journalists to become "negotiators and arbiters, not merely reporters."[40]

While Barbara Walters was mildly disciplined in 1987 by ABC for carrying a diplomatic message from the Middle East to President Reagan, there was no evidence that the networks were shying away from this linkage role as intermediary or power broker. In some cases, the creative diplomacy fashioned by the networks prompted full-page self-congratulatory advertisements in major newspapers. Proximity to government, foreign and domestic, and involvement in governmental affairs carried with it a special status the networks relished.

The intense competition between the networks to get an exclusive interview with Soviet General Secretary Mikhail Gorbachev before his December 1987 summit with President Reagan proved that network behavior showed no sign of change. When the Soviets selected NBC's Tom Brokaw, CBS News President Howard Stringer fired off a letter to the Soviet leader saying that CBS News was "shocked and disappointed that we have been denied a one-on-one interview." NBC claimed it was the "Network of Choice" and had launched an orchestrated campaign to get the interview as soon as Gorbachev took office. The whole affair looked more like an intramural competition for legitimacy and status than for news. If NBC could carry the first pre-summit words from the General Secretary's mouth to the American people, it would carry enormous prestige. The Gorbachev interview was just one more example of the status-seeking behavior at which the networks became so skilled during the television age.[41]

## PUBLIC POLICY INITIATIVES

On occasion, the networks have elevated themselves to a quasi–governmental role by attempting to solve complex public policy problems. In 1983, ABC joined with Harvard University to sponsor a symposium in Washington designed to find ways to increase voter participation. ABC reportedly spent several hundred thousand dollars to prepare and execute the event, including $25,000 to lure former Presidents Gerald Ford and Jimmy Carter to the conference. Not satisfied with the decor of the Senate Caucus Room where the Watergate hearings were held, the networks purchased new drapes, a new rug and a huge oval table and 40 cane-backed chairs.[42] ABC filled its new chairs with luminaries from the political and journalistic worlds, coming as close to a "congressional" environment as possible. ABC even hired just-retired House Rules Committee Chairman Richard Bolling to "chair" the proceedings.

When the conference began, journalists, politicians, and academics sat side by side discussing serious political issues. In this forum, ABC News President Roone Arledge had equal status with Senate Majority Leader Howard Baker. When the conferees voted on recommendations, the journalists and the politicians had equal votes. The aura was that of an official congressional proceeding except that it was in some ways better. Scores of network executives and technicians stood by to nudge the program toward perfection. Unlike a regular congressional hearing, this network forum made everyone look eloquent in the edited version. In addition, network television gave this relatively distant and esoteric topic a bigger audience than a real hearing could ever hope to achieve.

The ABC symposium represented a new type of production, one manufactured by corporate management, using the news division as a prop. It was a corporate adventure in influencing public policy that tried hard to capture the mantle of congressional legitimacy. According to this scenario, the American people could expect their media "representatives" not only to criticize public policy but to make it as well.

## POSTSCRIPT

As powerful and pervasive as the networks remain and as strong as their "representative" role has been, it is unlikely that they will ever dominate the political scene the way they have during the past half century. No longer does the American political system need them quite so badly. No longer is there a willingness to tolerate their arrogance and dominance. The network magic is fading. Alternatives like CNN and C-SPAN already exist to broadcast convention coverage, debates, news conferences, presidential speeches, and other events. Furthermore, bitter internal struggles within the networks over news budgets and coverage priorities have left the news divisions more humble and introspective.

As the future of network news is debated, American political institutions have an opportunity to reclaim some control over the system which they lost to the mighty networks during the past half century. Politicians now realize that the natural order does not have to include network dominance and intrusion.

## Chapter 7

# A New Political Communication Order

During the 1960s and 1970s, the three commercial television networks swaggered through the nation's capital as invincible conquerors, demanding proper respect and deference from those associated with the three constitutionally sanctioned branches of government. A phone call from a network anchor or a Washington Bureau Chief could rouse any congressman or cabinet level official in an instant. When media decisions were made in Washington, the networks figured at the top of the list.

In such an environment, it seemed quite natural that the networks should be so dominant and forceful in setting the rules for access and relegating the opposition to second-class status. It was, after all, a network prerogative to make such assignments. The opposition had no right to access, only the right to petition the networks. Yet, this power relationship, like all others in Washington, was destined for change.

Throughout the 1980s, the network share of the broadcasting audience took a long and deliberate slide, ending the decade near 60 percent, down from 90 percent just ten years earlier. Cable, independent stations, and VCRs were constantly tempting the viewer to turn away from the networks. In addition, management upheavals, ownership changes, and staff cutbacks at the networks took their toll on employee morale and network status. The networks' patina was fading as was their undisputable claim to the role of arbiters of political access. As technological forces and diversity in the marketplace shook the foundations of network control, a new political communication order was emerging in which the networks would not be the dominant players.

## THE NETWORK RATINGS SLIDE

As the penetration of cable passed 50 percent in the mid–1980s and America offered more than 1,000 television stations to its people, the networks could no longer maintain their iron grip on the television audience. Network defections to competitors, which had been no more than minor nuisances in earlier years, suddenly grew to mammoth problems. The network prime time share eroded from 91 percent in 1976–77 to 67 percent in 1988–89.[1] During the summer months, the networks' share went as low as 55 percent. In households that had cable (and therefore more programming choices), the network share had slipped to a paltry 52 percent.[2] In just one year, from 1985–86 to 1986–87, the networks lost 1,128,000 households in prime time while cable gained 906,000.[3] The networks were being saved from disaster by the 45 percent of Americans who could not afford or did not have access to cable television.

CBS Board member Newton Minow said he used to complain during the mid–1980s that charts used at network meetings listed only ABC, CBS, and NBC. When he asked about cable, there were only blank stares.[4] For years, the networks lived in their own self-contained solar system with enough resources to make them all very fat and happy. Real competition from cable, VCRs, and independent stations was a bold and unwelcome intrusion into that world. The first reaction was to ignore it, but eventually the networks faced reality.

The three over-the-air networks were dealt a sobering blow in the fall of 1987, when Nielsen began a more refined audience measurement system using "people-meters." These devices recorded the preferences of each individual who was watching a particular program rather than lumping everyone in the household together. Generally, the people-meters recorded fewer members of the households watching programs than under the old system. After only three months of being rated by the people-meters, network audiences were down 10 percent.[5] By January 1988, CBS executives were claiming that the introduction of the people-meters had cost the networks $40 to $50 million in lost advertising.[6] If the people-meters were hurting the over-the-air networks, they were a boon to cable networks. The Cable Advertising Bureau reported a 30 percent gain in prime time viewing on pay cable networks after the new audience measurement was introduced.[7]

## REAGAN RATINGS RECESSION

Regardless of the technique used to measure audiences, the network share eroded significantly from the late 1970s through the 1980s. As the networks lost their stronghold on entertainment programming, the au-

**Table 7.1**
**Presidential Share of Audience, 1969–86**

| President | Speeches Ave. Share | News Conferences Ave. Share | All Broadcasts* Ave. Share |
|-----------|---------------------|------------------------------|------------------------------|
| Nixon | 75% (22)** | 75% (7) | 76% (31) |
| Ford | 81% (10) | 76% (12) | 78% (26) |
| Carter | 74% (12) | 67% (35) | 69% (49) |
| Reagan | 62% (28) | 61% (32) | 62% (66) |

*The number of broadcasts in this category is greater than the sum of speeches and news conferences because it contains ceremonial events, State of the Union messages, and other presidential broadcasts not included in the other two categories.

**Parenthesis contain the number of presidential speeches used to calculate the average share.

diences for presidential addresses and opposition responses also dropped. For example, Ronald Reagan reached an average of only 61 percent of the people watching television during prime time compared to 77 percent for Jimmy Carter and 79 percent for Gerald Ford and Richard Nixon. In fact, the "great communicator" at his best seldom reached as large a share of the audience as some of his less-gifted predecessors (see Table 7.1).

During prime time, the declines in audience could mean millions of lost viewers. For example, President Reagan averaged 55 million viewers for his evening speeches compared to 69 million for President Carter. While President Reagan's prime time speech ratings were respectable in the beginning of his Administration (1981—75 percent share), by the time he ran for re-election in 1984, just over half of the viewers watching television (53 percent) were watching the President. Even during State of the Union messages, when audiences were traditionally higher than with addresses to the nation, the speeches slipped from nearly an 84 share in 1981 to just under a 50 percent audience share in 1989, meaning that more than 30 million Americans had defected to other programming during his presidency. Viewers were taking advantage of the growing alternatives on the dial, denying the networks a massive, captive audience.

Presidential shares were falling, in part, because of a steady decline in the overall network audience share that began in 1979. Yet, as Table 7.2 illustrates, the President's share of audience dropped from 78 percent

**Table 7.2**
**Comparison of Overall Network Prime Time Shares with**
**Presidential Broadcasting Shares, 1979–86**

| Year | Network Share | Presidential Share | Difference |
|------|---------------|--------------------|------------|
| 1979 | 91% | 78% | −14% |
| 1980 | 90% | 79% | −11% |
| 1981 | 85% | 74% | −12% |
| 1982 | 83% | 65% | −22% |
| 1983 | 81% | 61% | −24% |
| 1984 | 78% | 56% | −28% |
| 1985 | 77% | 56% | −27% |
| 1986 | 76% | 58% | −24% |

in 1979 to 58 percent in 1986, while the prime time network audience dropped at a slower rate, declining from 91 to 76 percent over the same period. During every year of Reagan's presidency, except the first, the President's share of audience was running at least 20 percent below that of the networks.

## NETWORK DEFECTORS

If viewers were not watching the President, what were they doing? An examination of the number of average audience households viewing television during nine prime time presidential appearances (State of the Union, addresses to the nation, and news conferences) in 1986 and 1987 confirmed that, while presidential speeches were causing millions of Americans to turn away from network programming, they were still watching television. There was no difference between the Houses Using Television (HUT) for presidential speech evenings and regular prime time evenings. On average, 11,135,021 fewer households viewed a presidential appearance than viewed the entertainment programs which were shown three weeks prior to and three weeks after the presidential speech in the same time slot. More than 16 million households defected when President Reagan spoke to the nation on Contra Aid to Nicaraguan rebels in March 1986, while only four million households defected when the President held a news conference in November of that year after the Iran arms scandal.

Fortunately for the networks, all but 181,000 of the more than 11 million defecting households returned to network programming immediately after the President finished his speech. A substantial number of Americans made a conscious decision to avoid just the President's message, watch an alternative program, then quickly return to network programming.

The Nielsen data in this study did not show specifically where the approximately 11 million households nationwide went for programming when the President spoke. Some anecdotal data showed that independent television stations as well as cable channels benefitted. During President Reagan's 1987 State of the Union message, overnight ratings in New York showed that independent station WNYW's audience doubled from a five to a ten rating and WOR's rose 75 percent when the President began to speak. WNYW's sales manager said that the increased ratings during presidential speeches were so routine that his station aired special movies and charged higher rates during presidential broadcasts, increasing the earnings of the station by more than $100,000 per night.[8]

When President Bush held his first prime time televised news conference early on a Thursday evening in June 1989, enough viewers defected from the delayed "Cosby Show" on NBC to send the hit series to its lowest ratings position of the year. Millions of viewers obviously went elsewhere when they saw the President appear on the screen rather than Bill Cosby. Likewise, when President Bush made his first televised address to the nation on September 5, 1989, only half of the American people watching television bothered to tune-in.

Rarely have independents and cable programmers found the networks in such a vulnerable position. Clearly, ratings for presidential television have been in a steady downward spiral. Furthermore, the decline has been more rapid than the erosion of network audience share. In 1975, a Nielsen study showed that President Ford's speeches actually attracted additional viewers to the networks. Presidential broadcasts are now driving millions of viewers away from the networks rather than attracting them as earlier Presidents had done.

By the mid–1980s, an entertainment program like "The Cosby Show" could attract more viewers on one network than the President did by appearing on all three simultaneously, marking a significant decline in the reach of a presidential speech. While presidents can still command 80-plus audience shares in times of crisis, gone are the days when network roadblocking automatically delivers a huge captive audience.

The variability in ratings during the Reagan Administration suggested that viewers were highly selective in their behavior. Anchoring the audience for presidential broadcasts was a core of active, information-seeking viewers, which could expand according to the perceived interest in a speech. Shopworn speeches exhorting voters to support unpopular policies drew record low audiences, while speeches involving crisis or scandal attracted millions more. Also active were those viewers determined to avoid political content; they quickly banished the President from their homes as they intently search for something more appealing.

The increased menu of attractive entertainment programming on cable, independent television, and video cassette would seem to offer a more plausible explanation for the ratings decline of presidential television than viewer attitudes toward a President or politics in general. It could also be that the address to the nation format, virtually unchanged from the early days of radio, has become outdated and no longer captivates audience attention. Viewers realize that they can skip over presidential addresses when they are broadcast live and still have an opportunity on the late evening news to get the essence of the speech. A commitment of 30 minutes to a political speech, especially a routine one, seems unrealistic for the public to make during this age of competing visual stimuli.

The sagging appeal of presidential broadcasts has been accompanied by a corresponding decline in interest for other types of political programming. None of the 1988 presidential primary programming drew well; key primary debates were among the lowest-rated programs of the week. The conventions were a ratings embarrassment to the networks. Even the ratings for the two Bush–Dukakis debates were disappointing. When viewers had a choice, they voted in favor of entertainment. That Americans have been avoiding all types of political content, not just the President, could be quite critical to the future of political broadcasting.

## CNN'S TIME TO SPARE

While most of the defectors from network television went to entertainment programming on either cable channels or independent stations, one non-entertainment cable network benefitted from the network decline and became a major journalistic force on the American political scene. When CNN went on the air in 1980, it was little threat to the networks or to anyone else. Less than ten years later, however, CNN's 1600 employees in 21 bureaus were producing a profitable news product available in 83 countries, making it one of the world's largest and most important sources of electronic news.[9]

CNN coverage of the Reagan assassination attempt in 1981, its full coverage of the party nominations in 1984 and 1988, and its exhaustive coverage of the space shuttle challenger disaster in 1986 all embellished its reputation and stature. The inclusion of a CNN anchor among the network principals who interviewed President Reagan before the Gorbachev–Reagan Washington Summit in 1987 was a symbolic acknowledgement that the new network had arrived. As its first decade came to an end, CNN could legitimately claim to be a respected competitor to the three commercial networks.

Not only did CNN have growing respectability but it had a sizable audience as well. CNN had a potential viewing audience in 1990 of nearly 55 of the 90 million households with television. A 1989 survey showed that CNN and its sister network "Headline News" averaged nearly 24 percent of the overall news-viewing audience in a 24-hour period; this compared to 28 percent for ABC, 18 percent for NBC, and 30 percent for CBS.[10] During an average week, CNN reaches more than 30 million households. More than 500,000 households regularly watch its prime time newscasts at 8:00 and 10:00 PM EST. Its highest rated program, "The Larry King Show," is regularly seen in between 700 and 900 thousand homes each night.[11]

CNN achieved some of its biggest audiences in 1987 during the first day of Oliver North's testimony before the Senate's Iran–Contra Committee when 4 percent of households using television watched the proceedings. The gavel-to-gavel coverage of the Iran–Contra hearings also raised CNN's prestige. CNN took advantage of the networks' failure to carry all of the hearings by promoting itself as "The News Leader." The promotions said that while the networks were reassessing the commitment to news, CNN was forging ahead, providing full coverage of the hearings. The irony was that one of the least powerful and least prestigious broadcast institutions was best equipped to supplant the networks as purveyors of presidential communication.

CNN scored a first in 1985 when it provided live television time to Defense Secretary Caspar Weinberger to address the nation on his budget proposals for military spending. Until then, this special kind of controlled access had been reserved exclusively for Presidents appearing on the three networks. Now, cable was using its own initiative to extend the franchise to cabinet officers as well. CNN followed the Weinberger address with time for the opposition, doing an interview with House Speaker Tip O'Neill.[12]

CNN possessed a valuable resource the networks could not duplicate—24 hours of news time. It had the luxury of running nearly 500 election stories in the two years following Ronald Reagan's election to the presidency and 16 hours of live election coverage in 1986.[13] Increasingly, CNN covered presidential speeches and events the networks simply could not afford to cover. For example, when President Reagan assembled his staff the day after the disappointing 1986 mid-term elections, only CNN was there to cover it live. Two months earlier, when the President told National Security Agency employees about how espionage threatens national security, only CNN could find the time to carry it live. When President Reagan emerged from the Reykjavik Summit to make his first public statement, only CNN could make a painless decision to carry it live. CBS risked the ire of thousands of angry football fans by interrupting a Chicago Bears game while ABC and NBC ignored the Reagan speech altogether in favor of sporting events.

The most convincing evidence of CNN's ascendence came on February 2, 1988, when CNN bore total responsibility for carrying President Reagan's address to the nation on Contra aid. When all three networks declined to cover the speech live, viewers had to rely on CNN. While CNN's coverage did not dent the ratings of the big three, it paid huge dividends in prestige. Moreover, the Reagan speech coverage showed CNN to be a viable vehicle for exclusive transmission of presidential communication.

In contrast to the networks' usual behavior, CNN volunteered airtime to the Democratic opposition. CNN Executive Vice-President Ed Turner immediately called the Democratic Leadership to give Speaker Wright and Majority Leader Byrd an opportunity to respond, which they gladly accepted. Turner said that, because "news is all we do," CNN did not have as many hang-ups about giving airtime as the big three networks.[14]

By routinely broadcasting presidential speeches that the networks did not have time to cover, CNN exposed the widening gap between their burgeoning commitment to public affairs and that of the networks. While the ascent of CNN in the political arena was a painful lesson for the networks, it was not unexpected. The networks jumped to the forefront of political access in the 1920s not because of any great journalistic expertise but because they were the only ones able to transmit a signal nationwide.

Journalistic expertise was an irrelevant factor in the coverage of presidential speeches; it was simply a matter of who had the transmission belt and the most broadcast time to spare. Now, a new transmission system was available through cable television which had fewer time and economic constraints than did network broadcasting. As a result, it was CNN and not the networks that televised the majority of candidate debates during the 1988 election. The one thing the networks had that the cable channels did not was near total penetration. By 1990, cable was still in less than 60 percent of American households. Cable would have to extend its reach significantly for CNN to become the principal purveyor of political information.

## A LAMB'S ROAR

Another ambitious competitor for presidential and opposition speeches has been C-SPAN, joining the networks and CNN as a member of the presidential pool. In addition to covering House and Senate proceedings and committee hearings, C-SPAN transmits a plethora of political material 24 hours a day on two channels to a potential audience of more than 45 million homes.[15] In 1988, C-SPAN carried 4,709 hours of programming, half of it live, including more than 1,000 hours of public policy conferences and nearly as many hours of campaign coverage and call-in shows all on a budget of $13 million.[16] A 1987 national survey conducted by the University of Maryland found that C-SPAN increased its viewership by 43 percent in just three years and that more than 27 million Americans were at least sampling C-SPAN programming.[17] A much smaller number had become "C-SPAN Junkies," spending hours in front of the television watching public affairs programming.

The first decade of C-SPAN history was a Cinderella story in which technology gave the fledgling cable channel a window of opportunity. When the Rules Committee considered televising the House of Representatives in 1976, ABC, CBS, and NBC basically wrote the Committee's proposal. Network engineers designed the lighting and camera placements. Washington Bureau chiefs aggressively lobbied. The big three dominated because the House had no alternative to the networks which were the only organizations capable of transmitting a television signal nationwide. Had Speaker Albert not intervened at the 11th hour to table the network-backed measure, it would have passed the House, and ABC, CBS and NBC would be running the system today.

Just two years later when the House again considered the broadcasting question, the networks no longer dominated. A technology that was not even mentioned during the 1976 debate, satellite transmission, did. The House decided to control the televising of its own proceedings and make the feed available to anyone who wanted it. Into that opportunity rushed the cable industry's new public affairs channel C-SPAN which took responsibility for beaming the unedited proceedings of the House live into homes throughout America. C-SPAN founder Brian Lamb believes that Congress was particularly responsive to cable during this time because members so disliked the dominance and arrogance of the three networks. They wanted new players in the game who would have a greater respect for Congress as an institution and for its members.[18]

Operating out of a small storefront office in an apartment building in Arlington, Virginia, as the public affairs arm of the cable industry, C-SPAN began in 1979 with little more than a desk and a satellite dish. Yet, with the support of the cable industry, Brian Lamb needed only those resources to bring coverage of the United States House of Representatives to millions of cable subscribers. Unlike the television networks, which required an extensive distribution system of affiliates and massive capital infusion to operate, a cable network could be started on a shoestring. C-SPAN had no pressure to gather an audience because as Lamb says, "the whole foundation of C-SPAN is not built around Nielsen numbers but around the commitment of an industry to provide a public service."[19]

For the first time in television news history, viewers could get extensive political information via television without relying on the networks. The American people no longer had to settle for a brief blip about Congress on the national news; they could see the unexpurgated version unfold live before their eyes. The networks had been bypassed, and the home delivery of political events had taken a giant step forward. Members of Congress were particularly pleased because they had an accessible video pipeline to the electorate for the first time. Within a few years, it became common for congressmen to encounter constituents in their districts who had seen them on C-SPAN speaking at a hearing or on the House floor. Nearly every congressman also had an opportunity during the year to appear on live C-SPAN call-in shows and answer questions from a national audience.

Still, by 1990 C-SPAN was available to just over half of the American television households and, ironically, was only just entering the coveted Washington market which was among the last major cities to be wired for cable. Working with an annual budget of less than $15 million in 1990, Brian Lamb said in financial terms his network is little more than a "gnat on an elephant's back."[20] Yet, the impact of C-SPAN has been considerable. In a fragmented television environment, C-SPAN is a major player, attracting more than its share of opinion leaders, government officials, and politically active citizens.

Like CNN, one advantage C-SPAN has over the networks is time. The two C-SPAN networks have a total news hole of 48 hours a day. C-SPAN once had the luxury of following a congressman through a day's work in real time, including a half-hour drive to the office with no audio except the congressman humming to himself. While other networks had to compress campaign coverage into brief segments on the nightly news, C-SPAN could easily present the entire speech. At the end of the 1988 elections, C-SPAN boasted that its average sound bite during the campaign was 22 minutes compared to nine seconds on the network evening news.

Having passed its first decade, C-SPAN is much more than a purveyor of House and Senate proceedings. It has expanded its coverage to every type of political and public policy event, making it a legitimate competitor to the networks on a number of fronts. In fact, House and Senate proceedings comprise less than 15 percent of C-SPAN programming. Leading officeholders and policymakers now consider an interview on a C-SPAN call-in show as a valid alternative to broadcast exposure. C-SPAN has also begun to expand its reach by covering events in foreign countries, and some countries have been interested in starting their own public affairs channel modeled after C-SPAN.

While a "for the record" cable network like C-SPAN will never attract huge audiences, its growth has been impressive. By 1990, the service was adding nearly 500,000 new subscribers per month and was serving nearly 3,000 cable systems. C-SPAN II, which has broadcast Senate proceedings since 1986, reached more than 20 million homes by 1990. While millions of Americans may not be hanging on the edge of their seats to watch the proceedings of Congress unfold, the availability of C-SPAN to nearly 60 million households makes it a viable vehicle for presidential and opposition communication. C-SPAN routinely carries all presidential speeches and opposition replies. C-SPAN's abundance of time has also allowed it to offer complete coverage of the Democratic and Republican national conventions at a time when the networks are retreating to partial coverage.

C-SPAN is a service sponsored by the cable industry, but it resembles the kind of government information channel envisioned by Senator Gerald Nye in 1929 to bypass commercial broadcasters and send unfiltered information directly to the American people. On a typical day, viewers can see every conceivable type of government forum on C-SPAN, from committee hearings to party caucuses. The mere presence of C-SPAN robs the networks of their traditional roles as exclusive broadcasters of record. With close to 60 percent of American homes now wired for cable, anyone interested in tuning in an important congressional hearing or a presidential speech could do so on C-SPAN, obviating the need for the networks to duplicate coverage. As C-SPAN's reach expands and the pressure on network time increases, a more important role for this public affairs cable channel is all but certain.

Brian Lamb believes that the dominance of the three commercial networks during the past half century was an aberration that disrupted a normal flow of public affairs information, overcentralized communication patterns, and deprived the American people of free choice. Lamb sees the future as a more normal state of affairs with viewers exercising greater choice and no one entity dominating the public affairs stage.[21]

## RESTLESS AND AMBITIOUS AFFILIATES

As the share of the networks' audience decreases, their relationships with their affiliates are changing. The networks want to compensate their affiliates less for carrying their programming and expect affiliates to preempt network programming less. Meanwhile, the affiliates want to loosen the iron grip the networks have had on them, and they expect loyalty to be rewarded financially. CNN's Ed Turner likens the affiliate–

network struggle to the "dissolution of an empire," with the outcome being a "loose commonwealth" of stations, which have much greater independence.[22]

There have been signs that some affiliates' news departments have already become competitors with their own networks. By the mid–1980s, some restless and ambitious affiliates started to assemble the firepower to challenge the hegemony of the all-powerful networks. The scene was reminiscent of the westerns where the Indians finally figured out that the white man's guns, once awesome and magical, would work just as well for them. The networks were being shown to be fallible. Since the beginning of television, affiliates had been heavily dependent on the network umbilical cord for programming nourishment. Only after local news acquired bigger budgets and satellite technology to send and receive distant signals did brief surges of independence appear possible. By the 1988 elections, most stations in major markets had joined consortia to feed stories to member stations via satellite. Local affiliates could bring their viewers live coverage of a political convention or a superpower summit without relying on the networks for help.

A pioneer in the affiliate rebellion has been Stanley Hubbard, the Minneapolis broadcaster who developed a consortium of stations linked by satellite vans called Continental U.S. (CONUS), which has dramatically increased the reach of local stations. With satellite vans located at nearly 100 locations throughout the nation, CONUS has national access to breaking stories, which all members of the consortium can use. Nearly 200 stations have also signed agreements with CNN allowing them to use CNN footage and reports.[23]

The iconoclastic Hubbard relished his role as David in the face of network Goliaths. He resented the arrogance of the networks and their view that nothing of value came from between the coasts. Hubbard wanted to prove that a satellite network based in the Midwest and run by local broadcasters could compete favorably with the broadcasting giants. CONUS quickly became a force in news broadcasting as Hubbard's satellite trucks dotted the landscape from coast to coast ready on a moment's notice to rush into breaking news. Many of Hubbard's partners developed a strong loyalty to CONUS, feeding it before their own networks when a major story broke. The networks had to start their own satellite affiliate services to stave off the momentum being generated by CONUS and CNN. Meanwhile, Hubbard began his own news network in 1989 which broadcast regular daily newscasts nationwide.

In November 1985, Hubbard used his station KSTP-TV in Minneapolis to bypass ABC to cover President Reagan's address to a joint session of Congress after the Geneva summit. On the night of the broadcast, Minneapolis-St. Paul viewers discovered that local anchors Stan Turner and Ruth Spencer had replaced ABC's Peter Jennings. As the Marine helicopter landed on the Capitol lawn and the President made his way to the rostrum of the House, it was Turner and Spencer, not Jennings, who gave a running commentary.[24]

After the speech, KSTP-TV viewers watched a panel of Minnesotans with foreign policy expertise provide a critique. Later, local anchors Turner and Spencer interviewed members of the Minnesota congressional delegation on the steps of the Capitol. The entire broadcast was done independently of the networks; the local station provided not only the anchors but the satellite feed as well. As Stanley Hubbard said after the speech, "I have nothing against network news but I just happen to think we did more of a service for the people of Minnesota than the network coverage."[25] When affiliates developed the capability to transmit and receive live pictures from almost anywhere, many speculated that network news was being severely threatened. Yet, most knowledgeable executives realized that budgetary constraints would eventually pull local stations back to a more realistic posture of healthy dependence on the networks for coverage of international events and perspective on the news. The competitive spirit had, however, been unleashed among affiliates, and the networks would have to offer much more to appease them. To satisfy the affiliates' voracious appetites for news, the networks found themselves constantly feeding the affiliates reports that had never been used by the networks. This practice, of course, meant that local stations would have the breaking news stories first, forcing the networks into the role of amplifying for viewers what their affiliates had already told them earlier.

It is difficult to predict whether the isolated instances of local coverage of presidential speeches and opposition replies reflect a long-term trend. If more and more stations follow the example of KSTP-TV in Minneapolis when it covered the President's address, the dynamics of those broadcasts could well change. Much of the power of presidential speeches is rooted in the unilateral force with which they are delivered electronically. Presidents know that their voices will flow instantaneously across America in basically the same form. Local station intervention could disrupt that flow, adding a cacophony of voices where only three, ABC, CBS, and NBC, could be heard before. Routinely substituting a local congressional delegation for the national opposition response could severely undermine the fledgling growth of the congressional opposition as the legitimate countervailing voice to the President.

## CROSSROADS

By the beginning of the 1990s, the networks found themselves at a crossroads, forced by economics and technology to make decisions that would affect their role as arbiters of access. Would the networks consider the prestige and the newsworthiness of presidential addresses sufficient to cover the losses in ratings and revenues generated by these broadcasts? Should the networks continue to be the primary purveyor of presidential communication or should they cede that role to organizations like CNN and C-SPAN which have more airtime and fewer economic pressures? What risks are involved if the networks downgrade their political communication role?

These questions flow into the broader framework of the networks' commitment to news. Some analysts predict that the networks will evolve into program services, producing entertainment for a global market. News would have a role only if it were profitable and exportable. Cable channels dedicated exclusively to news would dominate the information arena, and the networks would cover themselves by investing in that cable news structure. In such a scenario, the increased penetration of cable and the delivery of signals to the rest of the nation via direct broadcast satellites would obviate the need for over-the-air networks to serve as transmission belts for public affairs information.

Until the broadcast marketplace sorts itself out, there will continue to be great pressure on the commercial networks to serve both information and entertainment functions simultaneously. CNN's Ed Turner keeps this pressurized reality on the surface by referring to ABC, CBS, and NBC as the "entertainment networks."[26] Every day, network news divisions live in a world of fierce economic pressures where giving away prime time for news specials is a luxury they cannot easily afford. Even one access commitment can translate into millions of dollars on the bottom line.

As the financial success of the networks becomes more endangered, the political access question looms larger; some believe that the handling of this question could greatly determine the personality and role of network broadcasting in the twenty-first century. Specifically, the networks have to determine how important the special news coverage role, including presidential and opposition communication, is to their image and economic viability.

## REDRESSING THE BALANCE

Despite the current economic and technological pressures on the broadcasting marketplace, it is quite likely that the networks will continue their political access role into the next century. If the networks continue to give prominent attention to presidential addresses, they must also come to grips with the chronic opposition access problem. Since the beginning of broadcasting, discrimination against the opposition of both parties has been obvious. The networks' judgments have been arbitrary and inconsistent; their treatment of the opposition has been arrogant and heavy-handed. Such inequity raises serious questions about the networks' suitability for controlling the nation's political access system.

Without a guarantee of access, a change in administration, a change in opposition, or even a change in network executives can provide the catalyst for a reversal of coverage patterns, destroying any progress made in promoting institutional parity. The time has come for a permanent, equitable solution to a problem that has plagued commercial broadcasting almost since its beginning. The only debate should be whether the automatic reply should be voluntary or compulsory.

This study concludes, as Minow, Martin, and Mitchell concluded nearly two decades earlier, that the opposition in Congress, Democratic and Republican, deserves an automatic reply to the President. Anything less is unsuitable. The experience during the Reagan Administration proves that such a system can work. After every presidential radio speech for six years there was an automatic opposition reply. Even on television, the networks relied mostly on a de facto automatic reply policy. The system can work without hardship on broadcasters or intrusion into their decision-making apparatus. Such a policy has served several European parliamentary governments well for decades.

A permanent, automatic reply policy not only guarantees access to political parties but removes the networks from the imperial role of defining the opposition. Yet, this is a role that the networks still seem to cherish. ABC's and NBC's refusal to carry live the Democratic opposition reply to President Bush's first televised address in 1989, showed a fundamental lack of respect for the institutional role of the congressional leadership and demonstrated the networks' inherent compulsion to dominate the flow of political communication. Such action argues strongly for an automatic opposition reply.

The fairness doctrine was a compulsory rule designed to ensure that both sides of controversial issues were heard. Yet, this initiative helped the opposition little in its quest for parity with the President. In fact, the fairness doctrine actually hurt the opposition because it empowered broadcasters to define the opposition as they saw it. Such power to choose often froze out the congressional leadership from the airwaves.

When the fairness doctrine was repealed, no regulation outside of the "equal time" rule during campaign periods provided even the remotest protection to the opposition. The congressional leadership was left on its own to petition the networks. A regulation or statute requiring the networks to provide an automatic reply to the opposition would provide equality and continuity to a very tenuous and unpredictable system. The only alternative to government action would be self-regulation by the networks in which they collectively pledge to provide an automatic reply on a long-term basis.

Even guaranteed network access, however, will not solve the communication problems of the opposition. If the congressional leadership is to communicate effectively, it must give communication in general, and television in particular, a higher priority. The Rayburn legacy of media indifference and even contempt must give way to planned strategic communication initiatives to take full advantage of the leadership's platform as "loyal opposition" to the President. If congressional leaders are ever to serve as a viable opposition force, they must possess media skills and initiatives comparable to a President's.

In the next century, if not before, backbench Congressmen will demand that their leaders be accomplished communicators as well as legislators. Just as television changed the face of the presidency, it will change the first branch of the government as well. More sophisticated and persuasive Democratic replies during the Reagan Administration showed the advantage to be gained from a higher priority for televised replies. Eventually, the leadership will not be satisfied with just replying to a President and will demand time to initiate broadcasts. Perhaps the election of media savvy Richard Gephardt as Majority Leader of the House of Representatives was a sign that the leadership is catching up with the television age.

## DEPRESSURIZING THE ENVIRONMENT

During the 1990s, pressure will inevitably build for all three networks to discontinue covering news events simultaneously. An early test will be the 1992 political conventions when the networks are expected to scale back coverage significantly. Eventually, news events that fail to gather a huge audience may be rotated among the three principal networks.

Presidential addresses, which are as close to a three-network command performance as the networks have, should be among the last kinds of stories to be subjected to rotation. Despite their presence as a very real economic liability, there is a surprisingly strong reverence for coverage of the President at all three networks.

Crisis events and pivotal presidential speeches create a special bonding between the American people and the networks. Sacrificing that special bonding risks accelerating the transition into a post–network era of broadcast journalism. For more than one-half century, the networks have been a comforting, natural place for Americans to turn in times of crisis and a powerful force for shaping a national consensus. In the eyes of many network executives, like Tony Malara of CBS, there is a great symbolic value in having the President of the United States on the air. Malara said that presidential coverage is one proof that the networks remain as a key link between the people and their government. Losing that special entree to the American people, including presidential broad-casting, would rob network broadcasting of its heart and soul. Some maintain that such public service broadcasting is the essence of network broadcasting and should not be sacrificed at any cost.

Given this symbolic reality, it is unlikely that the networks will discard presidential speeches easily. Yet, as audiences for presidential speeches diminish and economic pressures increase, network managers must face these realities. Rotation would allow the networks to remain in the political access arena with minimum bottom-line impact. Fewer presidential broadcasts mean fewer schedule disruptions, more competitive prime time schedules, and added revenues. The Watergate and Iran–Contra hearings in which the networks eventually rotated coverage offer precedent for this behavior.

The public service need of broadcasting a President's message could clearly be satisfied by one network, and entertainment executives at the networks would welcome the change; resistance would come from the news divisions, which perceive journalistic advantages in covering all presidential speeches. If the President should say something newswor-thy, the networks want to be there live. As former CBS President Frank Stanton said when asked about the possibility of rotating coverage and possibly missing a newsworthy event, "I wouldn't want to be second, and I damn sure wouldn't want to be third."[27] Such an intense com-petitive spirit discourages rotation.

By the end of the 1980s, even some persons in news seemed more eager to experiment with alternatives that would minimize the drain on the bottom line. Veteran NBC correspondent and former news executive Tom Pettit, for example, saw no need for three-network coverage, "I think the networks would be in better service of this country if they did not march in lockstep so much. In theory, there's no reason why three networks have to carry the President. There's no reason why two have to. You can't deny him access altogether but there will be a time when we won't all blithely carry the President's remarks even if he has asked for it."[28]

As an example of how the simultaneity hold can be broken, only one of Florida's seven CBS television affiliates (WCTV in Tallahassee) carried President Reagan's pivotal news conference in March 1987, in the wake of the Iran arms scandal. The news conference conflicted with the Florida–Syracuse NCAA tournament basketball game. The program director of WTVX in Fort Pierce, Florida, reasoned, "There are three different ways you can see the President, but there's only one way you can see the Gators."[29] Presumably there were few complaints that some Florida CBS affiliates did not show the President; viewers still had a choice of ABC, NBC, or CNN.

As long as the networks were financially healthy and the downside risks affected everyone equally, simultaneous presidential coverage was no more than a minor nuisance. Now that time is real money, rotation seems a palatable alternative to the more severe measure of dumping presidential broadcasting altogether.

## NEWS BROADCASTERS OF RECORD

When the networks start to trim their political coverage further, as they have already done with political conventions and election coverage, they risk losing the loyalty and dependence of their viewers. The networks built an audience by assuring viewers that they would always be there first with the best coverage. Without that assurance, viewers will waiver, not knowing from one day to the next whether they can depend on the networks to cover an event. If the networks withdraw too far from the special news coverage arena, the temptation will be to drop out altogether.

The rotation of presidential speeches and news conferences by the networks would make cable channels like CNN and C-SPAN the broadcasters of record for presidential speech. No longer could viewers depend on ABC, CBS, and NBC automatically to carry every presidential utterance. By the end of the 1980s, CNN was already moving into the void left by partial network withdrawal from the transmission belt function.

Eventually CNN and C-SPAN's commitment to public affairs coverage should pay dividends in terms of viewer loyalty and dependence. The day is approaching when viewers will turn to CNN first rather than to the networks when a breaking story occurs or to C-SPAN first for the full visual text of a public affairs event. As the networks start to pass on more public affairs events and cable penetration approaches 70 percent, uncertainty will grow about the network commitment to political communication. Still, a cable news or public affairs channel, much like a government channel in other countries, must build its audience from a much lower base, drawing the politically active and interested to its door. Only in times of genuine crisis could an all-news or public affairs cable channel expect to draw a majority of Americans to a White House pronouncement.

## LONESOME VOICE

In the end, the disposition of presidential broadcasts may not be as important to broadcasters as to politicians. Presidents have a vested interest in attracting simultaneous network coverage of their speeches. As former President Richard Nixon advised President Bush, "Of all the institutions arrayed with and against a President, none controls his fate more than television. Unless a President learns how to harness its power, his Administration is in trouble from the very beginning."[30] At the top of the list, Nixon placed the oval office address as the most powerful instrument for "informing, educating, and persuading" and for going "over the heads of his critics" to "speak directly to the American people."[31]

But Nixon was referring to the presidential address in its prime—the blockbuster speech that could reach 90 percent of the American people at the same time. What about the challenge that George Bush and his successors face in communicating with an ever dwindling and distracted audience? When the networks bow further to technology and economic pressures, how effective can the traditional presidential address be? How can a President buried on a cable channel compete against a plethora of entertainment offerings?

The reality is that except in times of crisis no President will reach 90 percent of American households again. C-SPAN's Brian Lamb believes all Presidents "will have a very difficult time soliciting the American people's attention through television."[32] It will be a frustrating experience for Presidents because they will not be able to command the American people to listen to what they have to say. The lack of a captive audience has already deflated several presidential speeches from extraordinary events to very ordinary ones, drastically altering the political communication landscape.

If the networks pull the plug on presidential addresses or cannot deliver a respectable minority of voters to the television set, the presidential advantage of sending a controlled communication to a massive captive audience will be gone. Presidents could search for alternative communication vehicles, but the powerful persuasive impact of the presidential addresses would be lost. When roadblocked access becomes a relic of the past, gone will be the days when Presidents can routinely mobilize an entire nation on a controversial political issue in the same way their predecessors could. Presidential communication will be drowned out regularly by the cacophony of competing stimuli on more popular entertainment channels.

What we are approaching is a more democratic environment in which the viewer has ultimate authority over his television viewing. Presumably, viewers resented being held hostage to a presidential speech when it was the only programming on all three channels; they now welcome the greater freedom that accompanies the new political communication order. Americans only marginally active politically who were forcefed televised political content during the three decades prior to the 1980s, can now escape it completely with a single, easy stroke of the remote control.

Does a more democratic viewing environment serve the broader, long-term interests of the body politic? Does the government have an obligation to promote the most effective means of communicating with its citizens, even if it forces them to listen? Will a more inaccessible electorate be any less connected to its government and to the political process than one that participates regularly in a shared national communication experience?

There is also the question of whether the ability to have simultaneous communication with the majority of the electorate is a necessity for successful execution of the presidency in an electronic age. What effect would there be on the presidency if the persuasive powers of television were no longer available? Would the congressional opposition, previously a victim of denied access opportunities, be in a more advantageous position in the absence of roadblocked presidential speech?

## OPTIONS

Given the reality of decreasing audiences and the probability of network withdrawal of simultaneous coverage, Presidents should be searching for alternative formats to replace or supplement addresses to the nation. Viewers are no longer willing to sit patiently watching a President speak for 30 minutes while entertainment offerings abound on cable channels and recaps of the speech are readily available on the evening news.

Presidents should consider experimenting with shorter, "newsbreak" types of formats, which would give them two to five minutes to get their point across. These made for television mini-speeches could be sandwiched between network programs in a format that might be more attractive to network bean counters and viewing audiences as well. Longer versions of the speech could be broadcast on C-SPAN and CNN. Shorter speeches, however, are no guarantee of huge audiences. Sophisticated younger viewers, already masters at zapping and zipping commercials, could instantly banish a President into oblivion with minimal effort.

Presidents may have to create a sense of drama to lure recalcitrant viewers. Perhaps a debate similar to question time in the House of Commons in which Congress would confront the President face-to-face on a particular issue would make for compelling television. Such a format would at least recognize the importance of the legislative branch as a coequal partner to the President better than the presidential news conference which ordains the media as the "Loyal Opposition."

If the presidential address is the White House's most powerful weapon, Presidents must find a way to use this vehicle once again to reach a huge mass audience. It may mean bringing pay cable, direct broadcast satellite channels, and specialized channels into the fold as well as the major networks. Presidents should press cable and broadcast executives to reach a consensus for transmitting a limited amount of presidential and opposition television to the American people.

The options could range from single-channel coverage on C-SPAN to the ultimate roadblock—simultaneous coverage on every television outlet in America. Total saturation from MTV to TNT and everything in between would indeed rival any impact made by Roosevelt and Kennedy. Presidents could establish different levels of speeches: the most important rating universal coverage, others gaining partial coverage. The presumption would be that at least some presidential communication is important enough that every American watching television should be compelled to watch.

There is some precedent for such a roadblock on cable television. Most cable channels agreed a few years ago to telecast the industry's Ace Awards for outstanding programming live. While it is highly unlikely that the cable industry would support roadblocked access for presidential and opposition speeches, talk of reregulation of the cable industry creates a climate in which a positive response to congressional pressure is not out of the question.

The next few years will be a time of testing and experimentation for presidential television as economic and political pressures interract. The development of presidential and opposition access into the twenty-first century will no doubt affect the power of the "bully pulpit" and perhaps the balance of political power. The difference between reaching 1 percent of the electorate and 90 percent in one broadcast is a great one. Certainly, the nation has been conditioned to believe that massive audiences are the norm. Could it be, however, that the smaller, diverse, fragmented audiences of the future are the desired norm and best represent the spirit of free speech, democratic choice, and constitutional balance?

If the electronic media have helped to create the imbalance between the President and the Congress, perhaps they are the appropriate vehicles to push the pendulum back and provide the Congress with the powerful voice one would expect it to have in a representative democracy. The question, however, is whether political access is too important to be left to the structurally flawed network system that has blunted opposition access during the first 70 years of American broadcasting. At the very least, both the Congress and the national broadcast media should be questioning the status quo.

It is difficult to assess the full impact of network television on the presidential–legislative power struggle, but the past half century has certainly taken its toll on the opposition. Chronic relegation to second-class status in the shadow of presidential dominance has left the "Loyal Opposition" with its hands in its pockets and its eyes on the ground, unable to cope. Something has gone awry. The President is not as majestic and all-powerful and the opposition in Congress is not as feeble and inept as the networks would have us believe.

The smothered voice of the opposition should speak on a par with Presidents. Perhaps the next century will provide the American people with a television distribution system that is not quite so full of itself and that has more respect for balance in the constitutional system. We must strive for a system that encourages the voices of both Presidents *and* opposition leaders to flow far beyond the Potomac.

# Notes

## INTRODUCTION

1. "In Brief," *Broadcasting*, August 3, 1981, p. 102.
2. Ronald Reagan, Address to the Nation on Federal Tax Reduction Legislation, *Weekly Compilation of Presidential Documents*, July 27, 1981, p. 819.
3. "In Brief," p. 102.
4. John Weisman, "TV and the Presidency," *TV Guide*, March 20, 1981, p. 8.
5. See, for example, Rutkus, Denis S., "The Public Trustee Concept in Broadcast Regulation" (Washington, D.C.: Congressional Research Service, 1981), p. 59.
6. 47 USC 315 (A) (1976).
7. Editorializing by Broadcast Licensees, 13 FCC 1246, (1949).
8. Ibid.
9. The three phases mentioned in this section were adapted from a four phase description written by Denis S. Rutkus of the Library of Congress.

## CHAPTER 1

1. Erik Barnouw, *A Tower in Babel: A History of Broadcasting in the United States to 1933* (New York: Oxford University Press, 1966), pp. 145–46.
2. "Health of President Coolidge Conserved by Broadcasting," *New York Times*, February 24, 1924, sec. 8, p. 15.
3. Barnouw, *A Tower in Babel*, p. 146.
4. Elmer Cornwell, "Coolidge and Presidential Leadership," *Public Opinion Quarterly* 21 (Summer 1957): 269.
5. Louise M. Benjamin, "Campaign Policies, Broadcasters and the Presidential Election of 1924," Paper presented to the History Division of the Association for Education in Journalism and Mass Communication Annual Convention, San Antonio, August, 1987, p. 4.

6. Ibid., pp. 14–15.

7. "Health of President Coolidge Conserved by Broadcasting," sec. 8, p. 15.

8. Edward Chester, *Radio, Television, and American Politics* (New York: Sheed and Ward, 1969), p. 23.

9. "The First Sixty Years of NBC," *Broadcasting*, June 9, 1986, p. 50.

10. Ibid.

11. Barnouw, *A Tower in Babel*, pp. 189–90.

12. "Fifty to Broadcast Washington Fete," *New York Times*, June 11, 1927, p. 3.

13. "The First 60 Years of NBC," p. 51.

14. Murray Katzman, "News Broadcasting in the United States: 1920–1941," Unpublished Ph.D. Dissertation, New York University, 1968, p. 73.

15. Lewis Paper, *Empire: William S. Paley and the Making of CBS* (New York: St. Martin's Press, 1987), p. 25.

16. Helen Sioussat, *Mikes Don't Bite* (New York: L. B. Fischer, 1943), p. 33.

17. Erik Barnouw, *The Golden Web: A History of Broadcasting in the United States, Volume II—1933 to 1953* (New York: Oxford University Press, 1968), p. 3.

18. *New York Times*, November 4, 1928, p. 16.

19. Paper, *Empire*, p. 60.

20. Barnouw, *A Tower in Babel*, p. 199.

21. Ibid., p. 204.

22. Paper, *Empire*, p. 28.

23. "Station Proposed for Federal Use," *New York Times*, May 12, 1929, p. 3.

24. *New York Times*, December 28, 1930, p. 1.

25. Samuel L. Becker, "Presidential Power: The Influence of Broadcasting," *Quarterly Journal of Speech* 47, no. 1 (February 1961): 14.

26. Katzman, "News Broadcasting in the United States," p. 84.

27. Frank Stanton, Former President, CBS, Personal Interview, New York, January 24, 1985.

28. Martin Mayer, *Making News* (Garden City, NY: Doubleday and Co., 1987), pp. 108–10.

29. Orrin E. Dunlap, "Marconi Magic in the Home," *New York Times*, December 4, 1932, sec. 8. p. 10.

30. "Hoover to Speak Three Times on Radio Latter Part of May," *New York Times*, May 7, 1931, p. 1.

31. "Hoover Radio Record Surpasses Coolidge's," *New York Times*, May 11, 1931, p. 3.

32. Mayer, *Making News*, p. 112.

33. Paper, *Empire*, p. 69.

34. Barnouw, *The Golden Web*, pp. 18–20.

35. Mayer, *Making News*, pp. 112–13.

36. Katzman, "News Broadcasting in the United States," p. 106.

37. Ibid., p. 107.

38. Ibid., p. 97.

39. Ibid., p. 98.

40. Barnouw, *The Golden Web*, p. 7.

41. Chester, *Radio Television and American Politics*, p. 33.

42. James A. Farley, *Behind the Ballots* (New York: Harcourt Brace, 1938), p. 319.

43. Elmer Cornwell, *Presidential Leadership of Public Opinion* (Bloomington: Indiana University Press, 1965), p. 255.

44. Franklin D. Roosevelt, letter to M. H. Aylesworth, May 18, 1933, P.P.F. 447, Roosevelt Library.

45. Seymour H. Fersh, "The View from the White House: A Study of the Presidential State of the Union Messages" (Washington, D.C.: Public Affairs Press, 1937), p. 9, cited in Cornwell, *Presidential Leadership of Public Opinion*, p. 260.

46. "Government Monopolizes Radio, A Senator Charges," *New York Times*, January 19, 1934, p. 1.

47. Becker, "Presidential Power," p. 16.

48. Mayer, *Making News*, p. 111.

49. Turner Catledge, "Roosevelt Speech Politics, Says G.O.P.; Radio Reply Asked," *New York Times*, January 2, 1936, p. 1.

50. "NBC Allows Reply to Roosevelt Talk," *New York Times*, January 3, 1936, p. 3.

51. Ibid.

52. Sioussat, *Mikes Don't Bite*, p. 30.

53. Ibid.

54. David Halberstam, *The Powers That Be* (New York: Alfred Knopf, 1979), p. 38.

55. Ibid., p. 37.

56. Ibid.

57. "Radio Chains Bar Republican Skit but Party Gets Chicago Outlet," *New York Times*, January 14, 1936, p. 1.

58. "Topic of the Times," *New York Times*, January 20, 1936, p. 18.

59. Byron N. Scott, "Communication Act of 1934," *Congressional Record*, vol. 80, January 24, 1936, p. 973.

60. "Three Radio Bills Pushed," *New York Times*, January 19, 1936, sec. II, p. 1.

61. "Senator Drops a Bomb," *New York Times*, March 21, 1937, sec. 11, p. 10.

62. Stanley High, "Not-So-Free Air," *Saturday Evening Post*, February 11, 1939, p. 9.

63. Ibid.

64. Ibid., p. 77.

65. Chester, *Radio, Television and American Politics*, p. 34.

66. Ibid., p. 41.

67. Ibid., p. 63.

68. Barnouw, *The Golden Web*, p. 49.

69. Ibid.

70. Ibid., p. 50.

71. Ibid.

72. Rolf Kaltenborn, "Is Radio Politically Impartial," *The American Mercury*, June, 1946, p. 665.

73. Ibid., p. 666.

74. Barnouw, *The Golden Web*, p. 170.

75. Ibid., p. 169.

76. Barnouw, *The Golden Web*, p. 61.

77. Cornwell, "Coolidge and Presidential Leadership," p. 278.

78. Waldo Braden and Earnest Brandenburg, "Roosevelt's Fireside Chats," *Speech Monographs* 22 (November 1955): 293.

79. Sioussat, *Mikes Don't Bite*, p. 34.

80. "Two L.A. Stations Refuse to Air Programs," *Broadcasting*, October 1, 1936, p. 15.

81. "Battle Is on for Political Radio Time," *Broadcasting*, April 14, 1947, p. 80.

82. "CBS Declines to Air Jefferson Day Speech," *Broadcasting*, April 7, 1947, p. 26.

83. "Democrats Defend Jefferson Day Time," *Broadcasting*, April 21, 1947, p. 92.

84. Newton N. Minow, John B. Martin, and Lee M. Mitchell, *Presidential Television* (New York: Basic Books, 1973), p. 82.

85. "Applicability of the Fairness Doctrine in the Handling of Controversial Issues of Public Importance," *Fairness Primer* 29 F.R. 10416 (1964).

## CHAPTER 2

1. Samuel Becker, "Presidential Power: The Influence of Broadcasting," *Quarterly Journal of Speech* 47 no. 1 (February 1961): 17.

2. Edward Chester, *Radio, Television and American Politics* (New York: Sheed and Ward, 1969), p. 72.

3. Elmer Cornwell, *Presidential Leadership and Public Opinion* (Bloomington: Indiana University Press, 1965), pp. 267–68.

4. James F. Fixx, ed. *The Mass Media and Politics* (New York: Arno Press, 1972), p. 248.

5. *New York Times*, March 31, 1952, p. 18.

6. Chester, *Radio, Television and American Politics*, p. 105.

7. Cornwell, *Presidential Leadership of Public Opinion*, p. 271.

8. Ibid., p. 272.

9. Jack Gould, "TV: Hagerty's Role Discussed," *New York Times*, February 28, 1958, p. 45.

10. Newton N. Minow, John B. Martin, and Lee M. Mitchell, *Presidential Television* (New York: Basic Books, 1973), p. 35.

11. Sig Mickelson, *The Electric Mirror: Politics in an Age of Television* (New York: Dodd, Mead & Company, 1972), p. 163.

12. Chester, *Radio, Television, and American Politics*, p. 92.

13. Craig M. Allen, "TV and the 1956 Presidential Campaign: Insights into the Evolution of Political Television," Paper presented to the History Division, Association for Education in Journalism and Mass Communication, August, 1987.

14. Ibid.

15. "California Democratic State Central Committee," 40 FCC 501 (1960).

16. Kathleen Hall Jamieson, *Packaging the President: A History and Criticism of Presidential Campaign Advertising* (New York: Oxford University Press, 1984), p. 114.

17. Joseph P. Berry, Jr., *John F. Kennedy and the Media: The First Television President* (Lanham, MD: University Press of America, 1987), p. 142.

18. Ibid., pp. 108–9.

19. Ibid., p. 66.

20. Pierre Salinger, *With Kennedy* (New York: Avon Books, 1967), p. 83.

21. David Halberstam, *The Powers That Be* (New York: Alfred Knopf, 1979), p. 384.

22. Minow, Martin, and Mitchell, *Presidential Television*, p. 110.

23. "GOP Won't Talk Back," *Broadcasting*, April 15, 1963, p. 5.

24. "G.O.P. Gets Air Time to Answer Kennedy," *New York Times*, September 19, 1963, p. 14.

25. Ibid.

26. Fixx, *The Mass Media and Politics*, p. 268.

27. "GOP Gets Equal Time to JFK's Tax Message," *Broadcasting*, September 23, 1963, p. 30.

28. Ibid.

29. Minow, Martin, and Mitchell, *Presidential Television*, p. 44.

30. "The Brand That's Being Burned Into TV," *Broadcasting*, November 8, 1965, p. 54.

31. Minow, Martin, and Mitchell, *Presidential Television*, p. 44.

32. Ibid.

33. Juan Williams, *Eyes on the Prize* (New York: Viking Press, 1987), pp. 241–42.

34. Halberstam, *Powers That Be*, p. 433.

35. Halberstam, *Powers That Be*, p. 384.

36. Richard Salant, Personal Interview, New York, January 24, 1985.

37. Denis S. Rutkus, "The Johnson Presidency," Unpublished manuscript, 1985, p. 4.

38. "GOP Gets Rebuttal Time," *Broadcasting*, January 17, 1966, p. 10.

39. "Harsher Laws on Equal Time," *Broadcasting*, January 23, 1967, p. 72.

40. Ibid.

41. Ibid.

42. "LBJ's Message Gets Top Effort," *Broadcasting*, January 22, 1968, p. 64.

43. "Television," *New York Times*, January 26, 1968, p. 95.

44. "TV: Johnson's Address Gets Immediate Scrutiny," *New York Times*, January 18, 1968.

45. Minow, Martin, and Mitchell, *Presidential Television*, p. 56.

46. Ibid.

47. Denis S. Rutkus, "A Report on Simultaneous Television Network Coverage of Presidential Addresses to the Nation," Congressional Research Service, Library of Congress, January 12, 1976, pp. 8–9.

48. Ibid., p. 5.

49. Ibid, pp. 13–14.

50. Minow, Martin, and Mitchell, *Presidential Television*, p. 62.

51. Louis Harris, "President's Use of TV Helps," *Chicago Tribune*, September 3, 1970, p. 17.

52. Minow, Martin, and Mitchell, *Presidential Television*, p. 62.

53. Ibid, p. 86.

54. "Committee for the Fair Broadcasting of Controversial Issues," 25 FCC 2d 283 (1970), p. 304.

55. "Opening TV to the Political Outs," *Broadcasting*, June 29, 1970, p. 32.

56. Leonard Goldenson, Telegram to Democratic and Republican Congressional Leaders, August 17, 1970.

57. "Wild Outbursts of Political Demands," *Broadcasting*, July 13, 1970, p. 19.

58. "CBS Takes 'Opposition' Off the Air," *Broadcasting*, August 24, 1970, p. 34.

59. Newton N. Minow, and Lee M. Mitchell, "Incumbent Television: A Case of Indecent Exposure", *Annals of the American Academy of Political and Social Science* 425 (May 1976) pp. 74–87.

60. Columbia Broadcasting System v. FCC, United States Court of Appeals, District of Columbia Circuit, November 15, 1971, p. 1033.

61. Ibid., p. 1020.

62. "Applicability of the Fairness Doctrine in the Handling of Controversial Issues of Public Importance," Fairness Primer, 29 Fed. Reg. 10416 (1964).

63. Minow, Martin and Mitchell, *Presidential Television*, p. 134.

64. U.S. Senate, Hearings before the Communications Subcommittee on S.J. Res. 209, August 4, 5, and 6, 1970, pp. 9–10.

65. Ibid., p. 53.

66. Ibid., pp. 56–57.

67. Ibid., p. 10.

68. Ibid., p. 68. In this quote, Dr. Stanton was not referring to an opposition response but to an address by Chief Justice Burger which CBS planned to broadcast on a delayed basis, thereby denying him simultaneous access. Dr. Stanton said that by not broadcasting the Burger speech live, CBS was proving a "diversity of treatment [that]gives a greater exposure to the American people of the Chief Justice's remarks than all of us scheduling it as a live broadcast in the daytime."

69. Frank Stanton, former President of CBS, Personal Interview, New York, Janaury 24, 1985.

70. Minow, Martin, and Mitchell, *Presidential Televsion*, p. 104.

71. Frank Stanton, Former President of CBS, Personal Interview, New York, Janaury 24, 1985.

72. Raymond Timothy, Group Executive Vice-President of NBC, Telephone Interview, May 6, 1985.

73. Robert Cirino, *Don't Blame the People: How the News Media Use Bias, Distortion and Censorship to Manipulate Public Opinion*, (Los Angeles: Diversity Press, 1971), p. 210.

74. Everett H. Erlick, Senior Vice President and General Counsel of ABC, Inc., Letter to Senator Mike Mansfield, April 24, 1973.

75. Attachment to February 24, 1982 letter of Peter B. Kenney, Vice President of NBC, Washington, to Congressional Research Service.

76. Source material from this section comes from the author's participant observations while serving as Press Secretary to Speaker Carl Albert from 1972–1976.

77. Ibid.

## CHAPTER 3

1. Edward J. Epstein, *News from Nowhere*, (New York: Vintage Books, 1973), p. 253.

2. "President vs. Networks," *Newsweek*, October 28, 1974, p. 2.

3. Les Brown, "TV Networks, in a Shift, Air Ford at His Request," *New York Times*, October 16, 1974, p. L4.

4. Tom Wicker, "The Pulpit Magnified," *New York Times*, October 18, 1974, p. 42.

5. Arthur Taylor, Telegram to House Speaker Carl Albert and Senate Majority Leader Mike Mansfield, October 28, 1974.

6. John Weisman, "He Always Hits His Marks," *TV Guide*, May 31, 1975, p. 4.

7. Andrew Glass, "The Preening of the President—For Television," *New York Times*, March 16, 1975, p. 29.

8. David Broder, "Ford Carefully Rehearsed 'Make-or-Break' Speech," *Washington Post*, January 14, 1975, p. A3.

9. Les Brown, "Democrats Reach Low TV Audience," *New York Times*, January 25, 1975, p. B10.

10. Source material from author's participant observations.

11. Ibid.

12. William Lord, Telegram to House Speaker Carl Albert and Senate Majority Leader Mike Mansfield, October 13, 1975.

13. Denis S. Rutkus, "A Report on Simultaneous Television Network Coverage of Presidential Addresses to the Nation," Congressional Research Service, Library of Congress, January 12, 1976, pp. 8–9.

14. Carl Albert, Speaker of the U.S. House of Representatives, News Release, January 18, 1976.

15. Denis S. Rutkus, "Opposition Party Access to the Broadcast Networks to Respond to the President" (Washington, DC: Congressional Research Service, 1977), p. 16.

16. "No Prime Time for Ford," *Time*, October 20, 1974, p. 8.

17. Frank Sean Swertlow, "Two Networks Reject Request to Carry President's Speech," *TV Guide*, October 18, 1975, p. A1.

18. Ibid.

19. Ibid.

20. John Carmody, "Two Networks Decline to Carry Ford Speech," *Washington Post*, October 8, 1975, p. A1.

21. Swertlow, "Two Networks Reject Request to Carry President's Speech," p. A1.

22. Ibid.

23. Haynes Johnson, "Just How Will an Energy Program Affect Fred Doxsee?," *Washington Post*, April 21, 1977, p. A1.

24. Tom Shales, "No Network Nibbles for a Carter Speech," *Washington Post*, June 28, 1978, p. B1.

25. Gary Deeb, "CBS Deserves Kudos for Saying No to Carter," *Austin American-Statesman*, February 12, 1978, p. 21.

26. "Carter Gets Stood Up by CBS-TV," *Broadcasting*, February 6, 1978, p. 30.

27. Tom Shales, "Snaps, Crackles and Pops Over a Fireside Chat," *Washington Post*, February 3, 1978, p. D1.

28. "Carter Gets Stood Up by CBS-TV," p. 30.

29. Paul Klein et al., *Inside the TV Business*, pp. 190–91.

30. Shales, "Snaps, Crackles and Pops Over a Fireside Chat," p. D1.

31. Ron Nessen, "Two Views on Coverage of the President's Panama Canal Speech," *TV Guide*, April 1–7, 1978, pp. A5–6.

32. Ibid.

33. "Preempting the President," *New York Times*, February 9, 1978, p. A32.

34. Shales, "Snaps, Crackles and Pops," p. D1.

35. Ibid.

36. Deeb, "CBS Deserves Kudos for Saying No to Carter," p. 21.

37. Lester Crystal, Executive Producer, "MacNeil/Lehrer Newshour," Former President, NBC News, Personal Interview, New York, January 24, 1985.

38. Richard Salant, letter to Denis S. Rutkus, January 25, 1985.

39. Paul Klein et al., *Inside the TV Business* (New York: Sterling Publishing Co., 1979), pp. 190–91.

40. William Brock, Chairman, Republican National Committee, Telegram to ABC, CBS, and NBC News Executives, February 2, 1977.

41. David Gergen, "The 'Outs' Get a Chance to Reply," *Washington Star*, June 10, 1977, p. A11.

42. Bill Hart, "GOP Airs Its Energy Views on NBC Television Network," *First Monday*, June, 1977, p. 7.

43. Ibid.

44. Ronald Reagan, "Do the Networks Always Shortchange the 'Loyal Opposition'?," *TV Guide*, March 11, 1978, p. 5.

45. Figures were rounded to the nearest minute.

46. Reagan, "Do the Networks Always Shortchange the 'Loyal Opposition'?," p. 5.

47. Ibid.

48. Ibid., p. 6.

49. Ibid.

50. Tom Raum, "Republicans are Taking to Airwaves to Beam Home Their Arguments," Associated Press, January 30, 1986.

## CHAPTER 4

1. Thomas Griffith, "Being Too Easy on Reagan," *Time*, November 17, 1986, p. 88.

2. "Reagan Meets the Press," *USA Today*, November 19, 1986, p. 1.

3. Griffith, "Being Too Easy on Reagan," p. 88.

4. Ibid.

5. "I Love People," *Newsweek*, July 7, 1986, p. 16.

6. David Fuchs, Executive Vice President, CBS, Personal Interview, New York, June 27, 1986.

7. David Gergen, Former White House Communications Director, Personal Interview, Washington, D.C., March 6, 1985.

8. Robert McFarland, Washington Bureau Chief, NBC News, Personal Interview, Washington, D.C., March 6, 1985.

9. Lawrence Grossman, President, NBC News, Personal Interview, New York, June 26, 1976.

10. Gergen, March 6, 1985.

11. Robert Kaiser, "Blowing Smoke and Calling It Reality," *Washington Post*, October 17, 1982, p. B1.

12. Ibid.

13. William Leonard, Former President, CBS News, Personal Interview, Washington, D.C., March 4, 1985.

14. Tom Wicker, "The Pulpit Magnified," *New York Times*, October 18, 1974, p. 42.

15. Tom Pettit, Executive Vice President, NBC News, Personal Interview, New York, April 22, 1985.

16. Richard Wald, Vice President, ABC News, Former President, NBC News, Personal Interview, New York, April 22, 1985.

17. Newton N. Minow, John B. Martin, and Lee M. Mitchell, *Presidential Television* (New York: Basic Books, 1973), p. 21.

18. Edward J. Epstein, *News from Nowhere* (New York: Vintage Books, 1973), p. 253.

19. Ibid.

20. Kaiser, p. B1.

21. Richard Salant, Former President, CBS News, Former Vice Chairman, NBC, Personal Interview, New York, January 24, 1985.

22. Pettit, April 22, 1985.

23. Attachment to February 24, 1982 letter to Peter B. Kenney, Vice President, Washington, to Congressional Research Service.

24. Attachment to February 12, 1982 letter of Gene P. Mater, Senior Vice President, CBS Broadcast Group, to Congressional Research Service, Presidential Requests for Live Coverage, "CBS News Standards," November 16, 1978.

25. "Reagan on TV: He Must Ask," *New York Times*, March 17, 1986, p. A13.

26. George Watson, Robert McFarland, Jack Smith, and William Headline, "How the President Gets on the Air Live," Letter to the Editor, *New York Times*, March 25, 1986, p. 30.

27. Attachment to February 9, 1982 letter to Susan Povenmire, Assistant Director of News Information, ABC News, to Congressional Research Service.

28. CBS News, "Production Standards: Presidential Requests for Live Coverage," October 16, 1978.

29. Richard Salant, Memorandum to Arthur Taylor, John Schneider, and John Appel, CBS, November 4, 1974.

30. Ibid.

31. Salant, January 24, 1985.

32. Attachment to February 9, 1982 letter of Susan Povenmire.

33. Kaiser, p. B1.

34. "No Presidential Speech Pleased ABC–TV," *Lawton Constitution*, October 13, 1982, p. 20.

35. Wald, April 22, 1985.

36. Tony Schwartz, "Mixed Ratings for NBC," *New York Times*, October 14, 1982, p. 29.

37. "When a President Wants Air Time," (editorial), *Washington Post*, October 17, 1982, p. B6.

38. David Hoffman and Edward Walsh, "O'Neill Rebuffs Reagan Bid to Address House on Contras," *Washington Post*, June 24, 1986, p. 1.

39. Grossman, June 26, 1976.

40. Linda Greenhouse, "House Votes 221–209, to Aid Rebel Forces in Nicaragua; Major Victory for Reagan," *New York Times*, June 26, 1986, p. 1.

41. "CBS and ABC Rebuff Reagan," *New York Times*, October 14, 1987, p. 11.

42. George Watson, Washington Bureau Chief, ABC, Telephone Interview, February 3, 1988.

43. "White House Faults Networks for Skipping Reagan Speech," *Broadcasting*, February 8, 1988, p. 113.

44. Ibid.

45. Ibid.

46. Ann McFeatters, "Networks Didn't Kill Contra Vote," Scripps Howard Syndicate, February 10, 1988.

47. "The Futurist in Charge of NBC News," *Broadcasting*, February 29, 1988, p. 49.

48. Watson, February 3, 1988.

49. "Dead End," *Broadcasting*, February 15, 1988, p. 15.

50. Jessica Lee, "TV First: 3 Top Networks Reject White House Speech," *USA Today*, February 3, 1988, p. 4A.

51. Ibid.

52. Wald, April 22, 1985.

53. Pettit, April 22, 1985.

54. Fraser P. Seitel, *The Practice of Public Relations*, 2nd ed. (Columbus, OH: Merrill, 1984), p. 332.

55. Arthur R. Taylor, Telegram to Charles D. Ferris, Democratic Policy Committee, January 18, 1975.

56. Wald, April 22, 1985.

57. Ronald Reagan, "A Presidential Perspective on Radio," *Broadcasting*, September 8, 1986, p. 22.

58. Ron Nessen, "Always on Saturday?" *Washington Post*, August 20, 1986, p. A19.

59. Ibid.

60. Ron Nessen, "Two Views on Coverage of the President's Panama Canal Speech," *TV Guide*, April 1–7, 1978, pp. A5–6.

61. Grossman, June 26, 1986.

62. Les Brown, *Television: The Business Behind the Box* (New York: Harcourt, Brace, Jovanovich, 1971), p. 363.

63. Epstein, *News From Nowhere*, p. 114.

64. Brian Donlon, "CBS Delivers Returns, but Not Ratings," *USA Today*, November 6, 1986, p. 1.

65. "Election Coverage: The Long and the Short of it," *Broadcasting*, November 10, 1986, p. 50.

66. Ibid.

67. Ibid.

68. Ernest Leiser, "Bring Back the Instant News Specials," *TV Guide*, August 2, 1986, p. 39.

69. Desmond Smith, "Is the Sun Setting on Network Nightly News?" *Washington Journalism Reviews*, January 1986, p. 31.

70. Grossman, June 26, 1986.

71. Fred Friendly, *Due to Circumstances Beyond Our Control* (New York: Random House, 1967), p. 170.

72. Leonard, March 4, 1985.

73. Ibid.

74. Raymond Timothy, Group Executive Vice-President, NBC, Telephone Interview, May 6, 1985.

75. Ibid.

76. Wald, April 22, 1985.

77. McFarland, March 6, 1985.

78. Epstein, *News From Nowhere*, p. 116.

79. Ibid., p. 124.

80. Ibid., p. 115.

81. Stanton, January 24, 1985.

82. Ibid.

83. Edward Hudson, "Lorne Green, TV Patriarch, Is Dead," *New York Times*, September 12, 1987, p. 30.

84. Gergen, March 6, 1985.

85. Ibid.

86. Timothy, February 10, 1986.

87. John Carmody, "The TV Column," *Washington Post*, February 28, 1986, p. D10.

88. John Corry, "ABC Film on One-Armed Outfielder," *New York Times*, April 14, 1986, p. C18.

89. Timothy, May 6, 1985.

90. McFarland, March 6, 1985.

91. Ibid.

92. Gergen, March 6, 1985.

93. McFarland, March 6, 1985.

94. Barry Sussman, "But Mr. President, Americans Don't Like Ayatollah Khomeini," *Washington Post*, December 1, 1986, p. 37.

95. Ibid.

96. Kenneth T. Walsh and Dennis Mullin, " 'Spin Patrol' on the March," *Newsweek*, December 1, 1986, p. 17.

97. Ibid.

98. Ibid.

99. Griffith, "Being Too Easy on Reagan," p. 88.

## CHAPTER 5

1. On ceremonial occasions or with speeches dealing with marginally controversial issues, it made no sense for the opposition to request time. On other occasions, the opposition could not crystallize a position in time to request a reply.

2. Denis S. Rutkus, "President Reagan, The Opposition, and Access to Network Airtime" (Washington, D.C.: Congressional Research Service, 1984), p. 38.

3. Adam Clymer, "Democrats Hold Reagan's Theme Has Been Unfairness to the Needy," *New York Times*, January 27, 1982, p. A1.

4. Christopher Matthews, Press Secretary, Speaker Thomas P. O'Neill, Jr., Personal Interview, Washington, D.C., March 29, 1985.

5. Lawrence Grossman, President, NBC News, Personal Interview, New York, June 26, 1986.

6. Barbara Matusow, "Democrats Play Catch-Up in the Media Game," *Washington Journalism Review*, April, 1986, p. 14.

7. Ibid.

8. Lester Crystal, Executive Producer, "MacNeil/Lehrer Newshour" and Former President, NBC News, Personal Interview, New York, January 14, 1985.

9. David Fuchs, Executive Vice President, CBS, Personal Interview, New York, June 27, 1986.

10. Matthews, March 29, 1985.

11. Rutkus, "President Reagan, the Opposition and Access to Network Airtime," p. 45.

12. Charles T. Manatt, Letter to William Leonard, President of CBS News, August 1, 1981.

13. "CBS Wins in First Week of Post-Season Play," *Broadcasting*, April 28, 1985, p. 64.

14. John Carmody, "The TV Column," *Washington Post*, May 29, 1985, p. B6.

15. Chuck Conconi, "Personalities," *Washington Post*, June 17, 1985, p. D3.

16. "NBC's Week Begins with Thursday," *USA Today*, June 5, 1985, p. 3D.

17. David Burke, Executive Vice President, ABC News, Personal Interview, New York, January 25, 1985.

18. Tom Pettit, Executive Vice President, NBC News, Personal Interview, New York, April 22, 1985.

19. Lou Cannon and John Carmody, "Reagan Says ABC News Erred," *Washington Post*, February 28, 1986, p. A1.

20. Ibid.

21. Ibid.

22. John Weisman, "What TV Isn't Telling Us About Those Soviet Spokesmen," *TV Guide*, April 26, 1986, p. 4.

23. "Quello Calls for Better Journalism," *Broadcasting*, October 13, 1986, p. 76.

24. Rutkus, "President Reagan," p. 11.

25. Gene P. Mater, Senior Vice President, CBS Broadcast Group, Letter to Congressional Research Service, February 12, 1982.

26. Attachment to February 9, 1982, letter of Susan Povenmire, Assistant Director of News Information, ABC News, to Congressional Research Service.

27. Howell Raines, "Democrats: No Emmy, Please," *New York Times*, February 6, 1985, p. A22.

28. " 'Dynasty' Delays Democrats," *Ithaca Journal*, February 6, 1985, p. 9.

29. Burke, January 25, 1985.

30. Ibid.

31. " 'Dynasty' Preempts Democrats After Reagan Address Tonight," *Los Angeles Times*, February 6, 1985, p. 6.

32. John Curry, "ABC Rates 'Dynasty' Over Democrats," *USA Today*, February 6, 1985, p. 1.

33. Ibid.

34. Richard Salant, Former President, CBS News, Former Vice Chairman, NBC, Personal Interview, New York, January 24, 1985.

35. "Democrats Air A Bleak 'State of the Union'," *Congressional Quarterly*, January 20, 1982, vol. 40, p. 154.

36. George Watson, Letter to Democratic Congressional and Party Leaders, March 13, 1983.

37. Lawrence Grossman, Letter to the Democratic Congressional Leadership, February 25, 1985.

38. Grossman, June 26, 1986.

39. Ibid.

40. Steven V. Roberts, "Don't Touch That Dial . . . " *New York Times*, January 27, 1986, p. A16.

41. John S. DeMott, "Live Opposition," *Time*, February 9, 1987, p. 18.

42. Kenneth T. Walsh, "Sunset for a Presidency," *U.S. News and World Report*, February 9, 1987, p. 23.

43. James Reston, "Give TV Its Day," *New York Times*, June 4, 1986, p. 27.

44. Grace Wyndham Goldie, *Facing the Nation: Television and Politics, 1936–1976* (London: The Bodely Head, 1977, p. 186.

45. Joe S. Foote and Dennis K. Davis, "Network Visibility of Congressional Leaders, 1969–1985," Paper presented to the Political Communication Division of the International Communication Association, May 22–25, 1987, p. 6.

46. "For Democrats, the Medium's a Mess," *The New York Times*, December 10, 1984, p. B10.

47. Ibid.

48. Foote and Davis, p. 7.

49. "Reagan Draws the Line on Taxes . . . The Rise of Dan Rostenkowski," *U.S. News and World Report*, June 10, 1985, p. 17.

50. Rowland Evans and Robert Novak, "The Rise of Rosty," *Washington Post*, May 31, 1985, p. A23.

51. " 'Write Rosty' Blitz," *USA Today*, June 6, 1985, p. 1A.

52. John S. DeMott, "Live Opposition," p. 18.

53. Ronald Peters, Director, Carl Albert Congressional Studies Center, Telephone Interview, April 5, 1985.

## CHAPTER 6

1. Michael J. Robinson, "Television and American Politics, 1956–1976," *The Public Interest* (Summer 1977): 21.

2. Christopher J. Matthews, "Boss Tube: How the Networks Stole the Party," *New Republic*, December 16, 1985, p. 14.

3. Henry Fairlie, "How Journalists Get Rich," *The Washingtonian*, August 1983, p. 81.

4. Robert MacNeil, "Has Television Cast a Spell over Politics?" *TV Guide*, June 28, 1980, p. 5.

5. Max Kampelman, "The Power of the Press: A Problem For Our Democracy," *Policy Review*, Fall 1978, p. 7.

6. Jonathan Alter, "The Media in the Dock," *Newsweek*, October 22, 1984, p. 72.

7. Michael A. Ledeen, "Learning to Say 'No' to the Press," *The Public Interest*, no. 73 (Fall 1983): 114.

8. David Halberstam, *Powers That Be (New York: Alfred Knopf, 1979)*, p. 434.

9. "The People and the Press," *Times Mirror Corporation*, January, 1986.

10. Frank A. Reel, The Networks (New York: Charles Scribner and Sons, 1979), p. 89.

11. Jack Anderson, "TV Networks Reject Ford Interview," *Washington Post*, July 28, 1975, p. C23.

12. Eric Severeid, Former Commentator, CBS News, Personal Interview, Washington, D.C., March 5, 1985.

13. "Tilt to Left?: Interview with Don Hewitt," *U.S. News and World Report*, May 13, 1985, p. 65.

14. Neil Hickey, "TV *Must* Create Rebuttal Time," *TV Guide*, June 22, 1985, p. 25.

15. Ibid., p. 34.

16. William A. Henry, III, "Journalism Under Fire," *Time*, December 12, 1983, p. 76.

17. Ibid.

18. "Press Gets Bad News on its Image," *U.S. News and World Report*, April 22, 1985, p. 14.

19. "Public Critical of Intrusive Press Coverage in Political Campaign," *Broadcasting*, November 23, 1987, p. 77.

20. Clarke Taylor, "Network Anchors Mull Credibility of TV News," *Los Angeles Times*, November 28, 1984, p. 6.

21. "Speakers Claim Intrusive Tactics by Reporters Put Off Public," *Network News*, Associated Press Radio Newsletter, vol. 3, no. 7, 1984, p. 10.

22. "Watson Sees Rise in TV News Quality as Well as Quantity," *Broadcasting*, October 18, 1982, p. 51.

23. "NBC Affiliates Bask in Ratings Glory," *Broadcasting*, May 20, 1985, p. 90.

24. Michael Schudson, "The Politics of Narrative Form: The Emergence of News Conventions in Print and Television," *Daedalus* 111, no. 4 (Fall 1982): 105.

25. Irving Kristol, "Crises for Journalism: The Missing Elite," in G. Will, ed., *Press, Politics, and Popular Government* (Washington, D.C.: American Enterprise for Public Policy Research, 1972), p. 50.

26. John Weisman, "Who's Toughest on the White House and Why?" *TV Guide*, August 27, 1983, p. 10.

27. Kampelman, "The Power of the Press," p. 19.

28. Tom Bethell and Charles Peters, "The Imperial Press," *Washington Monthly*, November 1976, p. 29.

29. "The Right Way and the Wrong," *Broadcasting*, June 29, 1970, p. 90.

30. Haynes Johnson, "Just How Will An Energy Program Affect Fred Doxsee?" *Washington Post*, April 21, 1977, p. A1.

31. Richard K. Doan, "Emmy Awards Given to Two Comedy Series Cancelled by Networks," *TV Guide*, June 20, 1970, p. A1.

32. Severeid, March 5, 1985.

33. Don Hewitt, "TV's Circus: Conventions," *New York Times*, February 28, 1986, p. B4.

34. Joe S. Foote and Tony Rimmer, "The Ritual of Convention Coverage," in

William Adams, ed., *Television Coverage of the 1980 Presidential Campaign* (Norwood, N.J.: Ablex Publishing, 1983), p. 74.

35. Jack Valenti, "All Power to the Networks," *Washington Post*, August, 1984, p. A11.

36. "Live NBC Forum to Feature All 12 Presidential Candidates," *Southern Illinoisan*, November 28, 1987, p. 19.

37. William A. Henry, III, "Don Hewitt: Man of the Hour," *Washington Journalism Review*, May 1986, p. 26.

38. Steven V. Roberts, "The Global Village: A Case in Point," *New York Times*, February 20, 1986, p. B8.

39. Ibid.

40. "Brokaw Sees Media Moving Too Fast," *Broadcasting*, November 17, 1986, p. 76.

41. Dennis Hevesi, "How NBC Got Gorbachev Interview," *New York Times*, November 25, 1987, p. 24.

42. "ABC Turns Up Nose at Decor, Spruces Up Caucus Room," *The Washingtonian*, December 1983, p. 19.

## CHAPTER 7

1. "Cable TV Facts," Cable Advertising Bureau, New York, 1988, p. 13.

2. Ibid., p. 14.

3. Ibid., p. 16.

4. Newton Minow, Director, Annenberg Washington Program, Personal Interview, Washington, D.C., February 5, 1988.

5. Peter J. Boyer, "New TV Ratings Device Registers Fewer Viewers of Network Shows," *New York Times*, December 24, 1987, p. 1.

6. Peter J. Boyer, "CBS Cites New Meters for $40 Million in Costs," *New York Times*, January 19, 1988, p. 24.

7. Janet Stilson, "Study: Meters Show Improved Cable Ratings," *Electronic Media*, January 4, 1988, p. 4.

8. Rudy Taylor, Sales Manager, WNYW-TV, New York, Personal Interview, New York, February 6, 1987.

9. Scott Ticer, "Captain Comeback," *Business Week*, July 17, 1989, p. 106.

10. "Cable News Numbers," *Broadcasting*, May 11, 1987, p. 8. The ratings for total news viewing are greatly influenced by the amount of news programming a network airs. CNN, for example, with a 24-hour news service, has a cumulative news rating much more competitive with the networks than it does with regular head-to-head program ratings. Likewise, among ABC, CBS, and NBC, the network that airs the least hours of news programming per day will likely have a lower rating even though its individual programs may be highly rated.

11. Steve Haworth, Director, CNN Public Relations, Telephone Interview, August 30, 1989.

12. Warren Weaver, "As the Weinberger Turns," *New York Times*, February 13, 1985, p. A24.

13. Ibid.

14. Ed Turner, Executive Vice President, Cable News Network, Personal Interview, Atlanta, March 7, 1988.

15. "C-SPAN Subscriber Growth," *C-SPAN Update*, August 21, 1989, p. 1.

16. Ibid.

17. "Lawmakers on the Tube," *New York Times*, January 19, 1987, p. 10.

18. Brian Lamb, Chairman, C-SPAN, Personal Interview, Washington, D.C., August 9, 1989.

19. Ibid.

20. Lamb, August 9, 1989.

21. Ibid.

22. Turner, March 17, 1988.

23. John Weisman, "Nightly News Shows Under Siege—Will They Keep Their Clout," *TV Guide*, October 11, 1986, p. 10.

24. William J. Drummond, "Is Time Running Out for Network News?" *Columbia Journalism Review*, p. 52.

25. Desmond Smith, "You *Can* Go Home Again," *Washington Journalism Review*, June 1986, p. 47.

26. Turner, March 17, 1988.

27. Frank Stanton, Former President, CBS, Personal Interview, New York, January 24, 1985.

28. Tom Pettit, Executive Vice President, NBC News, Personal Interview, New York, April 22, 1985.

29. "President Pre-empted," *New York Times*, March 19, 1987, p. 46.

30. Richard Nixon, "Memo to President Bush: How to Use TV—and Keep from Being Abused by It," *TV Guide*, January 14, 1989, p. 26.

31. Ibid., p. 29.

32. Lamb, August 9, 1989.

# Bibliography

"ABC Turns Up Nose at Decor, Spruces Up Caucus Room." *The Washingtonian*, December 1983, p. 19.

Abel, Elie, ed. *What's News: The Media in American Society*. San Francisco: Institute for Contemporary Studies, 1981.

Albert, Carl. Speaker of the U.S. House of Representatives, news release, January 18, 1976.

Alter, Jonathan. "The Media in the Dock." *Newsweek*, October 22, 1984, p. 72.

———. "The Struggle for the Soul of CBS News." *Newsweek*, September 15, 1986, pp. 52, 54.

Alter, Jonathan, Luch Howard, and Nancy Stadtman. "In the Dock." *Newsweek*, October 22, 1984, p. 66.

*America's Watching: Public Attitudes Toward Television*. New York: Television Information Office, 1987.

Anderson, Jack. "TV Networks Reject Ford Interview." *Washington Post*, July 28, 1975, p. C23.

Anderson, Susan Heller. "For Executives at NBC, Belt-Tightening Begins." *New York Times*, November 7, 1986, p. 28.

"Applicability of the Fairness Doctrine in the Handling of Controversial Issues of Public Importance." *Fairness Primer*, 29 Fed. Reg. 10416 (1964).

Balutis, Alan P. "Congress, the President and the Press." *Journalism Quarterly* 53 (1976): 509–15.

———. "The President and the Press: The Expanding Presidential Image." *Presidential Studies Quarterly* 7 (1977): 244–51.

Barnouw, Erik. *The Golden Web: A History of Broadcasting in the United States, Volume II—1933 to 1953*. New York: Oxford University Press, 1968, p. 3.

———. *The Image Empire*. New York: Oxford University Press, 1970.

———. *A Tower in Babel: A History of Broadcasting in the United States to 1933*. New York: Oxford University Press, 1966, pp. 45–46.

———. *Tube of Plenty*. New York: Vintage Books, 1973.

Baroodi, Mike. Director of Public Affairs, The White House, Washington, D.C., Personal Interview, April 1, 1985.

"Battle Is on for Political Radio Time." *Broadcasting*, April 14, 1947, p. 80.

Becker, Samuel L. "Presidential Power: The Influence of Broadcasting." *Quarterly Journal of Speech* 47 no. 1 (February 1961): 14–17.

Benjamin, Louise M. "Campaign Policies, Broadcasters and the Presidential Election of 1924." Paper presented to the History Division of the Association for Education in Journalism and Mass Communication Annual Convention, San Antonio, August 1987, p. 4.

Bergreen, Laurence. *Look Now, Pay Later*. New York: Doubleday & Company, 1980.

Bernstein, Lester. "The Dishwasher League." *New York Times*, December, 9, 1986, p. 1.

Berry, Joseph P., Jr. *John F. Kennedy and the Media: The First Television President*. Lanham, MD: University Press of America, 1987.

"Best Guess: What Three Networks Took In, Kept in 1985." *Broadcasting*, May 5, 1986, p. 35.

Bethel, Tom, and Charles Peters. "The Imperial Press." *Washington Monthly* (November 1976): 29.

Blanchard, Robert E., ed. *Congress and the News Media*. New York: Hastings House, 1974.

Blau, Eleanor. "CNN's 'Businesslike' Anchor Getting Some Rave Reviews." *Southern Illinoisan*, February 25, 1989, p. 18.

Bonafede, Dom. "The Washington Post—Competing For Power with The Federal Government." *National Journal*, April 17, 1982, pp. 664–74.

Boyer, Peter J. "CBS Aides Say Network Will Cut Hundreds of Jobs." *New York Times*, May 6, 1986, p. C22.

———. "CBS Cites New Meters for $40 Million in Costs." *New York Times*, January 19, 1988, p. 24.

———. "CBS Explains Evening News Incident." *New York Times*, September 14, 1987, p. 20.

———. "For Many Who Remain, Sadness Turns to Anger Over CBS Dismissals." *New York Times*, March 9, 1987, p. 16.

———. "14 Reporters Among 215 Cut by CBS." *New York Times*, March 17, 1987, p. 13.

———. "NBC Cancels Magazine Show '1986'." *New York Times*, December 10, 1986, p. 26.

———. "NBC Head Proposes Staff Political Contributions." *New York Times*, December 9, 1986, pp. 1, 26.

———. "Networks May Rotate their Daily Coverage." *New York Times*, July 14, 1987, p. 7.

———. "New TV Ratings Device Registers Fewer Viewers of Network Shows." *New York Times*, December 24, 1987, p. 1.

———. "Shepherd Resigns as CBS Program Head." *New York Times*, April 25, 1986, p. C31.

———. " '60 Minutes Star Is Critical of CBS." *New York Times*, August 6, 1986, p. 19.

————. "Staff Cutback Is Begun at ABC News." *New York Times*, April 1, 1986, p. C20.

Braden, Waldo, and Earnest Brandenburg. "Roosevelt's Fireside Chats." *Speech Monographs* 22 (November 1955): 293.

"Brand That's Being Burned into TV, The." *Broadcasting*, November 8, 1965, p. 54.

Brewin, Bob. "VCRs: Bigger Than Box-Office." *The Village Voice*, March 11, 1986, p. 45.

Briggs, Asa. *Governing the BBC*. London: British Broadcasting Corporation, 1979.

British Broadcasting Corporation. *Aide Mémoire of 1947*, 1947.

————. *Aide Mémoire of 1969*, 1969.

Brock, William. Chairman, Republican National Committee, Telegram to ABC, CBS, and NBC News Executives, February 2, 1977.

Broder, David. "Ford Carefully Rehearsed 'Make-or-Break' Speech." *Washington Post*, January 14, 1975, p. A3.

"Brokaw Sees Media Moving Too Fast." *Broadcasting*, November 17, 1986, p. 76.

Brown, Les. "Democrats Reach Low TV Audience." *New York Times*, January 25, 1975, p. B10.

————. "Political Access to Television: A Double Standard." *New York Times*, October 26, 1974, p. 63.

————. "TV Networks, in a Shift, Air Ford at His Request." *New York Times*, October 16, 1974, p. L4.

————. *Television: The Business Behind the Box*. New York: Harcourt, Brace, Jovanovich, 1971.

Buck, Rinker. "What the Cutbacks Really Mean." *Channels*, September, 1986, p. 68.

Buckley, William F., Jr. "Let Presidents Have Their Say." *Washington Post*, May 13, 1983, p. A19.

Burke, David. Executive Vice-President, ABC News, New York, Personal Interview, January 25, 1985.

"CBS and ABC Rebuff Reagan." *New York Times*, October 14, 1987, p. 11.

"CBS Declines to Air Jefferson Day Speech." *Broadcasting*, April 7, 1947, p. 26.

CBS News. "Production Standards: Presidential Requests for Live Coverage." October 16, 1978.

"CBS Takes 'Opposition' Off the Air." *Broadcasting*, August 24, 1970, p. 34.

"CBS Wins in First Week of Post-Season Play." *Broadcasting*, April 28, 1985, p. 64.

"C-SPAN." *Broadcasting*, April 3, 1989, p. 62.

"C-SPAN: Documenting A Decade of Public Affairs." *Broadcasting*, April 3, 1989, p. 62.

"C-SPAN Stats." *Broadcasting*, September 14, 1987, p. 124.

"C-SPAN Subscriber Growth." *C-SPAN Update*, August 21, 1989.

"Cable News Numbers." *Broadcasting*, May 11, 1987, p. 8.

"Cable TV Facts." New York: Cable Television Advertising Bureau, 1989.

"California Democratic State Central Committee." 40 FCC 501 (1960).

Cannon, Lou, and John Carmody. "Reagan Says ABC News Erred." *Washington Post*, February 28, 1986, p. A1.

Carmody, John. "The TV Column." *Washington Post*, May 29, 1985, p. B6.

———. "The TV Column." *Washington Post*, February 28, 1986, p. D10.

———. "Two Networks Decline to Carry Ford Speech." *Washington Post*, October 8, 1975, pp. A2, 81.

"Carter Gets Stood Up by CBS-TV." *Broadcasting*, February 6, 1978, p. 30.

Cater, Douglas. *The Fourth Branch of Government*. Boston: Houghton Mifflin, 1959.

Catledge, Turner. "Roosevelt Speech Politics, Says G.O.P.; Radio Reply Asked." *New York Times*, January 2, 1936, p. 1.

Chaze, William L., Daniel Collins, and Ron Scherer. "Who Will Control TV?" *U.S. News & World Report*, May 13, 1985, pp. 60–68.

Chester, Edward W. *Radio, Television, and American Politics*. New York: Sheed and Ward, 1969.

Clymer, Adam. "Democrats Hold Reagan's Theme Has Been Unfairness to the Needy." *New York Times*, January 27, 1982.

Cohn, D. "Access to Television to Rebut the President of the United States: An Analysis and Proposal." *Temple Law Quarterly* 45 (1982): 141–201.

Columbia Broadcasting v. FCC, United States Court of Appeals. District of Columbia Circuit, November 15, 1971.

Columbia Broadcasting System v. Democratic National Committee. 412 U.S. 94, 1973.

Comstock, George. *Television in America*. London: Sage Publications, 1980.

Conconi, Chuck. "Personalities." *Washington Post*, June 17, 1985, p. D3.

———. "Rostenkowski Gets Good Numbers." *Washington Post*, June 17, 1985, p. D3.

Cornwell, Elmer E., Jr. "Coolidge and Presidential Leadership." *Public Opinion Quarterly* 21 (Summer 1957): 269.

———. "The President and the Press: Phases in the Relationship." *Annals of the American Academy of Political and Social Science*, 427 (1976): 53–64.

———. *Presidential Leadership of Public Opinion*. Bloomington: Indiana University Press, 1965.

Corry, John. "ABC Film on One-Armed Outfielder." *New York Times*, April 14, 1986, p. C18.

Cowan, Geoffrey. "Presidential Television." *UCLA Law Review*, 21 (1974): 1690–1714.

Crystal, Lester. Executive Producer, "MacNeil/Lehrer Newshour." Former President, NBC News, New York, Personal Interview, January 24, 1985.

Curran, Charles. *A Seamless Robe*. London: Collins, 1979.

Curry, John. "ABC Rates 'Dynasty' Over Democrats." *USA Today*, February 6, 1985, p. 1.

"Dead End." *Broadcasting*, February 15, 1988, p. 15.

Deeb, Gary. "CBS Deserves Kudos for Saying No to Carter." *Austin American-Statesman*, February 12, 1978, p. 21.

"Democrats Air a Bleak 'State of the Union.' " *Congressional Quarterly* 40 (January 20, 1982): 154.

"Democrats Defend Jefferson Day Time." *Broadcasting*, April 21, 1947, p. 92.

DeMott, John S. "Live Opposition." *Time*, February 9, 1987, p. 18.

Denton, Robert E. *The Primetime Presidency of Ronald Reagan*. New York: Praeger, 1988.

———, and Dan F. Hahn. *Presidential Communication*. New York: Praeger, 1986.

Doan, Richard K. "Emmy Awards Given to Two Comedy Series Cancelled by Networks." *TV Guide*, June 20, 1970, p. A1.

Donlon, Brian. "CBS Delivers Returns, but Not Ratings." *USA Today*, November 6, 1986, p. 1.

Douglas, Margaret. Assistant to the Director-General, British Broadcasting, London, England, Personal Interview, July 11, 1984.

———. Assistant to the Director-General, British Broadcasting Corporation, Telephone Interview, April 19, 1984.

Dreher, Carl. *Garnoff: An American Success*. New York: New York Times Book Co., 1977.

Drummond, William J. "Is Time Running Out for Network News." *Columbia Journalism Review*, p. 52.

Dunlap, Orrin E. "Marconi Magic in the Home." *New York Times*, December 4, 1932, sec. 8, p. 10.

" 'Dynasty' Delays Democrats." *Ithaca Journal*, February 6, 1985, p. 9.

" 'Dynasty' Preempts Democrats After Reagan Address Tonight." *Los Angeles Times*, February 6, 1985, p. 6.

Dzodin, Harvey. Director, Standards and Practices, ABC, New York, Personal Interview, April 21, 1985.

Editorializing by Broadcast Licensees, 13 FCC 1246 (1949).

Edwards, G. "The President, the Media and the First Amendment." *Presidential Studies Quarterly* 12 (1982): 42–47.

"Election Coverage: The Long and the Short of It." *Broadcasting*, November 10, 1986, pp. 50–52.

Ely, Caroline. "The Fast-Paced Canadian House." *C-SPAN Update*, January 27, 1986, p. 3.

———. "In Cable's Early Days, Ferris Was a Big Wheel." *C-SPAN Update*, August 5, 1985, p. 9.

Epstein, Edward J. *News from Nowhere*. New York: Vintage Books, 1973.

Erlick, Everett H. Senior Vice President and General Counsel, ABC Inc., Letter to Senator Mike Mansfield, April 24, 1973.

Evans, Rowland, and Robert Novak. "The Rise of Rosty." *Washington Post*, May 31, 1985, p. A23.

Fairlie, Henry. "How Journalists Get Rich." *The Washingtonian*, August, 1983, p. 81.

Farley, James A. *Behind the Ballots*. New York: Harcourt Brace Jovanovich, 1938.

Fersh, Seymour H. "The View from the White House: A Study of the Presidential State of the Union Messages." Washington, D.C.: Public Affairs Press, 1937, p. 9.

"Fifty to Broadcast Washington Fete." *New York Times*, June 11, 1927, p. 3.

"First Sixty Years of NBC, The." *Broadcasting*, June 9, 1986, pp. 49–64.

Fixx, James F., ed. *The Mass Media and Politics*. New York: Arno Press, 1972.

Foote, Joe S., and Dennis K. Davis. "Network Visibility of Congressional Leaders, 1969–1985." Paper presented to the Political Communication Division of the International Communication Association, May 22–25, 1986, p. 6.

———, and Tony Rimmer. "The Ritual of Convention Coverage." In *Television Coverage of the 1980 Presidential Campaign*. Edited by William Adams. Norwood, NJ: Ablex Publishing, 1983.

———. "Reagan on Radio." In *Communication Yearbook* 8, pp. 692–706. Edited by Robert Bostrum. Beverly Hills: Sage Publications, 1984.

"For Democrats, the Medium's a Mess." *New York Times*, December 10, 1989, p. B10.

"Ford Plans Press Talk; ABC Passes." Associated Press, October 9, 1975.

French, B. A. *The Presidential Press Conference*. Washington, D.C.: University Press of America, 1982.

Friendly, Fred W. *Due To Circumstances Beyond Our Control*. Random House: New York, 1967.

———. "If I Had My Career in Broadcast Journalism to Start Over Again in August, 1986..." Remarks to the Radio and Television News Directors Association. Salt Lake City, Utah, August 29, 1986, p. 9.

"Friendly Suggests CBS Cuts." *New York Times*, March 17, 1987, p. 13.

Fuchs, David. Executive Vice-President, New York, CBS, Personal Interview, June 27, 1986.

Gans, Herbert J. *Deciding What's News, A Study of CBS Evening News, NBC Nightly News, Newsweek and Time*. New York: Vintage Books, 1980.

Gergen, David. Former White House Communications Director, Washington, DC, Personal Interview, March 6, 1985.

———. "The 'Outs' Get A Chance To Reply." *The Washington Star*, June 10, 1977, p. A11.

Gibbs, Ellen Berland. "Back to the Bottom Line." *Washington Journalism Review*, July 1986, p. 52.

Glass, Andrew. "The Preening of the President—For Television." *New York Times*, March 16, 1975, p. 29.

Goldberg, Ralph. Assistant to the President, CBS News, New York, Personal Interview, January 24, 1985.

Goldenson, Leonard. Telegram to Democratic and Republican Congressional Leaders, August 17, 1970.

Goldie, Grace W. *Facing the Nation: Television and Politics, 1936–76*. London: The Bodley Head, 1977.

"Goodman's Goals for Broadcasting." *Broadcasting*, February 10, 1986, pp. 70–72.

"GOP Asks Air Time to Answer Kennedy." *New York Times*, September 19, 1963, p. 14.

"GOP Gets Air Time to Answer Kennedy." *New York Times*, September 20, 1963, p. 30.

"GOP Gets Equal Time to Answer JFK's Tax Message." *Broadcasting*, September 23, 1963, p. 70.

"GOP Gets Rebuttal Time." *Broadcasting*, January 17, 1966, p. 10.

"GOP Gets TV Time to Answer Johnson." *New York Times*, December 15, 1967, p. 29.

"GOP Won't Talk Back." *Broadcasting*, April 15, 1963, p. 5.

Gould, Jack. "TV: Hagerty's Role Discussed." *New York Times*, February 28, 1958, p. 45.

"Government Monopolizes Radio, A Senator Charges." *New York Times*, January 19, 1934, p. 1.

Graber, Doris, ed. *The President and the Public*. Philadelphia: Institute for the Study of Human Issues, 1982.

Graening, Susan, and Mark Mandernack. "Affiliates React to Cuts at CBS News." *Electronic Media*, March 16, 1987, p. 54.

Greene, Harold. *The Third Floor Front*. London: The Bodley Head, 1969.

Greenhouse, Linda. "House Vote 221–209, to Aid Rebel Forces in Nicaragua; Major Victory for Reagan." *New York Times*, June 26, 1986, p. 1.

———. "Message Spells Relief for Democrats." *New York Times*, June 19, 1987, p. 8.

Griffith, Thomas. "Being Too Easy on Reagan." *Time*, November 17, 1986, p. 88.

Grossman, Lawrence K. Letter to the Democratic Congressional Leadership, February 25, 1985.

———. President, NBC News, New York, Personal Interview, June 26, 1987.

Grossman, Michael B., and Martha J. Kumar. "The White House and the News Media: The Phases of Their Relationship." *Political Science Quarterly* 94 (1979): 27–53.

———. *Portraying the President: The White House and the News Media*. Baltimore: Johns Hopkins University Press, 1981.

Haight, Timothy R., and Richard A. Brody. "The Mass Media and Presidential Popularity: Presidential Broadcasting and News in the Nixon Administration." *Communication Research* 4 (1977): 41–60.

Halberstam, David. *The Powers That Be*. New York: Alfred Knopf, 1979.

Harmetz, Aljean. "Fox Plans a TV Program Service." *New York Times*, May 7, 1986, p. C30.

"Harsher Laws on Equal Time." *Broadcasting*, January 23, 1967, p. 72.

Hart, Bill. "GOP Airs Its Energy Views on NBC Television Network." *First Monday*, June, 1977, p. 7.

Hart, Roderick P. *The Sound of Leadership: Presidential Communication in the Modern Age*. Chicago: University of Chicago Press, 1987.

Hayworth, Steve. Director of Public Relations, CNN, Telephone Interview, August 30, 1989.

Headline, William. Washington Bureau Chief, Cable News Network; Former Assistant Washington Bureau Chief, CBS News, Washington D.C., Personal Interview, March 4, 1985.

"Health of President Coolidge Conserved by Broadcasting." *New York Times*, February 24, 1924, sec. 8, p. 15.

Henry, William A., III. "All Power to the Networks." *Washington Post*, August 1984, p. A11.

———. "Don Hewitt: Man of the Hour." *Washington Journalism Review*, May 1986, p. 26.

———. "Journalism Under Fire." *Time*, December 12, 1983, p. 76.

Hess, Stephen. *The Washington Reporters*. Washington, D.C.: Brookings Institute, 1981.

Hevesi, Dennis. "How NBC Got Gorbachev Interview." *New York Times*, November 25, 1987, p. 24.

Hewitt, Don. "TV's Circus: Conventions." *New York Times*, February 28, 1986, p. B4.

Hickey, Neil. "TV *Must* Create Rebuttal Time." *TV Guide*, June 22, 1985, p. 25.

Hiebert, Ray, et al. *Mass Media TV*. New York: Longman Inc., 1985.

High, Stanley. "Not-So-Free Air." *Saturday Evening Post*, February 11, 1939, p. 9.

Hoffman, David, and Edward Walsh. "O'Neill Rebuffs Reagan Bid to Address House on Contras." *Washington Post*, June 24, 1986, p. 1.

"Hoover Radio Record Surpasses Coolidge's." *New York Times*, May 11, 1931, p. 3.

"Hoover to Speak Three Times on Radio Latter Part of May." *New York Times*, May 7, 1931, p. 1.

"House Turns Investigative Eyes on Network News." *Broadcasting*, May 4, 1987, pp. 31–35.

Hudson, Edward. "Lorne Green, TV Patriarch, Is Dead." *New York Times*, September 12, 1987, p. 30.

"I Love People." *Newsweek*, July 7, 1986, p. 16.

"In Brief." *Broadcasting*, August 3, 1981, p. 28.

Jamieson, Kathleen Hall. *Packaging the President: A History and Criticism of Presidential Campaign Advertising*. New York: Oxford University Press, 1984.

John, Kenneth E. "Americans Oppose Government Restraints on the Media." *Washington Post National Weekly*, October 29, 1984, p. 38.

Johnson, Haynes. "Just How Will an Energy Program Affect Fred Doxsee?" *Washington Post*, April 21, 1977, p. A1.

Kaiser, Robert. "Blowing Smoke and Calling It Reality." *Washington Post*, October 17, 1982, p. B1.

Kaltenborn, Rolf. "Is Radio Politically Impartial?" *The American Mercury*, June 1946, pp. 665–69.

Kampelman, Max. "The Power of the Press: A Problem for Our Democracy." *Policy Review*, Fall 1978, pp. 7–39.

Kampelman, May W. "Congress, the Media and the President." In *Congress Against the President*. Edited by H. C. Manfield, Sr. New York: Academy of Political Science. *Proceedings of the Academy of Political Science*, 32. (1), 1975.

Katzman, Murray. "News Broadcasting in the United States: 1920–1941." Unpublished Ph.D. Dissertation, New York University, 1968, p. 73.

Klein, Paul, et al. *Inside the TV Business*. New York: Sterling Publishing Co., 1979.

Kling, Bill, and Jeremiah O'Leary. "White House Upbraids ABC for Soviet's TV Commentary." *The Washington Times*, February 28, 1986. p. 1A.

Kristol, Irving. "Crises for Journalism: The Missing Elite," In *Press, Politics, and Popular Government*. Edited by G. Will. Washington, D.C.: American Enterprise for Public Policy Research, 1972.

Lamb, Brian. Chairman, C-SPAN, Washington, D.C., Personal Interview, August 9, 1989.

Lamson, Carolyn. "Pool Position." *C-SPAN Update*, July 15, 1985, p. 1.

"Lawmakers on the Tube." *New York Times*, January 19, 1987, p. 10.

"LBJ's Message Gets Top Effort." *Broadcasting*, January 22, 1968, p. 64.

Ledeen, Michael A. "Learning to Say 'No' to the Press." *The Public Interest*, no. 73 (Fall 1983): 113–18.

Lee, Jessica. "TV First: 3 Top Networks Reject White House Speech." *USA Today*, February 3, 1988, p. 4A.

Leiser, Ernest. "Bring Back the Instant News Specials." *TV Guide*, August 2, 1986, pp. 39–40.
———. "The Little Network That Could." *New York Times Magazine*, March 20, 1988, p. 32.
Leonard, William. Former President, CBS News, Washington D.C., Personal Interview, March 4, 1985.
"Live NBC Forum to Feature All 12 Presidential Candidates." *Southern Illinoisan*, November 28, 1987, p. 19.
Lord, William. Telegram to House Speaker Carl Albert and Senate Majority Leader Mike Mansfield, October 13, 1975.
McFarland, Robert. Washington Bureau Chief, NBC News, Washington D.C., Personal Interview, March 6, 1985.
MacNeil, Robert. "Has Television Cast A Spell Over Politics?" *TV Guide*, June 28, 1980, pp. 5–8.
Malara, Tony. CBS President-Affiliate Relations, Las Vegas, Nevada, Personal Interview, May 1, 1989.
Manaheim, J. "The News Conference and Presidential Leadership of Public Opinion: Does the Tail Wag the Dog?" *Presidential Studies Quarterly* 11 (1981): 177–88.
Manatt, Charles T. Letter to William Leonard, President of CBS News, August 1, 1981.
Mater, Gene P. Senior Vice President, CBS Broadcast Group, Letter to Congressional Research Service, and Attachment, February 12, 1982.
Matthews, Christopher J. "Boss Tube: How the Networks Stole the Party." *New Republic*, December 16, 1985, p. 14.
———. Press Secretary, Speaker Thomas P. O'Neill, Jr., Washington D.C., Personal Interview, March 29, 1985.
Matusow, Barbara. "Democrats Play Catch-Up in the Media Game." *Washington Journalism Review*, April 1986, p. 14.
———. *The Evening Stars*. New York: Ballentine Books, 1983.
———. "Station Identification, Network Affiliates Loosen the Apron Strings." *Washington Journalism Review*, April 1985, pp. 28–33.
Mayer, Martin. *About Television*. New York: Harper & Row, 1972.
———. *Making News*. Garden City, NJ: Doubleday, 1987.
Meaney, Don. Former Washington Bureau Chief, NBC News, Washington D.C., Personal Interview, March 6, 1985.
Media, The. "C-SPAN Gets Large Budget Increase." *Broadcasting*, February 10, 1986, p. 67.
Mickelson, Sig. *The Electric Mirror: Politics in an Age of Television*. New York: Dodd, Mead & Company, 1972.
Minow, Newton. Director, Annenberg Washington Program, Washington D.C., Personal Interview, February 5, 1988.
———, John B. Martin, and Lee M. Mitchell. *Presidential Television*. New York: Basic Books, 1973.
———, and Lee M. Mitchell. "Incumbent Television: A Case of Indecent Exposure." *Annals of the American Academy of Political and Social Science* 425, no. 3 (Summer 1950): 74–87.

Mitchell, Lee M. "Government as Broadcasters—Solution or Threat?" *Journal of Communication* 28 (1978): 69–72.

Moyers, Bill. "Taking CBS News to Task." *Newsweek*, September 15, 1985, p. 53.

"Mr. Truman Steps Aside." *New York Times*, March 31, 1952, p. 18.

"NBC Affiliates Bask in Ratings Glory." *Broadcasting*, May 20, 1985, p. 90.

"NBC Allows Reply to Roosevelt Talk." *New York Times*, January 3, 1936, p. 3.

"NBC's Week Begins with Thursday." *USA Today*, June 5, 1985, p. 3D.

Nessen, Ron. "Always on Saturday?" *Washington Post*, August 20, 1986, p. A19.

———. "Two Views on Coverage of the President's Panama Canal Speech." *TV Guide*, April 1–7, 1978, pp. A5–6.

"Network Comparisons." *Broadcasting*, April 13, 1987, pp. 10–14.

"Network Critics Assail Move to 'Junk Entertainment' in TV." *Southern Illinoisan*, April 29, 1987, p. 13.

Nixon, Richard. "Memo to President Bush: How to Use TV—and Keep from Being Abused by It." *TV Guide*, January 14, 1989, p. 26.

"No Presidential Speech Pleased ABC–TV." *Lawton Constitution*, October 13, 1982, p. 20.

"No Prime Time for Ford." *Time*, October 20, 1975, p. 8.

O'Neill, Thomas P., Jr. Letter to Speaker and Senator Byrd, NBC News, February 25, 1985.

———. Letter to Lawrence K. Grossman, President, NBC News, March 11, 1985.

"Opening TV to the Political Outs." *Broadcasting*, June 29, 1970, pp. 32–34.

Ornstein, Norman, and Michael J. Robinson. "Where's All the Coverage? The Case of our Disappearing Congress." *TV Guide*, January 11, 1986, pp. 4–10.

Paletz, David L., and Robert M. Entman. "Presidential Power and the Press." *Presidential Studies Quarterly* 10 (1980): 416–26.

———, and Robert M. Entman. *Media Power Politics*. New York: Free Press, 1981.

———, and Richard J. Vinegar. "Presidents on Television: The Effects of Instant Analysis." *Public Opinion Quarterly* 41 (1977/78): 488–97.

Panitt, Merrill. "TV is Weakening the Presidency." *TV Guide*, November 26, 1983, pp. 43–46.

Paper, Lewis J. *Empire: William S. Paley and the Making of CBS*. New York: St. Martin's Press, 1987.

Pearce, Alan. *NBC News Division and The Economics of Prime Time Access*. New York: Arno Press, 1979.

"People and the Press, The." *Times Mirror Corporation*, January, 1986.

Peters, Ronald. Director, Carl Albert Congressional Studies Center, Telephone Interview, April 22, 1985.

Pettit, Tom. Executive Vice-President, NBC News, New York, Personal Interview, April 22, 1985.

Powell, Bill, and Jonathon Alter. "Civil War at CBS." *Newsweek*, September 15, 1986, pp. 46–50.

"Preempting the President." *New York Times*, February 9, 1978, p. A32.

"Presidential Rating." *Broadcasting*, December 5, 1983, p. 9.

Presidential Requests for Live Coverage. "CBS News Standards," November 16, 1978.

"President Pre-empted." *New York Times*, March 19, 1987, p. 46.

"President vs. Networks." *Newsweek*, October 28, 1974, p. 31.

"Press Gets Bad News on its Image." *U.S. News and World Report*, April 22, 1985, p. 14.

Provenmire, Susan. Assistant Director of News Information. Attachment to letter to Congressional Research Service, February 9, 1982.

"Public Critical of Intrusive Press Coverage in Political Campaign." *Broadcasting*, November 23, 1987, p. 77.

"Quello Calls for Better Journalism." *Broadcasting*, October 13, 1986, p. 76.

"Radio Chains Bar Republican Skit but Party Gets Chicago Outlet." *New York Times*, January 14, 1936, p. 1.

Raines, Howell. "Democrats: No Emmy, Please." *New York Times*, February 6, 1985, p. A22.

Ranney, Austin. *Channels of Power*. New York: Basic Books, 1983.

Rather, Dan. "From Murrow to Mediocrity?" *New York Times*, March 10, 1987, p. 25.

Raum, Tom. "Republicans Are Taking to Airwaves to Beam Home their Arguments." Associated Press, January 30, 1986.

"Reagan Draws the Line on Taxes . . . The Rise of Dan Rostenkowski." *U.S. News and World Report*, June 10, 1985, p. 17.

"Reagan Meets the Press." *USA Today*, November 19, 1986, p. 1.

"Reagan on TV: He Must Ask." *New York Times*, March 17, 1986, p. A13.

Reagan, Ronald. Address to the Nation on Federal Tax Reduction Legislation, *Weekly Compilation of Presidential Documents*, July 27, 1981, p. 819.

———. "Do the Networks Always Short Change the 'Loyal Opposition'?" *TV Guide*, March 11, 1978, pp. 4–8.

———. "A Presidential Perspective on Radio." *Broadcasting*, September 8, 1986, p. 22.

Reel, Frank A. *The Networks*. New York: Charles Scribner and Sons, 1979.

Reston, James. "Give TV Its Day." *New York Times*, June 4, 1986, p. 27.

———. "State of the Union?" *New York Times*, January 29, 1986, p. A23.

"Right Way and the Wrong, The." *Broadcasting*, June 29, 1970, p. 90.

Rivers, William L. "The Media as Shadow Government." *The Quill*, March 1982, pp. 11–15.

Roberts, Steven V. "The Global Village: A Case in Point." *New York Times*, February 20, 1986, p. B8.

———. "Don't Touch That Dial . . . " *New York Times*, January 27, 1986, p. A16.

Robinson, Michael J. "Television and American Politics, 1956–1976." *The Public Interest* (Summer 1977): 3–39.

———. "The Impact of Instant Analysis." *Journal of Communication* 27 (1977): 17–23.

Roosevelt, Franklin D. Letter to M. H. Aylesworth, May 18, 1933, P.P.F. 447, Roosevelt Library.

Rosenstiel, Thomas B. "Latest News at Networks: Cutting Costs." *Los Angeles Times*, November 22, 1985, p. 1.

Rosenthal, Andrew. "Watching Cable News Network Grow." *New York Times*, December 16, 1987, p. 12.

Rubin, Richard L. "The Presidency in the Age of Television." In *The Power to Govern: Assessing Reform in the United States*. Edited by R. M. Pious. Pro-

*ceedings of the Academy of Political Science*, 32 (2), 1981, pp. 138–52. New York: Academy of Political Science.

Rutkus, Denis S. "President Reagan, the Opposition and Access to Network Airtime." Washington, D.C.: Congressional Research Service, 1984.

———. "Opposition Party Access to the Broadcast Networks to Respond to the President." Washington, D.C.: Congressional Research Service, 1977.

———. "Presidential Television." *Journal of Communication* 26 (2) (1976): 73–78.

———. "A Report on Simultaneous Television Network Coverage of Presidential Addresses to the Nation." Washington, D.C.: Congressional Research Service, Library of Congress, January 12, 1976.

———. "The Johnson Presidency." Unpublished Manuscript, 1985.

———. Unpublished Manuscript, 1985.

Salant, Richard S. Letter to Denis S. Rutkus, January 25, 1985.

———. Memorandum to Arthur Taylor, John Schneider, and John Appel, CBS, November 4, 1974.

———. New York, New York, Personal Interview, January 24, 1985.

———. "When the White House Cozies Up to the Home Screen." *New York Times*, August 23, 1981, p. 25.

———. Former President, CBS News, Former Vice Chairman, NBC, Personal Interview, New York, New York, January 24, 1985.

Salinger, Pierre. *With Kennedy*. New York: Avon Books, 1967.

Schmidt, Benno, Jr. *Freedom of the Press vs. Public Access*. New York: Praeger Publishers, 1976.

Schneider, Greg. "The 90-Second Handicap, Why TV Coverage of Legislation Falls Short." *Washington Journalism Review*, June 1985, pp. 44–46.

Schudson, Michael. "The Politics of Narrative Form: The Emergence of News Conventions in Print and Television." *Daedalus* 3, no. 4 (1982): 97–112.

Schwartz, Tony. "Mixed Ratings for NBC." *New York Times*, October 14, 1982, p. 29.

Scott, Byron N. "Communication Act of 1934." *Congressional Record* 80 (January 24, 1936): 973.

Seitel, Fraser P. *The Practice of Public Relations*. 2d ed. Columbus, OH: Merrill, 1984.

"Senator Drops a Bomb." *New York Times*, March 21, 1937, sec. 11, p. 10.

Severeid, Eric. Former Commentator, CBS News, Washington, D.C., Personal Interview, March 5, 1985.

Seymour-Ure, Colin. "Presidential Power, Press Secretaries and Communication." *Political Studies* 28 (1980): 253–70.

Shales, Tom. "Looking Out for No. 1." *The Washington Post*, March 4, 1986, p. B1.

———. "No Network Nibbles for a Carter Speech." *Washington Post*, June 28, 1978, p. B1.

———. "Snaps, Crackles and Pops Over a Fireside Chat." *Washington Post*, February 3, 1978, p. D1.

Shibi, Hamin. *Presidential Television*. Columbia: University of Missouri, School of Journalism, 1976.

Sioussat, Helen. *Mikes Don't Bite*. New York: L. B. Fischer, 1943.

Smith, Desmond. "RCA and GE, Going for the Globe." *Washington Journalism Review*, March 1986, p. 37.

———. "Is the Sun Setting on Network Nightly News?" *Washington Journalism Review*, January 1986, pp. 30–33.

———. "You *Can* Go Home Again." *Washington Journalism Review*, June 1986, p. 47.

Smith, Hedrick. "For Democrats, The Medium's a Mess." *New York Times*, December 10, 1984, p. B10.

Smith, Jack. Washington Bureau Chief, CBS News, Washington, D.C., Personal Interview, March 5, 1985.

Smith, Sally Bedell. "Paley Sees a 'Tragedy' in a Hostile Shift at CBS." *New York Times*, May 1, 1985, p. D1.

Socolow, Sanford. Former Washington Bureau Chief, CBS News, Ithaca, New York, Personal Interview, November 8, 1985; and Telephone Interview, February 22, 1985.

"Speakers Claim Intrusive Tactics by Reporters Put Off Public." *Network News*, Associated Press Radio Newsletter, vol. 3, no. 7, 1984, p. 10.

Sperber, A. M. *Murrow, His Life and Times*. New York: Freundlich Books, 1986.

Spragens, William C. *From Spokesman to Press Secretary: White House Media Relations*. Washington, D.C.: University Press of America, 1980.

———. *The Presidency and the Mass Media in the Age of Television*. Washington, D.C.: University Press of America, 1978.

Stanton, Frank. "The Critical Necessity For an Informed Public." *Journal of Broadcasting* 3, no. 3 (Summer 1958): 193–204.

———. Former President, CBS, New York, Personal Interview, January 24, 1985.

"Station Proposed for Federal Use." *New York Times*, May 12, 1929, p. 3.

Stilson, Janet. "Study: Meters Show Improved Cable Ratings." *Electronic Media*, January 4, 1988, p. 4.

Storch, Charles. "Soft Ad Market Puts Network on Spot." *Chicago Tribune*, September 14, 1986, pp. 7–1.

Sussman, Barry. "But Mr. President, Americans Don't Like Ayatollah Khomeini." *Washington Post*, December 1, 1986, p. 37.

———. "Grenada Move Earns Reagan Broad Political Gains, Poll Shows." *The Washington Post*, November 9, 1983, p. A3.

———. "News on TV: Mixed Review." *Washington Post National Weekly*, September 3, 1984, pp. 36–37.

Swertlow, Frank Sean. "Two Networks Reject Request to Carry President's Speech." *TV Guide*, October 18, 1975, p. A1.

Taylor, Arthur R. Telegram to Charles D. Ferris, Democratic Policy Committee, January 18, 1975.

Taylor, Clarke. "Network Anchors Mull Credibility of TV News." *Los Angeles Times*, November 28, 1984, p. 6.

———. Telegram to House Speaker Carl Albert and Senate Majority Leader Mike Mansfield, October 28, 1974.

Taylor, Ruby. Sales Manager, WNYW, New York, Personal Interview, February 6, 1987.

Tebbel, John, and Sarah Miles. *The Press and The Presidency from George Washington to Ronald Reagan*. New York: Oxford University Press, 1985.

"Television." *New York Times,* January 26, 1968, p. 95.

*Television: 1989 Nielsen Report.* Northbrook, IL: A. C. Nielsen, 1989.

Thompson, Kenneth W. *Ten Presidents and the Press.* Washington, D.C.: University Press of America, 1983.

"Three Radio Bills Pushed." *New York Times,* January 19, 1936, sec. II, p. 1.

Ticer, Scott. "Captain Comeback." *Business Week,* July 17, 1989, p. 106.

"Tilt to Left?: Interview with Don Hewitt." *U.S. News and World Report,* May 13, 1985, p. 65.

Timothy, Raymond. Group Executive Vice-President, NBC, Telephone Interview, February 10, 1986.

———. Group Executive Vice-President, NBC, Telephone Interview, May 6, 1985.

"Topic of the Times." *New York Times,* January 20, 1936, p. 18.

Turner, Ed. Executive Vice-President, Cable News Network, Atlanta, Georgia, Personal Interview, March 17, 1988.

"TV Goes Gavel to Gavel on Iran Hearings." *New York Times,* January 18, 1986, pp. 45–46.

"TV: Johnson's Address Gets Immediate Scrutiny." *New York Times,* January 18, 1968.

"TVB Conferees Exude Cautious Optimism for 1987." *Broadcasting,* November 24, 1986, pp. 63–67.

"Two L.A. Stations Refuse to Air Program." *Broadcasting,* October 1, 1936, p. 15.

U.S. Congress. Joint Committee on Congressional Operations. Hearings, 91st Congress, 2nd Session, August 4, 5, and 6, 1970.

———. Joint Committee on Congressional Operations. *Congress and Mass Communications.* Hearings, 93rd Congress, 2nd Session. February 20, 21; March 20; April 9, 10, 1974. Washington: U.S. Government Printing Office, 1974.

———. Joint Committee on Congressional Operations. *A Clear Message to the People.* Committee Report No. 9539, 94th Congress, First Session, 1975.

Valenti, Jack. "All Power to the Networks." *Washington Post,* August 1984, p. A11.

Vanardos, Lane. Executive Producer, Special Events, CBS News, Carbondale, Illinois, Personal Interview, April 11, 1989.

WNET Television. "Unplugging the Electronic Presidency." Transcript of Behind the Line, WNET Television, New York, New York, November 14, 1974.

Wald, Richard. Vice President, ABC News; Former President, NBC News, New York, Personal Interview, April 22, 1985.

Walsh, Edward, and Milton Coleman. "President's Defense Appeal Finds Little Support on Hill Wary of Waste." *Washington Post,* February 28, 1986, p. A8.

Walsh, Kenneth T. "Sunset for a Presidency." *U.S. News and World Report,* February 9, 1987, p. 23.

———, and Dennis Mullin. " 'Spin Patrol' on the March." *Newsweek,* December 1, 1986, p. 17.

Watson, George, Robert MacFarland, Jack Smith, and William Headline. "How the President Gets on the Air Live." *New York Times,* March 24, 1986, p. 30.

———. Letter to Democratic Congressional and Party Leaders, March 13, 1983.

————. Washington Bureau Chief, ABC News, Washington, D.C., Personal
       Interview, March 5, 1985; Telephone Interview, February 3, 1988.
"Watson Sees Rise in TV News Quality as Well as Quantity." *Broadcasting*,
       October 18, 1982, p. 51.
Wear, Donald. Vice President-Policy, CBS, New York, Personal Interview, April
       22, 1985.
Weaver, Warren. "As the Weinberger Turns." *New York Times*, February 13,
       1985, p. A24.
Weisman, John. "CBS Cancels Late-Night Show on Daniloff." *TV Guide*, October
       11, 1986, p. A1.
————. "Changes at Top Boost Morale at CBS News." *TV Guide*, September 27,
       1986, pp. A1, A36.
————. "He Always Hits His Mark." *TV Guide*, May 31, 1975, pp. 3–6.
————. "Nightly News Shows Under Siege—Will They Keep Their Clout?" *TV
       Guide*, October 11, 1986, p. 10.
————. "Staff Stunned by NBC Decision to Cancel '1986.' " *TV Guide*, December
       20, 1986, p. A1.
————. "TV and The Presidency." *TV Guide*, March 20, 1982, pp. 4–8.
————. "What TV Isn't Telling Us About Those Soviet Spokesmen." *TV Guide*,
       April 26, 1986.
————. "Who's Toughest on the White House and Why?" *TV Guide*, August
       27, 1983, pp. 5–14.
West, Paul. "The Video Connection, Beaming It Straight to the Constituents."
       *Washington Journalism Review*, June 1985, pp. 48–49.
"When a President Wants Air Time" (editorial). *Washington Post*, October 17,
       1982, p. B6.
White, Paul W. *News On The Air*. New York: Harcourt, Brace and Company,
       1947.
"White House Faults Networks for Skipping Reagan Speech." *Broadcasting*, Feb-
       ruary 8, 1988, p. 113.
Wicker, Tom. "The Pulpit Magnified." *New York Times*, October 18, 1974, p. 42.
"Wild Outbursts of Political Demands." *Broadcasting*, July 13, 1970, pp. 19–21.
Williams, Juan. *Eyes on the Prize*. New York: Viking Press, 1987.
Wolfson, Lewis W. *The Untapped Power of the Press, Explaining Government to the
       People*. New York: Praeger, 1985.
"Wright Ponders PAC for NBC." *Broadcasting*, December 15, 1986, pp. 58–60.
" 'Write Rosty' Blitz." *USA Today*, June 6, 1985, p. 1A.

# Index

# About the Author

JOE S. FOOTE became interested in the presidential–opposition access question while press secretary to Speaker of the House Carl Albert from 1972–76. After receiving his Ph.D. from the University of Texas at Austin, Foote returned to Capitol Hill as Administrative Assistant to Congressman Dave McCurdy of Oklahoma. He was visiting professor at Cornell University before becoming Chair of the Department of Radio-Television at Southern Illinois University at Carbondale. Foote's research interests are political communication and television news. He also has strong international interests and has worked in Europe, Africa, and South Asia.